MAPS & MORE

Kerala

Colloquially known as Maramady, this annual bullock race held in Anandappalli near Pathanamthitta is a popular event

How to use this book

FACT FILE
District: Kollam
STD code: 0474
When to go: August to March-end

Quick information reference

Getting There

By Air
The nearest airport is Thiruvananthapuram International Airport, 38 km.

By Rail
The nearest railway station is at Thiruvananthapuram, 30 km. Neyyattinkara is 21 km.

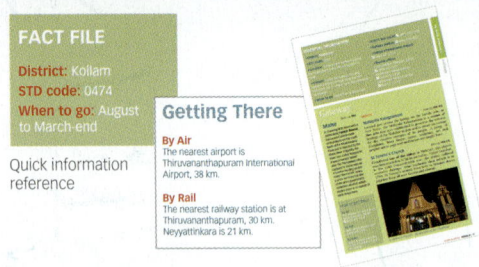

Sections

The book is divided into nine sections for easy reading and understanding. While the first section is an introduction, the next seven acquaint the reader with the three important cities, the backwaters, midlands, hills, river Nila and coastal Kerala. The last section is on wildlife.

Each section has an introduction followed by sights and attractions which are plotted on the accompanying map. Each sight has a specific grid number and can easily be located on the map. Although a few sights are not plotted, their grid number tells you their location.

Practical Information

The 'FACT FILE' gives the location, STD code and the best time to visit.

'Getting There' gives the closest and/or most convenient ways of reaching the destination by air, rail and road.

Tourist and forest department offices are also listed.

Resources

'Resources' lists out contact details of airports, airlines, railways, offices, houseboats, public holidays etc, along with places to stay which are given destination-wise.

Special Features

These features focus on certain interesting aspects of the region.

Icons

Specially designed and visually appealing icons appear throughout the text.

HOW TO USE MAP AND INDEX

1 Index is in alphabetical order with grid number to locate information in the map.

Sree Padmanabha Swamy Temple	A6
St Joseph's Cathedral	B2
Tagore Theatre	D2
Victoria Jubilee Town Hall	B2
Zoo	C1
WHERE TO STAY	
Comfort Inn Grand	1 B4
Horizon	2 C4
Jas	3 C4
KTDC Mascot	4 B1
Muthoot Plaza	5 B3
Pankaj	6 B4
Residency Tower	7 B4
Saj Lucia	8 A6

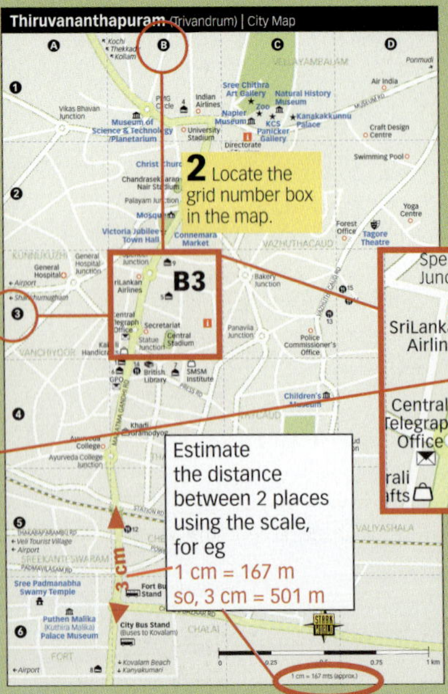

2 Locate the grid number box in the map.

3 Within the grid number box, locate* the name or number of the place.

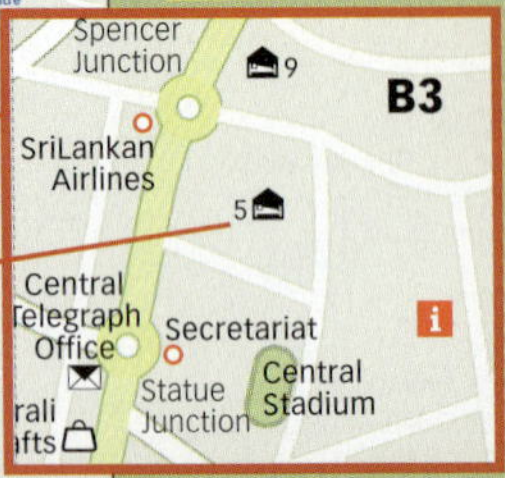

Estimate the distance between 2 places using the scale, for eg
1 cm = 167 m
so, 3 cm = 501 m

*The location of the place is indicated by the symbol next to the name. 'Where to Eat' and 'Where to Stay' information is shown by symbol with serial number. (eg Muthoot Plaza – 5 B3)

Refer **Back Flap** for Key to Symbols

MAPS & MORE

Kerala

Fact File
Capital : Thiruvananthapuram
Area : 38,863 sq km
Districts : 14
Population : 31,838,619
Literacy : 90.92%
Languages : Malayalam is the native tongue. English is also widely spoken.
Religions : Hinduism, Christianity and Islam
Time : GMT + 5.30
Currency : Indian Rupee
Climate : Tropical (22°C–34°C)
Figures: 2003

From the Publisher

Dear Reader,

Endowed with natural beauty as well as a diverse and fascinating populace, and blessed with a long history and a fascinating culture, Kerala is the destination of a lifetime. Our comprehensive guide to the State, *Stark World – Kerala*, unravelled its many mysteries, while attempting to capture the intoxicating essence of this exotic land.

Now we bring you *Maps & More – Kerala*, a portable, reader-friendly travel guide, to help you get around the State and enjoy its many marvels. Well-known tourist spots as well as remoter getaways are covered by the 30 maps spread across 140 pages. The book is divided into sections demarcating the State into *Backwaters*, *Midlands*, *The Hills*, *River Nila* and *Coastal Circuit*. There is also a section on Kerala's three largest *Cities* and another on *Wildlife*.

Specially commissioned by *Stark World*, the maps are unmatched in terms of quality – you can easily track down a location, a hotel, or even a shop! Interesting but succinct information accompanies each map, giving a feel of the destination, while leaving the rest for you to discover. The first in a series of concise travel books, *Maps & More – Kerala* will fit comfortably into your knapsack pocket. So travel light, and go forth and explore!

PN Shanavas
shanavas@starkworld.net

PS Your feedback and suggestions are most welcome.

SPONSOR

PUBLISHER
PN Shanavas

EDITOR
Akber Ayub

COPY EDITOR
Kajori Aikat

PROJECT CO-ORDINATOR
Robins V George

EDITORIAL CONTRIBUTORS
Aanchal Broca Kumar, Akhila Murthy

PHOTOGRAPHERS
Saibal Das, Joshy M Manjummel, Roopesh Pai, Jithendra M, Reju Rajan, Saji Chunda, Manoj Vasudevan, Sudhir Shivaram, PN Shanavas

PHOTOGRAPHY CO-ORDINATOR
Reju Rajan

DESIGN
The Leaf Design, Mumbai

GRAPHIC DESIGNER
Sony KT

IMAGING
J Madhu

GENERAL MANAGER
Sumit Chatterjee

DISTRIBUTION
Jose Varghese, Baiju Thomas

MANAGEMENT TEAM
Chairman : TK Harshan
Directors : PN Shanavas, BR Swarup
              Roy V Mathew, R Jaideep

CORPORATE OFFICE
61, 1st Main, 1st Cross, New Thippasandra, HAL 3rd Stage, Bangalore 560 075
Tel: +91–80–4125 5036, 6531 6748
Telefax: +91–80–4125 5037
Email: response@starkworld.net
www.starkworld.net

Copyright: Stark World Publishing Pvt Ltd. All rights reserved throughout the world. Printed and published by PN Shanavas on behalf of Stark World Publishing Pvt Ltd. Printed at Mytec Process Pvt Ltd, 204, IV Cross, Lalbagh Road, Bangalore 560 027 India.
No part of this book may be reproduced, stored in a retrieval system or transmitted in any form or means electronic, mechanical, photocopying, recording or otherwise, without prior written permission of Stark World Publishing Pvt Ltd. Brief text quotations with use of photographs are exempted for book review purposes only. Information has been obtained from sources believed to be reliable, but its accuracy and completeness, and the opinions based thereon, are not guaranteed. The maps in this book are for the convenience of tourists only. The publishers do not take responsibility for errors, if any. The territorial waters of India extend into the sea to a distance of twelve nautical miles measured from appropriate base line.
ISBN 81-902505-2-3 | 2006 Edition 1 | Reprint 2007

GUIDE MAPS

	page
Kerala State map	145

District Maps
Alappuzha	49
Ernakulam	27
Idukki	71
Kannur	104
Kasaragod	111
Kollam	46
Kottayam	56
Kozhikode	36
Malappuram	92
Palakkad	88
Pathanamthitta	63
Thiruvananthapuram	15
Thrissur	28
Wayanad	80

City Maps
	page
Ernakulam	22
Kochi & Ernakulam	21
Kozhikode	33
Thiruvananthapuram	11

Destination Maps
Fort Kochi & Mattancherry	24
Kovalam	98
Munnar	74
Kumily, Thekkady & Periyar Tiger Reserve	66
Varkala	101

Circuit Maps
Backwaters	42
River Nila	86

Velliamkallu is a rugged spur of granite off Payyoli coast, close to Kozhikode

Contents

Kerala
page: 6-9

- A Chequered History 6
- Unlike Any Other Place 7
- Amazing Waterways 7
- Mottled Midlands 7
- Ecological Hotspots 8
- The Western Ghats................... 8
- Art, Culture and Celebrations .. 8
- Ayurveda 9
- Architectural Heritage.............. 9

Cities
page: 10-38

- **Thiruvananthapuram**   **10**
  - Getaway – Ponmudi 17
- **Kochi**   **18**
  - Getaway – Thrissur 29
  - Kodungallur 30
  - Guruvayur 31
- **Kozhikode**   **32**
  - Getaway – Mahe 37
  - Thalassery............ 38

Backwaters
page: 40-53

- Kollam...................................... 44
- Alappuzha 48
- Kumarakom 52

Midlands
page: 54-67

- Kottayam 55
- Pala 58
- Kanjirapally 60
- Pathanamthitta....................... 62
- Kumily and Thekkady................ 65

The Hills
page: 68-83

- Thenmala 69
- Idukki 70
- Munnar 72
- Peermede 76
- Vagamon 77
- Nelliyampathy.......................... 78
- **Wayanad**   **79**
  - Vythiri...................................... 79
  - Sulthan Bathery 82
  - Kalpetta 82
  - Mananthavady 83

River Nila
page: 84-95

- Palakkad 89
- Ponnani 91
- Cheruthuruthy 94

Coastal Circuit
page: 96-112

- Kovalam 97
- Varkala 100
- Kannur 103
- Nileswaram............................ 107
- Kasaragod 109

Wildlife
page: 114-121

- Neyyar Wildlife Sanctuary....... 114
- Peppara Wildlife Sanctuary 115
- Shenduruney Wildlife Sanctuary................................. 115
- Periyar Tiger Reserve............. 116
- Idukki Wildlife Sanctuary 116
- Eravikulam National Park 117
- Chinnar Wildlife Sanctuary 117
- Thattekkad Bird Sacnctuary .. 118
- Chimmini Wildlife Sanctuary .. 118
- Peechi-Vazhani Wildlife Sanctuary................................. 119
- Parambikulam Wildlife Sanctuary 120
- Silent Valley National Park...... 120
- Wayanad Wildlife Sanctuary ... 121
- Aralam Wildlife Sanctuary 121

Resources
page: 132-143

- Accommodation 132
- Houseboats............................ 139
- Useful Information 140
- Index–Places and Tourist Attractions 141
- Index–Places-Location on the Map 142

Special Features

- Snake Boat Races 42
- Houseboats.............................. 47
- Toddy shops............................. 53
- Letters, Latex and Lakes......... 57
- Kerala Kalamandalam............. 87

MAPS & MORE **KERALA** | 5

Kerala
A million shades of green...

A little pond nestles atop the Chembra peak, the highest in hilly Wayanad

Global acclaim

Conde Nast Traveller – Declared Kerala 'one of the 10 best destinations in the world'.

National Geographic Traveler – Selected Kerala as 'one of the 50 destinations of a lifetime'.

Time – Featured Kerala in its 'Travel Watch' section.

The Weekend Financial Times, London – Celebrated Kerala's 'dreamy lagoons, curving waterways, damp paddy fields, swaying greenery and singularly beautiful people' in a cover story.

Geo Saison, Germany – Called Kerala the 'Mecca of the oldest and holistic health system'.

Three Sixty Degrees, UK – Unveiled the delights of a boat trip in Kerala.

Travel Agent, USA – Featured Kerala in a cover story as 'a place unlike anything else that Americans have experienced elsewhere in India'.

A Chequered History

Enraged by the arrogance and excesses of the early Kshatriya kings, Lord Vishnu assumed the form of Parasurama (avatar of Rama with the axe), and swore to annihilate 21 generations of them. However, once this mission was accomplished, rivers of blood began to flow over the land, making it unsuitable for Brahmins to live on. Overcome with remorse, Parasurama threw his axe into the sea. Where it landed, the waters dutifully receded to create a narrow strip of land, forming Kerala. This myth may be fanciful, but it is a fitting explanation nonetheless for the birth of a land that has come to be known as **'God's own country'**. The sobriquet is not linked to the myth however, but to the captivating charms of the region.

The name 'Kerala' is derived from *keralaputra* or the 'Land of the sons of the Cheras', who were the very first rulers of Kerala. Wars have raged over this coveted land since very ancient times. The neighbouring Cholas engaged the Cheras in battle since as early as 985 AD. Later, local principalities emerged as power centres. Foremost among them was a group of Samoothiri Brahmins, who soon gained control of the region's **famed spice trade**. The new rulers (later anglicised as 'Zamorins'), who established their capital in the port city of Kozhikode, grew to be the wealthiest in the entire sub-continent and had trade links with the Arabs, Jews, Romans and the Chinese. Later, the Portuguese, who first came as traders, began to covet the land more than its spices. Subsequently, the Dutch and later, **the British**, waged endless wars against the Portuguese and the local rajas. By the early 17th century, the British had gained control over vast stretches of the land and the spice trade. They went on to rule the subcontinent for over 200 years until India gained independence in 1947.

Unlike Any Other Place

The beaches of Kerala had begun to attract European guests of the Travancore kings from the early 1930s, although tourism had been an unknown concept then. However, within three decades, the coast began to see a transformation. Kovalam is a typical example. It had been little more than a sleepy coastal village until the 1960s, when backpackers and 'hippies' began to discover the charms of its southern beaches. Before long (1972), the State Tourism Department took over the summer palace of the Travancore royal family, the Halcyon Castle, and converted it into the first five-star hotel in Kovalam. Today, Kovalam has few equals as a seaside tourist destination. The story is similar in other parts of Kerala – the famous backwaters, the virgin forests and the green hills.

Amazing Waterways

Kerala has an **extensive network of waterways** that lace the interior coastline, from Hosdurg in the north to Thiruvananthapuram in the south, covering a distance of 560 km. Besides the large inland lakes that dot the land, the backwaters include the entire network of canals, estuaries and water bodies formed by the inimitable craftsmanship of nature. The waterways pulsate to a different beat, and are characterised by a lifestyle and ethos non-existent elsewhere in the country.

Kumarakom is typical of this water world. With its backdrop of rich green paddy fields and still grey waters, the region is resplendent in scenic beauty. The many resorts that have sprung up in and around Kumarakom have transformed this once quiet and peaceful settlement into a much sought after destination.

Mottled Midlands

The midlands too, are not to be ignored. Except for the absence of sandy beaches, this region appears to be an encapsulation of all that Kerala stands for. It is known for its undulating hills, flat valleys with extensive rubber plantations, a tract of forest that is **one of the finest wildlife reserves in the country**, panoramic backwater stretches, lush paddy fields, and a vibrant trading community with great economic clout.

Boats laden with goods negotiate the waterways

Bare facts about the backwaters

The 205-km-long waterway from Kollam to Kottapuram (near Kodungallur), running nearly parallel to the coastline, facilitates inland transport, cargo movement as well as backwater tourism.

Alappuzha, Kollam and Kumarakom are the three most popular backwater destinations.

Extensive paddy and plantation crops grow several feet below sea level at Kuttanad.

There are plenty of options for tourists ranging from short cruises costing a couple of hundred rupees to package holidays on houseboats costing as much as Rs 30,000 a day.

Annual snake boat races are much-awaited events, popular with both locals and tourists.

Ecological Hotspots

There is plenty for nature lovers and wildlife enthusiasts to do in Kerala, such as exploring the innumerable national parks and wildlife resorts. Located along the western corner of the Nilgiris, **Silent Valley National Park** constitutes one of the last vestiges of an undisturbed tropical evergreen rainforest. With an unbroken ecological history, continuously evolving for millions of years, this is a unique region. It has been termed an ecological island, one that contains immense biological and genetic wealth. Thanks largely to its difficult terrain and remote location, Silent Valley remains pristine and untouched.

Getting ready to portray Bhadrakaali, the demon goddess, in a Mudiyettu performance

Places such as Thekkady conjure up images of nature at its purest – undulating hills, crisp, clean air, and spice-scented plantations. Then there are the **elephants** – one of India's finest wildlife reserves is situated in Thekkady's Periyar forests. The first in the State to promote environmental tourism, Thekkady continues to beckon the adventurous traveller. Many other well protected pockets of wildlife elsewhere in the State draw visitors for the variety of local fauna and the captivating greenery.

A medley of art and dance forms

The most prominent among the ritual arts is the *theyyam* of northern Kerala and the *padayani* of south-central Kerala.

Celebrated classical dance forms include Kathakali, *mohiniattam* and *koodiyattam*.

Solo dance forms such as the *ottanthullal* have a strong element of ridicule and social criticism.

The traditional martial arts form, *kalarippayattu*, is more popular in the north than in other parts of the State.

Margamkali, of the Syrian Christians, is a women's dance form that uses circular formations similar to *thiruvathirakali* and celebrates the legend of St Thomas in Kerala.

The Western Ghats

Virgin beaches, languid backwaters and lush tropical vegetation are not the only attractions of Kerala. There are regions with cool climes and hilly environs that wait to be savoured. The Western Ghats offer cool, misty mountains, undulating meadows and picturesque valleys where vast areas are given over to plantations of tea, coffee and cardamom. The rolling High Ranges form a demarcating line at the eastern edge of Kerala, separating the State from its neighbours. The dense forests, extensive ridges and deep ravines of the Ghats have always sheltered Kerala from mainland invaders. These highlands, with their meandering roads and magnificent waterfalls, have also bestowed upon this region an ambience that is completely different from the State's other scenic locales. Remote yet easily accessible from any part of Kerala, each destination here is known for its own quaint charm.

Art, Culture and Celebrations

Art and culture have always been integral to Kerala. The pluralist aspect reflected in the art forms of the State is rooted in the rituals of its indigenous people. Among the dance forms that have evolved from ancient customs, the

8 | KERALA MAPS & MORE

most prominent are surely the ***theyyam*** of northern Kerala and the ***padayani*** of south-central Kerala. Although ***koodiyattam*** and **Kathakali** are classical forms once favoured by the elite, they now represent quintessential dance forms of the region. An interesting feature of the dances of Kerala, excluding the folk forms, is **the strong influence of *kalarippayattu***, a physical discipline that was followed irrespective of gender.

Kerala is also a land with a variety of celebrations that transcend regional and religious boundaries. What stands out is the thread of harmony that runs through the different ceremonies and rituals. The most spectacular event of all, **Onam**, epitomises a newfound vigour and optimism about life. The festival celebrates the return of King Mahabali, who is believed to visit his subjects every year. To convince their beloved king that Kerala is still the land of milk and honey, people decorate their homes and celebrate to the fullest, sometimes even faking prosperity, to present a happy façade for their king.

Ayurveda

Ayurveda, the Science of Life, is perhaps the oldest and definitely, the most holistic, medical system available to the contemporary world. Although it is practised all over India, Kerala is perhaps the only State where this science still follows age-old traditional laws. Situated in the tropical region, the State has an unparalleled **wealth of herbs and natural vegetation**. Although similar plants are perhaps found in the Himalayas, those found in Kerala have a special potency due to the State's unique geographical position and tropical climate. What is more, the hot and humid climatic condition of the region is regarded as specially favourable for ayurvedic treatments. In fact, the practitioners of Ayurveda in Kerala have evolved their own special formulations that are considered particularly efficacious.

Architectural Heritage

Kerala possesses a distinctive architectural style. Tiled roofs and gables, with spires, are ubiquitous. However, structures rarely rise above the first floor. Wood was used extensively not only on doors and windows, but even to make solid, carved walls. The numerous palaces, temples, churches and mosques dotting the State showcase this traditional style. However, the heavy solid wood with brass embellishments, used earlier on doors and windows, is rarely used these days, if at all.

The mountain of herbs

Agasthyakoodam, a legendary herbal mountain near Neyyar Dam, 20 km south of Thiruvananthapuram, is considered a treasure trove of medicinal herbs. It is here that Agasthya, the great sage, developed the Siddha system of medicine. This mountain and the surrounding Western Ghats, 1,500 m above sea level, constitute a hotbed of biodiversity. Eight per cent of the plant species found here are native to the region. The healing system that has originated from this mystic mountain gave birth to a potent branch of Ayurveda in southern Kerala.

Medicated rice packs heat specific parts of the body for a variety of benefits in a treatment called Njavarakizhi

The Padmanabha Swamy Temple is believed to be 2,000 years old

Thiruvananthapuram
The languorous capital

Getting There

By Air
The nearest is Thiruvananthapuram International Airport, 6 km
☎ 0471–250 1424

By Rail
The Thiruvananthapuram railway station is connected to all major metros
☎ 0471–232 1568

By Road
The KSRTC (☎ 0471–232 3886) and city bus stands connect to most towns in Kerala. Long-distance buses also operate from here.

The name 'Thiruvananthapuram' means the 'abode of Anantha' – referring to the sacred snake god on whom Lord Vishnu reclines. The British found the name too much of a mouthful and anglicised it to 'Trivandrum'. The capital of Kerala, this unpretentious city is clean, green and has a leisurely feel to it. The Padmanabha Swamy Temple that holds the deity of the royal family of Travancore is an important landmark.

This city was built on seven low hills, a similarity it famously shares with Rome. It has an interesting mix of commercial streets, tree-lined avenues, historical and modern buildings, ancestral homes and a long coastline washed by the Arabian Sea. There are no large industries, but Thiruvananthapuram does have its share of professionals and businessmen, and with the advent of the IT industry, a rising population of 'techies'. However, the Secretariat and the government offices still form the backbone of the town.

SIGHTS

Sree Padmanabha Swamy Temple   (Map pg 11, A6)

Located in the old walled fort area in the heart of the city, the Padmanabha Swamy Temple is a grand edifice that devotees believe has protected the town from all ills. Architecturally the east-facing structure is a mix of Chola, Pandya and indigenous Kerala styles. Access to the sanctum

SIGHTS AND ATTRACTIONS	Grid
Children's Museum	C4
Christ Church	B2
Connemara Market	B2
Kanakakkunnu Palace	C1
KCS Panicker Gallery	C1
Mosque	B2
Museum of Science & Technology/Planetarium	B1
Napier Museum	C1
Natural History Museum	C1
Puthen Malika (Kuthira Malika) Palace Museum	A6
Sree Chithra Art Gallery	C1
Sree Padmanabha Swamy Temple	A6
St Joseph's Cathedral	B2
Tagore Theatre	D2
Victoria Jubilee Town Hall (VJT Hall)	B2
Zoo	C1

WHERE TO STAY		
Comfort Inn Grand	1	B4
Horizon	2	C4
Jas	3	C4
KTDC Mascot	4	B1
Muthoot Plaza	5	B3
Pankaj	6	B4
Residency Tower	7	B4
Saj Lucia	8	A6
South Park	9	B3

WHERE TO EAT		
Arya Nivas	10	C5
Aryas (veg)	11	B5
Azad Restaurant	12	B5
Buddha's Delight	(see 1)	B4
Coffee Beanz	13	C3
Kalavara	14	B4
Park Field Gardens	15	D3
Sindhoor	16	D3
Swathi	(see 4)	B1
Terrace Green	(see 9)	B3
Tiffany's	(see 5)	B3

10 | KERALA MAPS & MORE

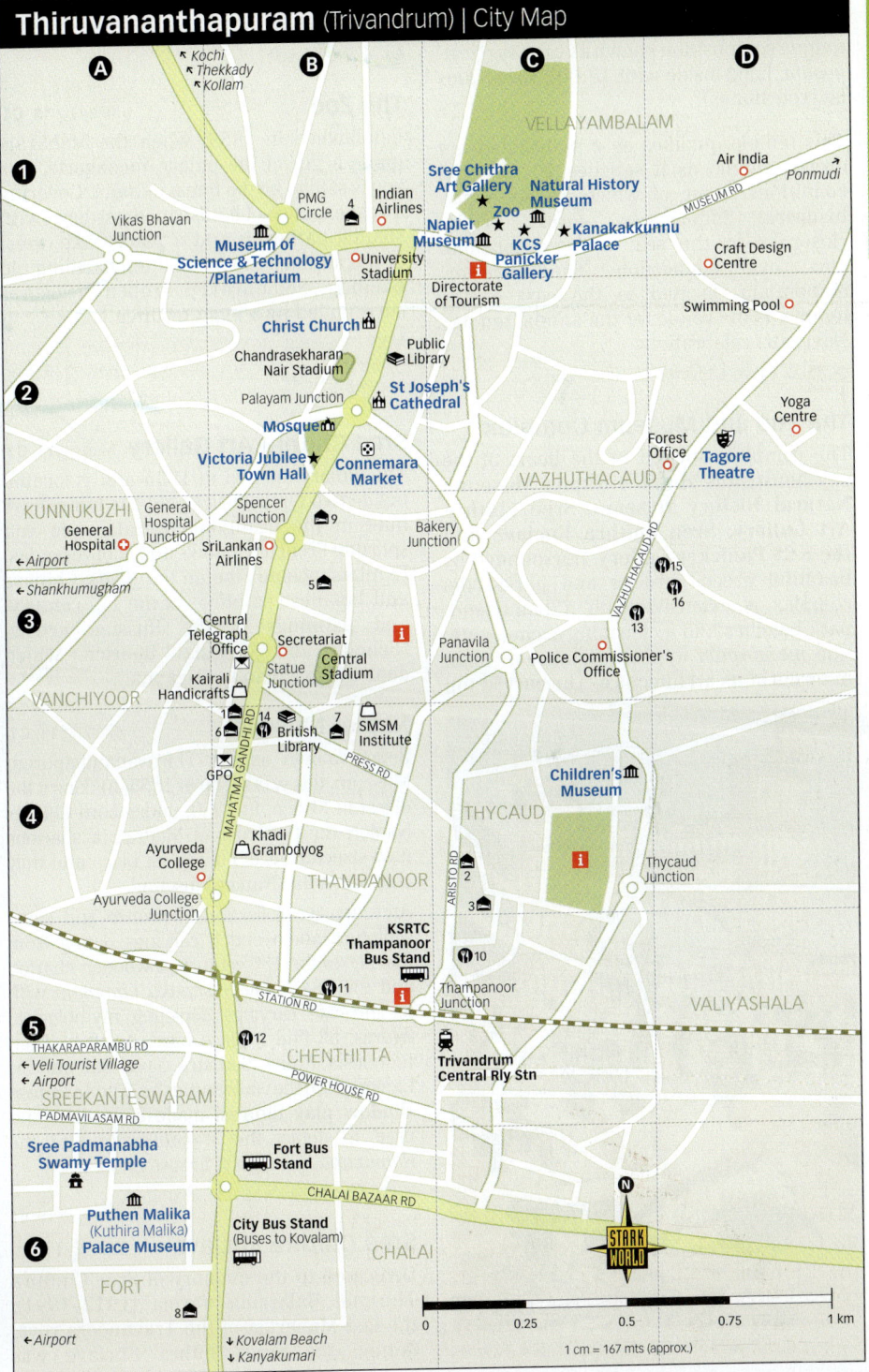

is through the distinctive *ottakkal* (single stone) *mandapam*. The idol is made of a unique composition known as *katu-sarkara-yogam*, lined inside with 12,008 *salagrams* (sacred stones).

This temple qualifies as a mahakshetram (great temple) as it satisfies 10 essential conditions, some of which are antiquity, historical importance, forest origin, closeness to the sea, elevated location, and royal connection. The navaratri mandapam, located to the east of the temple, is the venue for the annual ten day Navaratri celebrations.

Note: Entry is restricted to Hindus.

The Zoo and Museum Complex

The complex situated in the heart of the city houses the **zoo**, the **Napier Museum, Natural History Museum, Sree Chithra Art Gallery, Sree Chithra Enclave and the KCS Panicker Gallery**. Surrounded by beautiful green gardens and parks, the complex is extensive with a bandstand, park benches and a charming arched gate. The *mandapam* appears Southeast Asian in terms of its architecture. The curved top rafters and the granite base are reminiscent of a Hindu temple.

📞 *0471–231 6275*

The Zoo (Map pg **11**, **C1**)

Established in 1859, when the Maharaja made a gift of the palace menagerie, this zoo is said to be the finest in India. Covering a vast expanse of landscaped gardens, with shaded pathways and a placid lake, most of the animals are housed in charming old buildings. Some are kept in open enclosures surrounded by a moat or ditch.

Note: Walking around the extensive grounds could be tiring. Carry enough drinking water. Polythene bags are banned inside.

Sree Chithra Art Gallery (Map pg **11**, **C1**)

The gallery opened in 1935 and is located inside two typical brick-and-tile bungalows built in the traditional Kerala style and sporting French windows and cool verandas. Exhibits include Tibetan *thankhas*, Chinese and Japanese paintings of the 17th century, and paintings of the Russian artists, Nicholas and Svetoslav Roerich, which depict Himalayan landscapes.

Napier Museum (Map pg **11**, **C1**)

Better known as the Thiruvananthapuram Museum, this was set up in 1855, making it the oldest in Kerala. In 1880, under Lord Charles Napier, the Governor of Madras, a spacious new structure was built in its place and duly christened the 'Napier Museum'.

An extensive collection of bronze and stone sculpture and wooden carvings dating from the 11th to the 18th century, a wooden chariot, and the 1847-built *pushpaka vimanam* with its intricate carvings depicting mythological figures, all find a place here. Artefacts from Indonesia, China, Sumatra, Java, Bali and Sri Lanka adorn the walls and aisles. The **Javanese shadow play figures**, made of leather, and used to depict the *Mahabharata* and the *Ramayana*, are sure to arouse interest.

Note: Photography is not permitted.

Sree Chithra Enclave (Map pg **11**, **C1**)

Dedicated to the memory of Sree Chithra Thirunal Balarama Varma (1912–1991), the last Maharaja of the Travancore royal family, the Sree Chithra Enclave was

Cooking on the streets during Attukal Pongala festival

12 | KERALA MAPS & MORE

OTHER ATTRACTIONS IN THE COMPLEX

» **KCS Panicker Gallery**
Traces the work of KCS Panicker, nominated as one of the nine eminent artists of India. The gallery gives an insight into the evolution of the style and range of a versatile and directional artist.

» **Natural History Museum**
Housed in a modern building, it has separate sections such as the skeleton gallery, animal gallery, bird gallery and museum. An index gallery allows students to compare the limbs and organs of different species and study their functions. The taxidermy section also has some excellent specimens.

opened in 1993. An **audio-visual presentation** explains the evolution of the Travancore State and its geographical and socio-cultural history. Other exhibits include personal belongings and artefacts used by the royalty.

Kerala State Science and Technology Museum (Map pg **11**, **B1**)

First established in 1984, it opened to the public 10 years later, and today, houses more than 300 exhibits on science and technology. There are galleries on a variety of subjects including electricity, electronics, mechanics, computer science, and biomedical and solar energy. In 1997, the museum expanded to include a children's science park.

0471–230 6024

The Napier Museum – a blend of local and colonial styles

Methan Mani, the clock tower near Sree Padmanabha Swamy Temple

Priyadarshini Planetarium (Map pg **11**, **B1**)

The **GM-II star field projector** in the planetarium can project most of the constituents of the visible universe. It can also simulate the star-studded night sky over any location in the world, on any day up to 12,500 years in the past or the same number of years into the future.

0471–230 6024

Puthen Malika (Map pg **11**, **A6**)

Located in the East Fort, this charming two-storied palace with its 80 rooms and open verandas was built in the Kerala style by Maharaja Swathi Thirunal in 1844. It earned the name 'Kuthira Malika' or 'Horse Palace' on account of the wooden horses carved along the entire length of the exterior lintel on the upper floors.

Now converted into a museum, the Puthen Malika houses paintings belonging to the Travancore kings. Ornate woodcarvings on the ceiling, huge chandeliers, Belgian glass mirrors and pieces of marble sculpture embellish its interiors. Exhibits include life-sized Kathakali images, well-preserved palanquins of yesteryears and the armoury of kings. Portraits of all the kings who ruled Travancore adorn its walls; the 140-year-old Bohemian crystal throne and another

Veli Tourist Village

made of ivory recall the grandeur of a bygone era. The first floor holds porcelain artefacts, paintings, sundials, solar clocks and sculpture.

☎ 0471–247 3952

Aakulam Tourist Complex (Map pg **15**, **B3**)

Situated on the banks of the backwaters at Aakulam, 10 km away from the city, this tourist complex offers a range of exciting activities – boating facilities similar to the Veli Tourist Complex, a swimming pool open to men, women, children and beginners (with separate time slots for each), a musical dance fountain as well as a children's park. A snack bar offers refreshments.

☎ 0471–244 3043

Veli Tourist Village (Map pg **15**, **B3**)

A popular picnic spot, this village complex is located 12 km away from the city where the Veli Lake merges with the Arabian Sea. The small stretch of beach formed in between disappears under water when the lake floods over – a natural phenomenon locally known as *pozhi murikkal*.

A large garden holds works of sculpture by the eminent artist, **Kanayi Kunhiraman**. The floating pontoon bridge across the lake and the **boating facilities** also draw visitors. The open-air auditorium, with the sea as its backdrop, provides a venue for cultural performances and art festivals.

☎ 0471–250 0785

Vyloppilly Sanskrithi Bhavan

Commissioned in 2001 as homage to the great Malayalam poet, the late Vyloppilly Sreedhara Menon, the Bhavan consists of a cluster of pleasing buildings scattered over tranquil, green grounds. The *padipura* or gateway, and the *koothambalam* or **traditional theatre**, with its wooden flooring and distinctive lamps, are interesting. Kathakali recitals are held regularly. The Kerala Council for Historical Research (KCHR) also functions from here.

Note: There are regular cultural programmes on Monday evenings, starting 6 pm. Entry is free

☎ 0471–231 1842

OTHER STRUCTURES IN THE BHAVAN

» **Kalamandapam** An open-air venue for staging folk art.

» **Art Gallery** Exhibits the paintings of famous artists of Kerala.

» **Library** Dedicated to the memory of the late PN Panicker, a pioneering Malayalam writer. Also has a research and documentation facility.

» **Ranga Mandapam** An open-air auditorium with a seating capacity of nearly 2,000. It is a popular venue for cultural gatherings and shows (video projections).

» **Nritha Mandapam** A work of art in stone, built in honour of the famous danseuse, the late Kalamandalam Kalyanikutty Amma.

Beemapalli (Map pg **15**, **B4**)

The Beemapalli Dargah Shareef, located 12 km from the city, is dedicated to **Bee Umma**, a pious Muslim woman with great spiritual powers, who is said to have migrated from Saudi Arabia centuries ago to preach Islam.

A weekend on the Shankhumugham Beach

Thiruvananthapuram (Trivandrum) | District Map

IN AND AROUND — Thiruvananthapuram

DON'T MISS
» Methan Mani
The clock tower near Sree Padmanabha Swamy Temple has a clock with the face of a Muslim with goats on either side. Inspired by Dutch know-how, it was manufactured locally.

SIGHTS AND ATTRACTIONS	Grid
Agasthyakoodam (peak)	D2
Aakulam (tourist village)	B3
Anjengo (fort)	A2
Beemapalli (mosque)	B4
Chowara	C4
Koyikkal Palace	C3
Neyyar Wildlife Sanctuary	D3
Padmanabhapuram Palace	D5
Peppara Wildlife Sanctuary	D2
Ponmudi (hill station)	C2
Poovar	C4
Sivagiri Mutt	A2
Veli (tourist village)	B3
Vizhinjam	C4

BEACHES
Shankhumugham	B3
Kovalam	C4
Varkala	A2

WATERFALLS AND DAMS
Aruvikkara Dam	C3
Meenmutti waterfalls	C2
Neyyar Dam	D3

MAPS & MORE **KERALA** | 15

The annual 10-day Uroos festival commemorates the saint and her son, Sayyidussaheed Maheen Aboobaker, both of whom are buried here. Religious discourses and cultural programmes are held in the evenings on these days. In a ritual known as Chandanakkudam, devotees make offerings of coins in earthen pots or *kudams*.

Shankhumugham Beach (Map pg 15, B3)

People converge at this beach in the evenings to watch fiery sunsets. Across the road, there is a single-storey building with a high roof that houses an indoor sports centre with teakwood flooring and wooden galleries, probably the oldest in the State. Boxing championships are regularly held here. On the spacious veranda outside, a branch of the popular **India Coffee House** serves up traditional filter coffee and South Indian snacks.

The beach plays a crucial role in the bi-annual **Aarattu ceremony** when the deity, Lord Padmanabha, is taken in a procession for a ritual bath in the sea, escorted by caparisoned elephants and horses.

Padmanabhapuram Palace (Map pg 15, D5)

With 14 palaces spread across six and a half acres, the complex presents a unique example of the architectural skill and expertise of ancient Kerala. The original structure was a small palace, to which successive rulers made their own modifications. It reached its

Padmanabhapuram Palace

present form at the end of the 18th century. The *oottupura* or dining hall, the main palace known as *thai kottaram*, the ritual hall or *homapura*, the multi-storied *upparikka malika*, the *indravilasam* palace, the *navaratri mandapam* in the Vijayanagar style, the Archaeological Museum, and the *thekke kottaram* are some of the best known structures. Of the 127 rooms that were once in use, only 27 are now maintained on a regular basis.

ESSENTIAL INFORMATION

» **District:** Thiruvananthapuram (earlier Trivandrum).

» **STD Code:** 0471

» **Location:** At the southern end of Kerala, 87 km short of Kanyakumari (the southern tip of India).

» **Climate:** Tropical, cool in the high ranges and hot in the plains. Annual rainfall – 150 cm from June to October.

» **When to go:** November to February, when it is coolest (22°C to 32°C).

» **KSRTC bus stand:** ☎ 0471–232 3886

» **Private bus stand:** ☎ 0471–232 3886

» **Railway station:** ☎ 0471–232 1568

» **Thiruvananthapuram International Airport** ☎ 0471–250 1424

» **Kerala Tourism Office**
Park View, Thiruvananthapuram 695 033
☎ 0471–232 1132 (Toll free 1–600–444–747)
✉ 0471–232 2279 @ info@keralatourism.org
🌐 www.keralatourism.org

» **KTDC Tourist Reception Centre**
Station Road, Thampanoor,
Thiruvananthapuram 695 001
☎ 0471–233 0031

Getaway

Ponmudi
(Map pg **15**, **C2**)

Situated close to Thiruvananthapuram, this hill station is a quiet haven ideal for walks and treks. Winding, wooded paths and spice and tea plantations give it a lovely green cover. Wild orchids grow profusely on hillsides.

Getting There

By Air
The nearest is Thiruvananthapuram International Airport, 65 km.

By Rail
The Thiruvananthapuram railway station is well connected to all towns in the State and cities across India.

By Road
Buses ply regularly from the KSRTC bus stand (Thiruvananthapuram) through Vithura.

SIGHTS

Meenmutti Waterfalls
(Map pg **15**, **C2**)

Located 15 km before Ponmudi, where the Kallar River falls from a height.

Agasthyakoodam Mountains
(Map pg **15**, **D2**)

This spectacular peak near Ponmudi rises to a majestic 1,890 m to form a sharp cone. Ideal for trekking from December to February.

Note: Contact for trekking - Wildlife Warden, Thiruvananthapuram Wildlife Division 0471–236 0762

Aruvikkara Dam and Devi Temple
(Map pg **15**, **C3**)

The dam across the Karamana River, 17 km from the city, forms a reservoir that meets the city's water needs. The ancient **Bhagavathi Temple** sits on a rock, overlooking a waterfall.

Koyikkal Palace/ Numismatics Museum
(Map pg **15**, **C3**)

Located at Nedumangadu, this palace, once the abode of the Perakam dynasty, houses a Numismatics and Folklore Museum with some rare artefacts.

0472–281 2136

Misty hillsides at Ponmudi

Chinese fishing nets at Fort Kochi

Kochi
The bustling port city…

Getting There

By Air
Cochin International Airport at Nedumbasserry, 34 km.
☎ 0484–261 0115

By Rail
Ernakulam Town (☎ 0484–239 5198) and Ernakulam Junction (☎ 0484–237 5431) both serve as railheads and are well connected to the whole of Kerala and to other major cities in India.

By Road
The KSRTC bus stand (☎ 0484–236 0531) in Ernakulam offers daily services to all major cities in the State. NH 47 runs through Ernakulam.

A small area that was once bequeathed to a member of the royal family, Kochi later expanded to form a kingdom and then the State of Cochin. It gradually developed into a centre of trade and colonial rule, and eventually, shrank in size, but not in stature, as it evolved into the modern town of Kochi as we know it today.

The great flood of the Periyar River in 1341 created a natural harbour in Kochi. The Chinese and the Arabs are believed to be the first traders to visit this port, heralding a wave of subsequent visitors – the Portuguese, the Dutch and the British. The latter made it their administrative headquarters and changed the town's name to **Cochin**. Kochi offered, in abundance, **the finest spices** – pepper, ginger, cardamom, cloves and turmeric – to the world, a reputation that continues even to this day. Voyagers also coveted the fine ivory, sandalwood, perfumes and gold that was brought into this market town.

Boasting the largest port in the State, present-day Kochi is also one of the premier industrial, trading and commercial centres of southern India, where a diverse pool of cultures and histories blend to enhance its eclectic spirit. Ernakulam, the upmarket part of town, is where the buzz is. Alive with shopping centres, movie houses, offices, hotels, plush buildings, roadside eateries and exotic restaurants, it is an amalgamation of the old and the new – surely **the face of modern Kerala**.

Highlights

Known as the Queen of the Arabian Sea, Kochi's charms are manifold. From the Chinese fishing nets and heritage buildings of Fort Kochi to the old spice markets of Mattancherry and the cosmopolitan atmosphere of Ernakulam, buzzing with hotels, cinema halls shops and restuarants, the city combines the finest in tradition and modernity.

Hill Palace – the erstwhile residence of the King of Cochin is now Kerala's largest archaeological museum

Rainbow Bridge, Marine Drive

Ernakulam (Map pg **22**)
SIGHTS

Marine Drive (Map pg **22**, **A2**)
This scenic strip offers a spectacular view of the backwaters and the harbour and is packed with buildings ranging from corporate offices and banks to luxury hotels, cinema halls, restaurants, cafés and supermarkets. The drive is the **most popular hangout for the locals**.

MG Road (Map pg **22**, **C3**)
Mahatma Gandhi Road is the lifeline of the city. Lined with every type of commercial enterprise from garment showrooms and jewellery shops to a host of restaurants, it remains the most expensive piece of real estate in the city.

Broadway (Map pg **22**, **A2**)
Located in the heart of the city, Broadway is bound by a maze of alleys and crossroads. Before MG Road usurped its position as the main street, Broadway, parallel to Shanmugham Road, was the widest in town, hence its name. The narrow street and crossroads on its flanks are choc-a-block with shops selling everything under the sun from shoes, clothes, medicine, furniture, curios and kitchenware to spices, gold, hardware, electronics and books.

Shiva Temple (Map pg **22**, **B5**)
Popularly known as 'Ernakulathappan', the god of this temple is associated with the name of city. Lord Shiva, the chief deity, faces west towards the sea, considered a rarity. The Shiva and Parvati idols, found in *kirathamurthy* form, are claimed to be *swayambhoo* or 'self-created'.

The annual eight-day festival celebrated during January-February concludes with the Arattu procession when the image of the deity is taken for a ritual bath in the temple pool accompanied by caparisoned elephants.

☎ 0484–237 0415, 236 9804

Note: Entry is restricted to Hindus

Hill Palace Museum (Map pg **27**, **B3**)
This one-time residence of the Raja of Cochin at Thripunithura has been converted into the **largest archaeological museum in Kerala**. The hill-top palace, built in 1865, and consisting of 49 buildings, stretches across 52 acres of lush greenery. Exhibits displayed in its 18 galleries include the royal throne and chairs, pictures of the rulers of Cochin, Thanjavur paintings, 14th century wood-carvings, inscriptions, megalithic remains, crown, ornaments, and mural paintings. Jewellery, porcelain and epigraphy artefacts are housed in separate galleries.

Ancient musical instruments, clay sculpture, bronze and silver items of the 14th, 15th and 16th centuries, imported horse carts for the king, stone sculpture from the 10th to the 18th century, and rock-cut weapons of the Stone Age constitute some of the other exhibits.

Kerala Lalitha Kala Akademi (Map pg 22, B6)

The two-acre property in the heart of the city where the Maharaja of Cochin once held his durbars is now known as the Durbar Hall grounds. These grounds were also used for football games, exhibitions, military parades and processions from the nearby Shiva Temple. The one-time Parikshit Thampuran Museum situated here has been converted into an academy that showcases contemporary arts.

Museum of Kerala History (Map pg 27, A3)

The brainchild of the industrialist and philanthropist, R Madhavan Nair, this museum at Edapally is 10 km from the city and showcases the history of the State from the Neolithic Age to the modern period through pieces of sculpture. The one-hour **light and sound show** emphasises the richness of Kerala's past. The gallery of paintings holds 200 pieces of art by contemporary Indian artists and world masters. The **Gallery of Miniatures** is a treasure trove of Indian miniature painting.

Chottanikkara Temple (Map pg 27, B4)

This temple enshrines the Goddess Bhagavathi in three forms – Saraswati (the goddess of learning), draped in white; Bhadrakaali (the fierce and destructive form), dressed in crimson; and Durga (the divine mother), in blue.

Devotees flock to this popular pilgrim centre, and those seeking liberation from torment and mental illness often dance themselves into a frenzy. A **tree nearby is covered in long iron nails**, hammered in by devotees using their foreheads to render troublesome spirits permanently immobile. In the nine-day Makam Thozhal festival, held in February-March, prospective brides and young girls pray for a happy married life.

Note: Entry is restricted to Hindus.

Fort Kochi (Map pg 24, 27-A5)

SIGHTS

Santa Cruz Basilica (Map pg 24, B2)

A monumental structure with a brilliant blue dome, the basilica was built by the Portuguese in 1506 and recognised as a cathedral by Pope Paul

Kochi & Ernakulam | City Map

DON'T MISS

» **Chinese Fishing Nets**
These cantilevered contraptions, lining the Fort Kochi estuary, snare a meagre catch that is sold to beachfront eateries. Chinese fishing nets are also used in Kochi's backwaters.

20 | KERALA MAPS & MORE

SIGHTS AND ATTRACTIONS	Grid
Bishop's House/	
Indo-Portuguese Museum	A4
Bolghatty Island	C1
Durbar Hall & Grounds	D3
Dutch Cemetery	A3
Marine Drive	D2
Mattancherry Palace Museum	B3
Pardesi Synagogue	B4
Parikshith Thampuran Museum	D3
Santa Cruz Basilica	A3
St Francis Church	A3
Vallarpadom Island	B1
Vypeen Island	A2

WHERE TO STAY		
Casino	1	C3
Circle Manor	2	F1
Cochin Tower	3	E1
Gokulam Park Inn	4	E1
Harbour View Residency	5	E4
KTDC Bolgatty Palace	6	C2
Le Meridien	7	E5
Taj Malabar	8	B3
The Renaissance	9	F1
Trident Hilton	10	C3

WHERE TO EAT		
Black Pearl	(see 9)	F1
Chinese Garden	11	F3
Fen Fang	12	E3
Fort Kochi	(see 1)	C3
Pepper	(see 8)	B3
Periyar	(see 4)	E1
Seafood Grill	(see 10)	C3
Tharavad	(see 1)	C3
The Rice Boat	(see 8)	B3
The Thai Pavilion	(see 8)	B3
The Travancore	(see 10)	C4
Zingara	13	E4

BEACHES AND LAKES	
Fort Kochi Beach	A2
Vembanad Lake	B2

MAPS & MORE **KERALA** | 21

DON'T MISS

» **St Francis Church**
Beautifully engraved Dutch and Portuguese tombstones; the ancient rope-operated fans hanging from the ceiling are a rarity.

SIGHTS AND ATTRACTIONS	Grid
Durbar Hall & Grounds	C5
Ernakulathappan (Shiva) Temple	B5
Fine Arts Hall	B6
Marine Drive	A2
Parikshith Thampuran Museum	B5
TD Temple	B2

WHERE TO STAY

Abad Atrium	1	C2
Abad Metro	2	C3
Abad Plaza	3	C2
Avenue Regent	4	C6
Bharath Tourist Home (BTH)	5	B5
Hotel Grand	6	C4
Metropolitan	7	D5
Taj Residency	8	A3
Woodlands	9	C5
Woods Manor	10	C4
Yuvarani Residency	11	C5

WHERE TO EAT

Ambiswamy (Veg)	12	C6
Bimbi's (Veg)	13	C5
Ceylon Bake House	14	C6
Chariot	15	C3
Chicago Restaurant	16	C3
Coffee Beanz	17	A3
DD Food Court	18	C6
Indian Coffee House	19	C5
Luciya's Food Court	20	D3
Pavilion	(see 6)	C4
Peter's Bakery	21	C3
Sree Krishna Inn	22	C6
The Attic Steakhouse	23	A2
The Bubble Café	(see 8)	A3
Utsav	(see 8)	A3

LAKES

Vembanad Lake	A6

IV in 1558. Demolished in 1795 by the British, a new building was commissioned at the same site in 1887 by Bishop Dome Gomes Ferreira and later proclaimed a basilica by Pope John Paul II in 1984.

St Francis Church (Map pg **24**, **A2**)

This is India's first European church built in 1503 by a group of Portuguese Franciscan friars. The history of the church encapsulates the European struggle for power in India. Regular services are conducted through the week in English and Malayalam. The Portuguese explorer, **Vasco da Gama**, was buried here in 1524. Although his remains were taken back to Lisbon 14 years later, the tombstone remains intact.

Dutch Cemetery (Map pg **24**, **A3**)

The derelict granite and red laterite stone tombs of Dutch traders and soldiers lie serenely in a bed of heather bush and thistle under a green canopy. A mute yet sublime remnant of the once thriving European community in Kochi, the Dutch Cemetery, consecrated in 1724, now lies mostly in ruins.

Bishop's House/Indo-Portuguese Museum (Map pg **24**, **B3**)

Resting atop a small hillock close to the Parade Ground, this quaint structure with its grand driveway was built by the Portuguese in 1506 for their governor. Today, it is the residence of the Bishop of Kochi. In the adjacent Indo-Portuguese Museum, precious artefacts collected from various churches are displayed.

Fort Kochi Beach (Map pg **24**, **A2**)

Overlooking the Arabian Sea, with its legendary Chinese fishing nets dotting the foreground, Fort Kochi beach offers views of fiery sunsets. A colourful **carnival on New Year's Day** is a major draw. A novelty here is the waterfront shacks that offer the catch of the day prepared according to taste. Massive granite embankments have been built to arrest sea erosion along the shore.

The Dutch Cemetery near Fort Kochi Beach

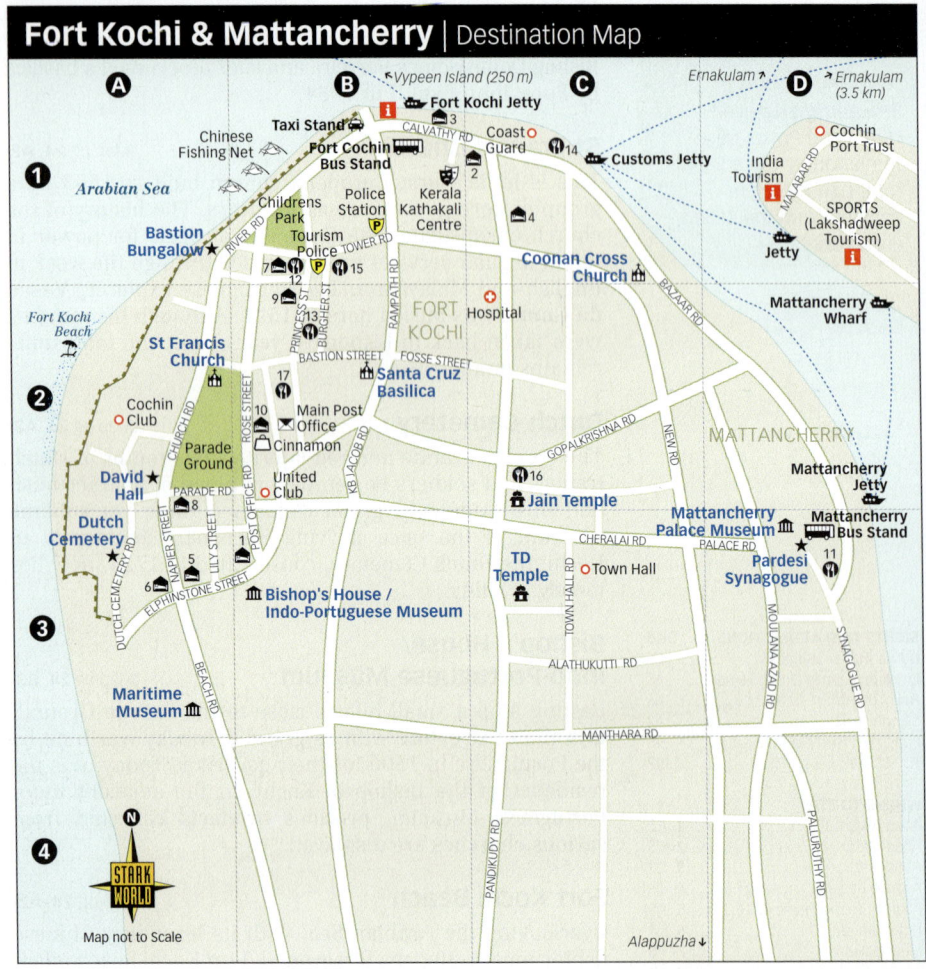

SIGHTS AND ATTRACTIONS	Grid
Bastion Bungalow	A1
Bishop's House/ Indo Portuguese Museum	B3
Coonan Cross Church	C1
David Hall	A2
Dutch Cemetery	A3
Jain Temple	C2
Maritime Museum	A3
Mattancherry Palace Museum	D3
Pardesi Synagogue	D3
Santa Cruz Basilica	B2
St Francis Church	A2
TD Temple	C3

WHERE TO STAY		
Ann's Residency	1	B3
Ballard Bungalow	2	C1
Brunton Boatyard	3	B1
Casa Linda	4	C1
Fort Heritage	5	A3
Kimansion	6	A3
Koder House	7	B1
Malabar House	8	A2
Old Courtyard	9	B2
Trinity Malabar Escapes	10	B2

WHERE TO EAT		
Ann's Residency	(see 1)	B3
Casa Maria	11	D3
Chariot Beach	12	B1
Elite	13	B2
Fort House	14	C1
Kashi Art Cafe	15	B1
Malabar Junction	(see 8)	A2
Rahmutullah (Kayees)	16	C2
Teapot-A Tea Room	17	B2
The History	(see 3)	B1

BEACHES
Fort Kochi Beach A2

DON'T MISS

» World's Oldest Pepper Exchange
Established in 1957, close to the spice market at Mattancherry, this is the only spice exchange in the country.

» Dutch Palace
Sweeping arches, a carved wooden ceiling and intricate murals add to the mystique of this old palace built in the traditional Kerala *naalukettu* style.

24 | KERALA MAPS & MORE

Maritime Museum (Map pg **24**, **A3**)

Established in 2001 to create awareness of India's maritime history, the museum actually consists of two bunkers, as carefully preserved as the exhibits, which have been converted into galleries. One is devoted to the maritime heritage of India through the ages, whereas the other showcases **shipbuilding activities in India, beginning from the Indus Valley civilisation to modern times**.

Mattancherry (Map pg **24, 27-A4**)

SIGHTS

Pardesi Synagogue (Map pg **24**, **D3**)

Constructed in 1568, this synagogue was destroyed in 1662 by cannon fire during a Portuguese raid and was rebuilt two years later when Kochi came under the Dutch yoke.

The 19th century glass chandeliers from Belgium, painted blue willow-patterned Chinese floor tiles from the 18th century, and the gallery for women with its slender gilt columns are interesting features. A 4th century copper plate carries the Maharaja's inscription in Malayalam, but in the unique *kannadiezhuthu* script that is decipherable only with the aid of a mirror.

Clock tower (Map pg **24**, **D3**)

Built in 1760 by Ezekiel Rahabi, an affluent Jewish businessman, the clock tower stands next to the synagogue. This is a great mystery as Jewish tradition does not have the custom of ringing bells.

Made 200 years after the synagogue, the clock has **four faces** – the one facing the Maharaja's palace showed time in Malayalam, another etched in Roman numerals was meant for the traders, the third side that faced the synagogue was in Hebrew, and the fourth side was kept mysteriously blank. Although it stopped working after the 1930s, the World Monument Fund has recently restored it.

Antique Shops in Jew Street (Map pg **24**, **D3**)

With the return of the Jews to Israel, their dwellings fell into disrepair and many were torn down to make way for newer

Displays crowd a shop window in Jew Street

structures. Anything that could be salvaged – **woodwork, furniture, artefacts, vessels and brass work** – of both utility and aesthetic value, found their way into antique shops that sprang up in the meandering alleys of Jew Town. Increasing demand, spurred on by tourism, brought traditional and contemporary bric-a-brac from all over the country into these shops.

Spice Market (Map pg **24**, **D3**)

Jew Street in Mattancherry is saturated with the smell of ginger, cardamom, cloves and pepper, thanks to the spice market that still survives. Trucks feed pushcarts that transport sackloads of spices in and out of the warehouses that line the narrow streets. Traders haggle frantically as workers dry, sort and pack the spices for retail.

Thirumala Devaswom Temple (Map pg **24**, **C3**)

Built in 1599, the temple houses the idol of Venkatachalapathi Thirumala Devar, believed to be responsible for the prosperity of the **Konkani community** that flourished in trade and commerce. Both temple and idol have had a chequered history and have been plundered and restored time and again.

Note: Entry is restricted to Hindus. Men have to wear a mundu.

Willingdon Island (Map pg **21**, **C4**)

This man-made island lies nestled in the backwaters between mainland Ernakulam and Mattancherry. Named after the Viceroy of India, Lord Willingdon, the 775-acre island was created from soil dredged up while deepening Kochi's harbour in 1928. The man responsible for this engineering feat was a visionary, Sir Robert Bristow.

The island is home to the Cochin Port Trust and the headquarters of the Southern Naval Command. There are also top-end luxury hotels such as the Taj Malabar, Trident Hilton and Casino Hotel.

A cluster of four other islands – **Vypeen, Gundu, Vallarpadom** and **Bolgatty** – crowd the creek where the large Vembanad Lake flows into the Arabian Sea.

SIGHTS
SNC Maritime Museum

This museum was established in 1989 to display the different maritime activities of the Indian naval forces. The star attraction is the *vallom* (boat) made of **a single piece of wood**, the *thampakam*. Once owned by the Raja of Ambalappuzha, it is said to be over 300 years old.

AROUND KOCHI

» Cherai Beach (Map pg **27**, **A2**)
Located on the northern end of Vypeen Island, about 25 km from the city, this is an idyllic beach without the crowds. Beach resorts abound.

» Athirappally Waterfalls (Map pg **28**, **D4**)
Amid lush green foliage at the entrance of the Sholayar forests, the Chalakudy River tumbles down to the dark granite below, a charming sight.

» Bhoothathankettu (Map pg **27**, **D2**)
Located 50 km from Ernakulam town, Bhoothathankettu is a scenic dam site with boating facilities and is surrounded by a vast virgin forest.

» Kumbalangi (Map pg **27**, **A4**)
A tiny village facing the Kochi backwaters in the western part of city, it is the first eco-friendly tourist village in India Kalagraamam, the artists' village, is a major attraction.

» Chendamangalam (Map pg **27**, **A2**)
Known for its unique geography, Chendamangalam, 42 km from Ernakulam, has three rivers, seven inlets, hillocks and vast green plains. This land was once the home of the Paliath Achans, the prime ministers of the rajas of Kochi. Their residence, the Paliam Palace, houses a collection of historical documents and relics.

ESSENTIAL INFORMATION

» **District:** Ernakulam

» **STD Code:** 0484

» **Location:** 218 km north of Thiruvananthapuram.

» **Climate:** Humid throughout the year. Torrential rains during the monsoons (June to September) follow the scorching heat of summer (March to June).

» **When to go:** September to February.

» **KSRTC bus stand:** 0484-236 0531

» **Ernakulam Town Railway Station**
0484- 239 5198

» **Ernakulam Junction Railway Station**
0484-237 5431

» **Cochin International Airport**
0484-261 0115

» **Department of Tourism**
Government of Kerala, Main Office, Shanmugham Rd (near St Theresa's College), Ernakulam 0484-236 0502

» **KTDC Tourist Reception Centre**
Opp Hotel Taj Residency, Shanmugham Rd, Ernakulam 0484-235 3234

» **District Tourism Promotion Council**
Old Collectorate Building, Park Avenue Rd, Ernakulam 0484-236 7334

Ernakulam | District Map

SIGHTS AND ATTRACTIONS	Grid
Chendamangalam (historical place)	A2
Chottanikkara (temple)	B4
Edapally (Museum of Kerala History)	A3
Fort Kochi	A4
Kaladi (Adi Shankaracharya Temple)	B2
Kodanad (elephant training centre)	C2
Kumbalangi (model tourism village)	A4
Malayattoor (church)	C2
Mattancherry (historical place)	A4
Thattekkad Bird Sanctuary	D3
Thripunithura (Hill Palace Museum)	B3
Veega Land (amusement park)	B3
Vypeen Island	A3

BEACHES AND LAKES
Cherai Beach	A2
Vembanad Lake	B4

DAMS
Bhoothathankettu Dam	D2

DON'T MISS

» Kumbalangi
Just 25 km from Kochi, Kumbalangi, a tiny village facing the Kochi harbour, was the first designated ecotourism village in India. Homestays abound.

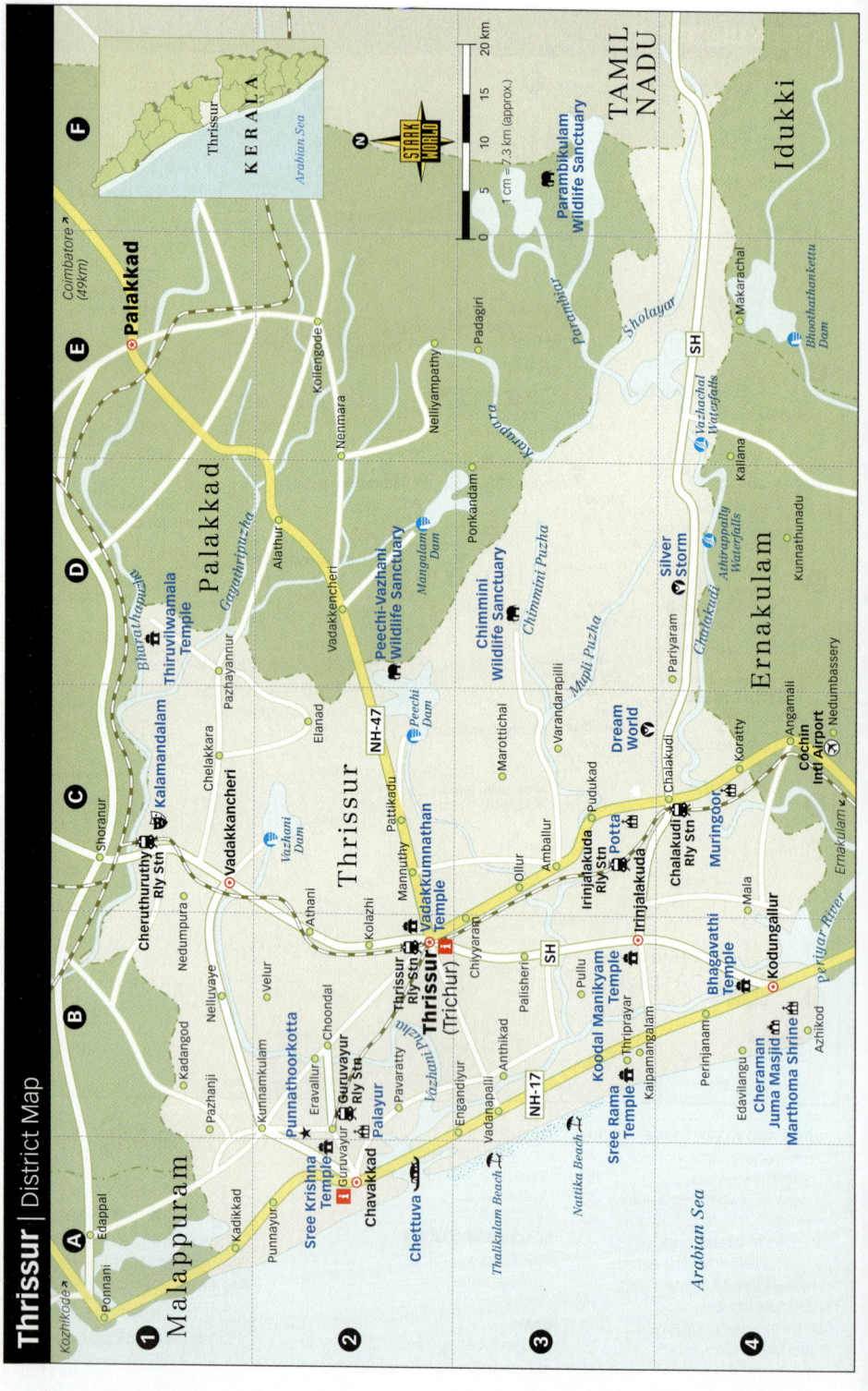

Getaway

Thrissur
(Map pg **28**, **B2**)

Thrissur is considered the cultural capital of the State. Home to several prominent art institutions, this is where the extravagant Pooram festival is held annually.

Getting There

By Air
The nearest is Cochin International Airport, 58 km
☎ 0484–261 0115

By Rail
Thrissur is an important railhead of the Southern Railways and is connected to all major towns in Kerala and the major cities of India ☎ 0487–242 3150

By Road
Well connected by highways with Thiruvananthapuram and Coimbatore. The KSRTC bus stand operates long distance and inter-State services ☎ 0487–242 1842

SIGHTS

Sakthan Thampuran Palace (Map pg **28**, **B2**)
Of historical, architectural and cultural importance, this palace of the erstwhile Maharaja of Cochin has been converted into a heritage museum. It has the **largest collection of excavated megalithic material in Kerala**.

The State Museum and Zoo (Map pg **28**, **B2**)
Built in 1885 and covering an area of 13.5 acres, the Art Museum, the Natural History Museum and the zoo are located at Chembukavu.

Vadakkumnathan Temple (Map pg **28**, **B2**)
One of the most revered temples in Kerala, a lofty stone wall and four imposing *gopurams* enfold the Vadakkumnathan Temple and its cover of sacred medicinal trees. In a unique ritual, ghee, or clarified butter, is poured over the Shiva *linga* every day.

Basilica of Our Lady of Dolores (Map pg **28**, **B2**)
With its three-storied façade and even higher steeples towering above the town's skyline, this is claimed to be the **largest and highest church in Asia**. It is adorned with Gothic towers and an array of 15 altars and church bells imported from Germany.

Martha Mariyam Chaldean Church (Map pg **28**, **B2**)
What makes this church distinctive is the absence of idols or pictorial representations of Christ. A cross is the only symbol here. This is a church that still follows the old rites and holds Mass in Syriac.

Lourdes Cathedral (Map pg **28**, **B2**)
This is one of three most important churches in Thrissur. Established in 1885, it was given the status of a cathedral in 1891. A flight of steps from the altar leads to an **underground prayer chamber**.

The crowds at Thrissur Pooram

SIGHTS AND ATTRACTIONS Grid
Bhagavathi Temple B4
Cheraman Juma Masjid B4
Chettuva Backwaters A2
Chimmini Wildlife Sanctuary D3
Dream World (amusement park) C3
Irinjalakuda (Koodal
Manikyam Temple) B3
Kerala Kalamandalam
(centre for arts) C1
Marthoma Shrine B4
Muringoor (retreat centre) C4
Palayur Church B2
Parambikulam Wildlife Sanctuary F3
Peechi-Vazhani Wildlife Sanctuary ... D2
Potta (retreat centre) C3
Punnathoorkotta (elephant
training centre) B2
Silver Storm (amusement park) D4
Sree Krishna Temple (Guruvayur) A2
Thiruvilwamala Temple D1
Sree Rama Temple (Thriprayar) B3
Vadakkumnathan Kshetram B2

WATERFALLS AND DAM
Athirappally Waterfalls D4
Peechi Dam C2
Vazhachal Waterfalls E4

BEACHES
Nattika Beach B3

Getaway

Kodungallur
(Map pg 28, B4)

The ancient port town of Kodungallur, once called 'Cranganore', echoes with the tales of an illustrious past in which legends and history become one.
A busy port town once, it is a quiet, picturesque place today, with a bustling fishing centre at nearby Azhikode. The town's ancient shrines beckon the devout.

SIGHTS

Cheraman Perumal Juma Masjid (Map pg 28, B4)
This mosque is believed to have been built in the seventh century at the behest of King Cheraman Perumal, who embraced Islam and later went to Mecca. Rebuilt and renovated over the years, the masjid still retains some of its original interiors.

Mar Thoma Pontifical Shrine (Map pg 28, B4)
Located at a vantage point on the edge of the backwaters at Azhikode Jetty, this shrine was built to commemorate the arrival of St Thomas the Apostle at Kodungallur. Built in the form of a semicircle, the small church in the centre is flanked by statues of the saints.

Kurumba Bhagavathi Temple (Map pg 28, B4)
Kali is the main idol of this temple complex. The majestic six-foot-high wooden image of Kali, her eight hands with their deadly weapons, and face covered by a mask, is **carved out of a jackfruit tree**. Bharani and Thalappoli are the famous annual festivals and attract pilgrims.

Kodungallur Bharani festival

Shiva Temple (Map pg 28, B4)
The Mahadeva Temple, dedicated to Shiva, is located in the same area as the Cheraman Juma Masjid. Inside the enclosure are a large multi-tiered metal lamp and a porch adorned with carvings dedicated to the heroes of the *Ramayana*. The shrine is a fine example of Kerala's famous temple architecture.

Koodalmanikyam Temple, Irinjalakuda (Map pg 28, B3)
Bharata, Rama's brother, is the deity of this temple. It is an **architectural marvel** with imposing gateways, round sanctum sanctorum and a marvellous *koothambalam*. Exquisite woodcarvings and granite friezes on the outer walls and the murals on the other walls are distinctive.

Sree Rama Temple, Thriprayar (Map pg 28, B3)
Built in the same architectural style as the Vadakkumnathan Temple, the exquisite sculpture here is noteworthy, as are the 24 panels of woodcarvings and several ancient murals. The circular sanctum sanctorum has several sculptural representations of scenes from the great epic, the *Ramayana*.

Getting There

By Air
The nearest is Cochin International Airport, 38 km
0484–261 0115

By Rail
The nearest railhead is Irinjalakuda, 15 km
0480–288 1243

By Road
About 35 km from Thrissur, at the intersection of the SH (linking Thrissur) and NH 17. Buses are available from Shakthan Thampuran bus stand.

Getaway

Guruvayur
(Map pg **28**, **B2**)

Guruvayur is a noted pilgrim centre. Even its local name, 'Bhuloka Vaikuntha', means 'the place where the spiritual world meets the earth', referring to its status as a holy town. Devotees throng the small town during the pilgrimage season.

Getting There

By Air
The nearest is Cochin International Airport, 90 km
0484–261 0115

By Rail
Thrissur is the nearest major station, 30 km
0487–242 3150

By Road
Well connected by private and KSRTC buses. Frequent trips to Thrissur.

SIGHTS

Sree Krishna Temple
(Map pg **28**, **A2**)

An air of piety pervades the atmosphere around the Sree Krishna Temple in Guruvayur where thousands of devotees wait in long queues for a fleeting glimpse of Guruvayurappan. It is **Kerala's largest shrine** and South India's second largest revenue earner. A 33.5-m tall gold-plated *dwajasthambha*, or flagstaff, stands in front of the temple.

Note: Entry is restricted to Hindus.

Punnathoor Kotta
(Map pg **28**, **B2**)

The palace grounds of the erstwhile Punnathoor rajas, it is home to more than 60 elephants, all gifted by devotees, and the only one of its kind in the world.
0487–255 6004

Palayur Church
(Map pg **28**, **B2**)

This is said to be the oldest among the churches established by St Thomas the Apostle, who is believed to have arrived in Kerala in 52 AD. Numerous life-sized granite statues depicting the life of the saint adorn the entrance of this building.

Krishnanattam, a sixteenth-century classical art form, is staged within the Sree Krishna Temple premises

Moplah women in their traditional finery

Kozhikode
A warm and friendly ambience...

Getting There

By Air
Calicut International Airport, 25 km
☎ 0483–271 1314

By Rail
Kozhikode railway station connects to all major cities
☎ 0495–270 3822

By Road
NH 17 and State highways connect the city to all destinations in Kerala and in the neighbouring states.
(KSRTC Bus stand ☎ 0495–272 3796)

Vasco da Gama landed in Kozhikode in 1498, thus putting it on the world map. Today, this great port of yesteryears is popular for its historical sites, unique culture, and warm and friendly ambience. Despite the urban sprawl, this charming coastal city is awash in glorious history.

The Arabs, who were the earliest traders to visit the shores of Kozhikode, called it 'Kalikut', a name later anglicised to 'Calicut' by the Europeans. The Italian explorer, Marco Polo, eulogised its virtues, whereas the Arab traveller and chronicler, Ibn Batuta, called it 'one of the great ports of the Malabar District where traders from all parts are found'. In the wake of the Portuguese, followed the Dutch, French and the British, who waged ceaseless war against the Zamorin kings, and later, among themselves, to gain control over this '**Jewel of the Malabar**'.

Adding to the sizeable Muslim population of Kozhikode today, are two other communities – the Hindus and the Christians. Ancient temples, mosques and churches are found all over, keeping alive rituals and traditions that go back a long time. The legacy of the broad-minded, tolerant Zamorin kings, once the town's rulers, lives on in the lanes and by lanes, in the bazaars and business hubs, through myriad events and festivals, and in the attitude of the ever accommodating local populace.

Highlights

Lacking the cosmopolitan air of a large city, Kozhikode carries its history on its sleeve. Many celebrated landmarks dot its landscape, while pockets of urban sprawl and the buzz of business lend it a modern air, albeit with a dash of endearing rusticity.

A plaque on the beach at Kappad commemorates the arrival of Vasco da Gama in Kozhikode

Kozhikode (Calicut) | City Map

SIGHTS AND ATTRACTIONS	Grid
Church of South India	C3
COMTRUST (Weaving Factory)	B3
English Church	B2
Kuttichira Tank	B4
Light House	A3
Mananchira Square	B3
Mishkal Mosque	B4
Mother of God Cathedral	B3
Planetarium	C2
Tali Temple	C4

WHERE TO STAY		
Asma Tower	1	D3
Beach Hotel	2	B3
Calicut Towers	3	C2
Fortune	4	B1
Hyson Heritage	5	B3
Maharani	6	D3
Malabar Gate	7	D4
Malabar Palace	8	C3
Sea Queen	9	B3
Taj Residency	10	B3

WHERE TO EAT		
Abi's Food Shop	11	B3
Bombay Restaurant and Bakery	12	B3
Coral Reef	(see 10)	B3
Dakshin	13	C3
Indian Coffee House	14	C4
Malabar Court	(see 4)	B1
Mamas 'n' Papas	15	A3
Mezban	(see 1)	D3
New Cochin Bakery	16	C3
New Top Form	17	C4
Paragon	18	B3
Sagar	19	C2
Zains	20	B3

BEACHES		
Kozhikode Beach		A3

DON'T MISS

» COMTRUST
Set up in 1844 by pioneering German missionaries from the Basel Mission, this factory is busy producing world-class upholstery.

» SM Street
SM Street, or Sweet Meat street, bustles with shops selling almost everything under the sun – as well as the famed halva, a soft glutinous delicacy.

MAPS & MORE KERALA | 33

SIGHTS

Beach Road (Map pg 33, A3)

A stretch of nearly 3 km skirting the beach, this boulevard is quiet during the heat of day, except for the marine aquarium at the northern end, which draws a few visitors. At sundown, people wander on to the promenade, and pushcarts, vending an assortment of snacks and eatables, emerge from the adjoining streets. Scattered beachfront eateries and ice cream parlours too, stir to life.

Note: Take a walk to Dolphin's Point at dawn to spot frolicking dolphins.

Mananchira Square (Map pg 33, B3)

The heart of the city and the hub of shopping and local transport, this square is surrounded by important landmarks such as the bust of the renowned Malayalam writer, SK Pottekkad, the popular SM Street, swarming with shoppers, and the pleasing brick-and-tile public library.

Note: Sweet Meat Street is choc-a-bloc with shops selling almost everything you might want to lay your hands on and is known specially for its famed halva, a glutinous local sweet dish.

Mishkal Mosque (Map pg 33, B4)

An architectural and historical landmark, the mosque was constructed by the rich Arab businessman and ship-owner, Nakhooda Mishkal, nearly 700 years ago. Built extensively out of wood, it is supported on 24 carved pillars and sports 47 doors. The intricate carvings on the ceilings and doors, *gopuram* style entrance arches, and the absence of minarets is reminiscent of **Kerala's temple architecture**.

The elegant façade of the Mother of God Cathedral

Mother of God Cathedral (Map pg 33, B3)

This 18th century Gothic cathedral, built by Jesuit missionaries, has a 200-year-old portrait of St Mary adorning its walls. The shrine stands as a tribute to **Italian expertise** (Italian architects are believed to have designed it) and Indian skill.

The adjoining cemetery holds old gravestones such as that of the first Catholic missionary of Kozhikode, Rev Pedro de Covilhany, who arrived here on May 20, 1498.

☎ 0495–236 6301

Tali Temple (Map pg 33, C4)

Built in the 14th century by the Zamorin king, Manavikraman, on the site of an earlier temple, this shrine is located about one and a half kilometres east of Mananchira Square close to Palayam market. It has elaborate carvings on wooden roofs and intricate bas-relief on the walls of the sanctum sanctorum. The temple is the venue of **Revathi Pattathanam**, an annual cultural and intellectual event.

☎ 0495–270 3610

CSI Church (Map pg 33, C3)

Built in 1842 as the **largest Basel Mission church** in the Malabar region, this shrine in the heart of the city is today's CSI Church. The architecture is a **mix of European and Kerala styles**. The church has a three-tiered turret atop the arched entrance porch and the main hall, and a cluster of rooms to the back and sides, all with peaked, tiled roofs. It owns the only pipe organ among all the dioceses in Kerala – a gift from St Ayden's Church in England.

☎ 0495–272 4572

Muchundipalli (Map pg 33, B4)

Constructed in the 13th century, this is the **oldest mosque in the city**, and has a stone slab inscribed in the ancient *vattezhuthu* (early Malayalam) script, narrating the story of a Zamorin king's donation of land. The building stands on a plinth, 1.5 m tall, and sports a double-tiered roof with an ornamental gable. the outer walls have elaborate beams that support a coffered ceiling with intricate and beautiful woodcarvings.

Planetarium and Science Centre (Map pg 33, C2)

This 250-seater planetarium at the city's Jaffar Khan Colony is a must-see. The sophisticated **Zeiss projector** simulates the night sky.

The entomology section, '**Giants of Nature**', at the Regional Science Centre, has huge working models of garden insects, bugs and arthropods that simulate natural movements and is popular with visitors.

0495–277 0571

Pazhassiraja Museum and Art Gallery (Map pg 36, B4)

Built in 1812, it was known as the East Hill Bungalow, but was later renamed in 1980 after Pazhassiraja Raja Kerala Varma of the Kottayam royal family. On display is a **rare collection** of copies of ancient murals, bronzes, old coins, excavated earthenware, models of temples and megalithic monuments such as rock-cut caves, crypts, umbrella stones and burial urns.

Next door is the art gallery, which exhibits an excellent collection of paintings by Raja Ravi Varma and his uncle, Raja Rama Varma. The Krishna Menon Museum is also located here.

0495–238 4382

Valayanadu Devi Kshetram (Map pg 36, B4)

This old shrine, located in Valayanadu, Govindapuram, was built in the 14th century. The most important festival of the temple, held in the Malayalam month of Makaram (December-January) and lasting eight days, attracts hundreds of devotees.

Note: Entry is restricted to Hindus.

Kallai (Map pg 36, B4)

A once bustling centre of Malabar's timber trade, this town is on the banks of the Kallai River, 6 km from the city. Kallai has its own old-world charm and you can still see timber being rolled into the river from the few timber yards along the banks. Logs are sent down along the gently flowing river from as far away as Nilambur in the Western Ghats.

AROUND KOZHIKODE

» KIRTADS (Map pg 36, B4)
The Kerala Institute for Research, Training and Development Studies of scheduled castes and scheduled tribes works with the objective of promoting the development of the marginalised sections of society.

» Beypore (Map pg 36, B5)
A coastal village, it is known for its boat-building expertise, a tradition that goes back 1,500 years. Boats constructed at Beypore are known to have sailed to various corners of the globe.

» Tasara Creative Weaving Centre (Map pg 36, B5)
This centre creates works of art in handloom – rugs, durries, wall hangings and bedspreads. People also stay here for extended periods to learn painting, designing and weaving.

» Payyoli Beach (Map pg 36, A3)
The endangered Olive Ridley turtles come to lay eggs in this secluded palm-fringed beach during November-December. One and a half kilometres north, the sand bank at the estuary of the Moorad River is a haven for birds.

» Kappad Beach (Map pg 36, B4)
A plaque proclaims that this is where Vasco da Gama first set foot on Indian soil. Historians are of the opinion, however, that he actually landed at the nearby Panthalayini Kollam.

» Kadalundi (Map pg 36, B5)
Consisting of 25 acres of mudflats at the Kadalundi river estuary, this is a wetland habitat for migratory and terrestrial birds and a haven for environmentalists. It is about 25 km from Kozhikode.

» Panthalayini Kollam (Map pg 36, B3)
According to some accounts, Vasco da Gama first landed on Indian soil in this historical village north of Koyilandi. Once frequented by Roman ships, the legendary Ibn Batuta referred to the town as 'Fandaraina'.

» Velliamkallu (Map pg 36, A3)
An adventurous boat ride takes you to this massive rock formation looming up from the sea, 36 km from Kozhikode, off the Payyoli Beach. Strangely shaped rocks, sitting on equally odd-looking boulders, bear the marks of cannon balls from numerous wars.

Kozhikode | District Map

DON'T MISS

» Mananchira Square
The heart of the city, it is surrounded by important landmarks. The bustling Sweet Meat Street, popular with locals, is close at hand.

SIGHTS AND ATTRACTIONS	Grid
Beypore (uru making)	B5
Chevayur (KIRTADS-Museum)	B4
East Hill (Museums and Art Gallery)	B4
Kadalundi Bird Sanctuary	B5
Kallai	B4
Kodakkal (Umbrella Stone)	B3
Lokanarkavu Temple	A2
Panthalayini Kollam	B3
Tasara (weaving centre)	B5
Thikkodi Light House	A3
Velliamkallu Island (Sacrifice Rock)	A3

BEACHES

Beypore Beach	B5
Kappad Beach	B4
Kozhikode Beach	B4
Payyoli Beach (Theeram)	A3

WATERFALLS AND DAMS

Peruvannamuzhi Dam	B2
Thusharagiri Waterfall	D3

36 | KERALA MAPS & MORE

ESSENTIAL INFORMATION

» **District:** Kozhikode (earlier Calicut)

» **STD Code:** 0495

» **Location:** Towards the northern part of the State about 8 hrs from Bangalore by road.

» **Climate:** Humid throughout the year. Summers (March through May) are hot. Monsoons set in around June and extend to September.

» **When to go:** September to December

» **KSRTC bus stand:** 0495–272 3796

» **Railway station:** 0495–270 3822

» **Calicut International Airport**
0483–271 1314

» **Tourist offices**
Kozhikode railway station
0495–270 2606
Calicut International Airport
0483–271 1314
DTPC
0495–272 0012

IN AND AROUND Kozhikode

Getaway

Mahe
(Map pg **104**, **C5**)

A charming little town with a distinctively French flavour, it is located 58 km north of Kozhikode and is bisected by the Mahe River. Originally the town was called 'Mayyazhi'; it was renamed 'Mahe' after the Frenchman who captured it. Mahe was an important trading centre under the French. Today a union territory, it is free of the strict government control on alcohol, which means there is no dearth of wine shops here.

Getting There

By Air
The nearest is Calicut International Airport, 58 km
0483–271 1314

By Rail
Connected to Kannur (0497–2705555) in the north and Kozhikode (0495–270 3822) in the south.

By Road
Mahe is well connected by NH 17 to Kannur and Kozhikode.

SIGHTS

Malayala Kalagramam
(Map pg **104**, **C5**)

Located just across the bridge on the Kerala side, in New Mahe, the Malayala Kalagramam is a **centre of fine arts** that was established to preserve the cultural heritage of the Malabar region and to create an avenue for the creative energies of its people. A range of disciplines, from dance, music, sculpture, art and graphic art to yoga and meditation are taught here.

St Teresa's Church
(Map pg **104**, **C5**)

Considered **one of the oldest** in Malabar, this church was first erected in 1736 by an Italian, Father Dominic. In the 1760 Franco-British war, the shrine suffered extensive damage. Abbe Duchenin then rebuilt it in 1788. St Teresa's annual feast, held in October, draws pilgrims from all over Kerala and abroad.

St Teresa's Church – all spruced up for Christmas

MAPS & MORE **KERALA** | 37

Getaway

Thalassery
(Map pg **104**, **C5**)

This historical coastal town is located 45 km north of Kozhikode at the site of the first British settlement on the Malabar Coast. It is also famous for its three c's – circus, cake and cricket.

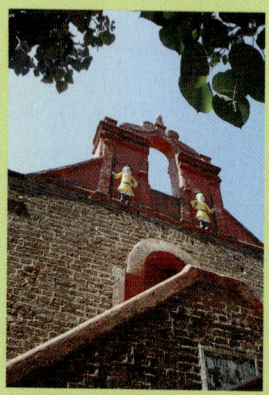

The lofty walls of the famous Thalassery Fort

Getting There

By Air
The nearest is Calicut International Airport, 64 km
☎ 0483–271 1314

By Rail
Thalassery station is served by all trains that pass through Kannur
☎ 0490–234 4131

By Road
The town is well connected by road to all major destinations to the north and south. The nearest KSRTC bus stand is Kannur.
☎ 0497–270 5960

SIGHTS

Thalassery Fort
(Map pg **104**, **C5**)

Built in 1708, on a headland facing the sea, the Thalassery Fort has massive laterite walls, turrets and bastions on the flanks. **Secret tunnels that lead to the sea** are now blocked and the small lighthouse on the flank also lies disused. Old cellars, in which pepper was once stored, hark back to the times when Thalassery was the hub of a lucrative pepper trade.

Dharmadom Island
(Map pg **104**, **C5**)

This lush, palm-fringed island covers five acres and is locally called *pacha thuruth* (green island). It sits beyond the confluence of the Anjanakandi and Thalassery rivers, just 100 m from the sandy beach of Dharmapattanam, itself cut off from the mainland by rivers on three sides and the sea to the west.

Muzhappilangad Beach
(Map pg **104**, **C5**)

Situated 8 km north of Thalassery, this **drive-through beach** – nearly 4 km of tightly packed wet sand – allows vehicles to whiz by. Black rocks strewn across the palm-fringed shore offer protection against the currents and shallow waters make it ideal for swimming.

Odathil Palli
(Map pg **104**, **C5**)

The rulers donated a piece of land in the heart of Thalassery, just half a kilometre from where the fort stands today, to a rich Arab merchant who built a mosque on the site. This shrine is nearly 500 years old and displays a mix of Hindu and Islamic architecture.

The serene Muzhappilangad Beach

38 | KERALA MAPS & MORE

Vasco da gama
1498

Stock Images | Customised Publishing | Online Guides | Travel Films | Travel Magazines | Theme Guides | Destination Books

Kerala

Your journey begins here.

STARK WORLD

www.starkworld.net

Backwaters
Amazing waterways...

Highlights

A network of interlinked canals, lakes, streams and estuaries that run just inland of the long coast, sometimes separated from the sea only by narrow sand banks, form the backwaters of Kerala. People live all along its banks, cultivating the fertile lands, and sustaining themselves through diverse vocations ranging from fishing, coir making, and toddy tapping to transporting men and goods along this labyrinthine water world.

Trading on the tranquil waterways

Kerala is a land of copious rainfall. Once the earth is saturated, the overflow runs into canals and streams, the rolling water surging ceaselessly through hills and mountain passes to flow into the forty odd rivers in the State. This labyrinthine network of rivers, canals, streams and lagoons constitute the famous backwaters of Kerala.

Innumerable water bodies from minor tanks to large lakes such as the Vembanad give life to this **unique eco-system**. Two permanent outlets to the sea – and many breaches in the narrow sand banks in between – provide drainage to the seven large lakes in the area.

Cultivation, fishing, coir and toddy making sustain the local populace, who live on slivers of land just large enough to accommodate a thatched house and a boat shed. Everything from bathing and washing clothes to cleaning fish is done on the banks. Small bridges span the canals intermittently, but since larger ones are few, paddle boats and dugout canoes constitute the chief mode of transportation. In many cases, they provide the only link between remote, isolated villages and crowded towns.

National Waterway No. 3, from Kollam to Kottapuram, covers a distance of 205 km and runs almost parallel to the coastline of southern Kerala, thus facilitating both cargo movement and backwater tourism. Regular ferry services connect most locations on either bank. Further north,

Striking in their serenity, the enchanting backwaters of Kerala

ferries run by the government criss-cross the length of Vembanad Lake, connecting Kochi with neighbouring tongues of land.

Paddy Fields below sea level

To prevent the ingress of sea water, a barrage has been built across the Vembanad Lake near Kumarakom. During the dry season, water levels may actually drop a few feet below sea level in the backwaters. Paddy is grown extensively on backwater-reclaimed loamy soil, secured by the endlessly long dikes bordering acres of land. Paddy cultivation below the sea level is perhaps a unique phenomenon.

Backwater Tourism

A leisurely boat ride along these unique waterways remains one of the most memorable experiences of a traveller. Offering charming picture-postcard scenes of the interplay between earth and water, a trip to the backwaters of Kerala is a must. Traditional punted boats, or the more elaborate *kettuvalloms*, are the recommended means of travel. The reflection of lines of slender coconut trees in the water, tropical greenery, and the vignettes of life along the banks, are all classic Kerala.

Coir Making

Coir making is an important vocation in the region, as it is in many villages throughout Kerala. The process begins with the fibrous husk of the coconut that is extracted after the nut is removed. Mounds of husk are kept submerged in water for up to nine months. This allows the stuff to rot and the tightly fused fibres open up. Next, the softened husk is pounded with an iron rod or fed into a de-husking machine to separate the fibre. Finally, the mass is fed into a combing machine that separates individual fibres and discards the pith. The loose fibres are dried in the sun and bundled into bales. These are later twisted on a simple machine to form ropes.

Toddy shops on stilts

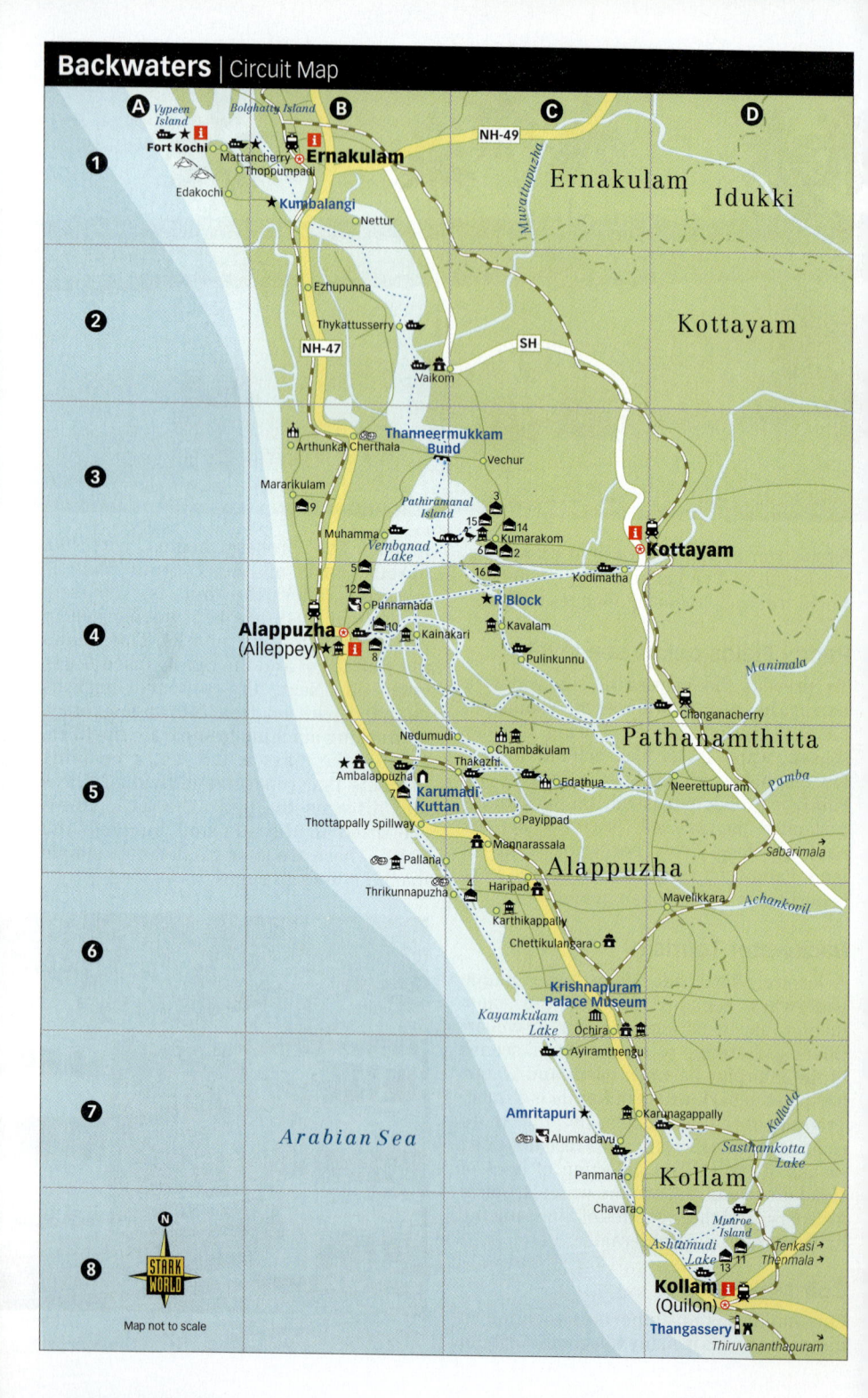

Backwaters | Circuit Map

42 | KERALA MAPS & MORE

SIGHTS & ATTRACTIONS	Grid
Alappuzha	B4
Ambalappuzha (Temple, Kunjan Nambiar Memorial	B5
Amritapuri (Mata Amritanandamayi math)	C7
Arthunkal (church)	B3
Bolghatty Island	A1
Chambakulam Church	C5
Chettikulangara (temple)	C6
Edathua Church	C5
Fort Kochi	A1
Haripad Temple	C6
Karumadi Kuttan (Buddha's statue)	B5
Krishnapuram PalaceMuseum	C6
Kumarakom (backwaters, bird sanctuary)	C4
Kumbalangi (model tourism village)	B1
Mannarassala Temple	C5
Mattancherry	A1
Munroe Island	D7
Ochira (temple)	C6
Pathiramanal (island)	B3
R Block	C4
Thanneermukkam Bund	B3
Thangassery (fort, lighthouse)	D8
Vaikom Temple	B2
Vypeen Island	A1

WHERE TO STAY		
Ashtamudi Lake Resort	1	D7
Backwater Ripples	2	C3
Coconut Lagoon	3	C3
Coir Village	4	C6
Kayaloram	5	B4
Kumarakom Lake Resort	6	C3
Kuttanad Resort	7	B5
Lake Palace	8	B4
Marari Beach Resort	9	B3
Palm Grove	10	B4
Palm Lagoon	11	D8
Punnamada Resort	12	B4
Saraovaram	13	D8
Taj Garden Retreat	14	C3
Waterscapes	15	C3
Whispering Palms	16	C4

LAKES	
Ashtamudi Lake	D8
Kayamkulam Lake	C6
Sasthamkotta Lake	D7
Vembanad Lake	B3

Snake Boat Races

At one time, boats were the only mode of transport in the backwaters. The advent of roads changed that. Much later, tourism heralded another change – rice boats metamorphosed into houseboats, and the slender snake boats, or *chundan vallom*, used by local kings to ferry soldiers during waterfront wars, spawned a new sport, the boat race. Over 100 ft long, the raised prow of this boat stands 10 ft above water and resembles a snake's hood.

Boat races are occasions of great excitement and entertainment that allow the oarsmen to prove their awesome physical prowess to the thousands gathered to watch. Most of these races are held in the water-logged Kuttanad region of Alappuzha.

As one story goes, when Jawaharlal Nehru visited Kerala in 1952, four traditional chundan valloms went to receive him. A mock snake boat race was also organised. Nehru was so fascinated that once he returned to Delhi, he sent a gleaming silver trophy for a boat race, duly named after him. Since then, the race has become a most prestigious one. Even today, boats race a one and a half kilometre stretch in four columns. The annual Nehru Trophy boat race begins during the harvest festival of Onam in August. Powered by over 100 muscular oarsmen, the slender crafts streak across the Punnamada Lake in Alappuzha, accompanied by feverish drumbeats and the cheers of thousands of spectators.

Powered by many oarsmen, the chundan participates in the Nehru Trophy boat race

Getting There

By Air
The nearest is Thiruvananthapuram International Airport, 70 km
☎ 0471-250 1424

By Rail
The Kollam railway junction is connected to all major towns in Kerala ☎ 0474-274 6194

By Road
Kollam is well connected by three national highways – NH 47, NH 208 and NH 17. Private and KSRTC buses frequently ply to all cities, towns and villages in Kerala.

Ferry Services
A government ferry service, operating from near the bus stand, connects all villages and towns along the backwaters.

FACT FILE

District: Kollam

STD code: 0474

When to go: August to March-end

For information contact
District Tourism Promotion Council
✉ Near KSRTC bus stand
☎ 0474-275 0170
🕐 7.30 am to 9 pm

A fisherman, ready with his net and fish basket

Kollam

(Map pg **46**, **B3**)

Eulogised by travellers such as Marco Polo and Ibn Batuta (who called it one of the leading trade capitals of the Old World), Kollam is where the famed network of waterways begins. The Ashtamudi Lake, known as the gateway to the backwaters, covers about 30 per cent of Kollam. From here, a 130 km long system of interlinked canals and lakes snakes up all the way to the north.

Coconut husk is soaked for months before processing into coir

Kollam is also regarded as the hub of **cashew processing** and the centre of the **fisheries industry** in Kerala. Moreover, over 2,000 factories and industrial units churning out products as diverse as coir, chemicals, ceramics, minerals and seafood make it the most industrialised district of the State.

SIGHTS

Alumkadavu Boat Building Yard (Map pg **46**, **A2**)
Located on the northern backwaters of Kollam, near Karunagappally, the famous *kettuvalloms*, or houseboats, are crafted here. Known as a boat-building and repairing centre, Alumkadavu is also popular as the ideal location to watch coir being made.

Mata Amritanandamayi Ashram (Map pg **46**, **A2**)
Vallikavu, the birthplace of the famous spiritual guru, Mata Amritanandamayi, is now known as Amritapuri and is a beehive of activity as the **headquarters of the**

Mata Amritanandamayi Trust. The 5-acre plot holds a self-contained township that includes a post office, bank, library and charitable dispensary.
Note: Accommodation and vegetarian food is free for devotees 📞 *0476–289 6399*

Ashtamudi Backwaters (Map pg **46**, **B3**)

The many cruises organised by DTPC is the finest way to explore these backwaters. The highlights of a one-day houseboat trip could include visits to Panmana Beach, a coir-making unit, and the houseboat-building yard at Alumkadavu. A day-night cruise entails a night stay on the Ashtamudi Lake.
Note: Charges range from Rs 4,000 to Rs 16,350 for two, including meals.

Ochira Parabrahma Temple (Map pg **46**, **A1**)

This temple has neither a structure to house an idol, nor an idol to worship. Ochira is dedicated to the formless, infinite 'Para Brahma', the Absolute and Supreme Principle.

The annual festival, Ochirakali, held during June-July, commemorates the historic battle between the Kayamkulam and Chempakasseri rajas.

Sasthamkotta Dharmasastha Temple (Map pg **46**, **B2**)

This is one among the many temples in Kollam dedicated to Lord Ayyappa. The

The pageantry of Ochirakali

monkeys that once colonised the surrounding woods were believed to be loyal followers of the ruling deity, Dharmasastha, and hence, are revered by devotees. A 10-day annual festival includes the colourful Kettukazhcha procession, various folk art performances and an elephant procession.
Note: Entry is restricted to Hindus.

Thangasseri (Map pg **46**, **B3**)

Located south of Kollam, Thangasseri, or 'gold village', was once the hub of a flourishing trade that used gold as currency, thanks to the early European traders. This picturesque settlement has a chequered history, dating back to the 14th century. The town's 144-ft lighthouse, built by the British, dates back to 1519. Thangasseri celebrated its 500th anniversary in 1999.

Thevally Palace (Map pg **46**, **B3**)

Standing on a promontory in central Kollam, this palace overlooks the scenic

Life moves at a gentle pace in the Ashtamudi Backwaters

Kollam (Quilon) | District Map

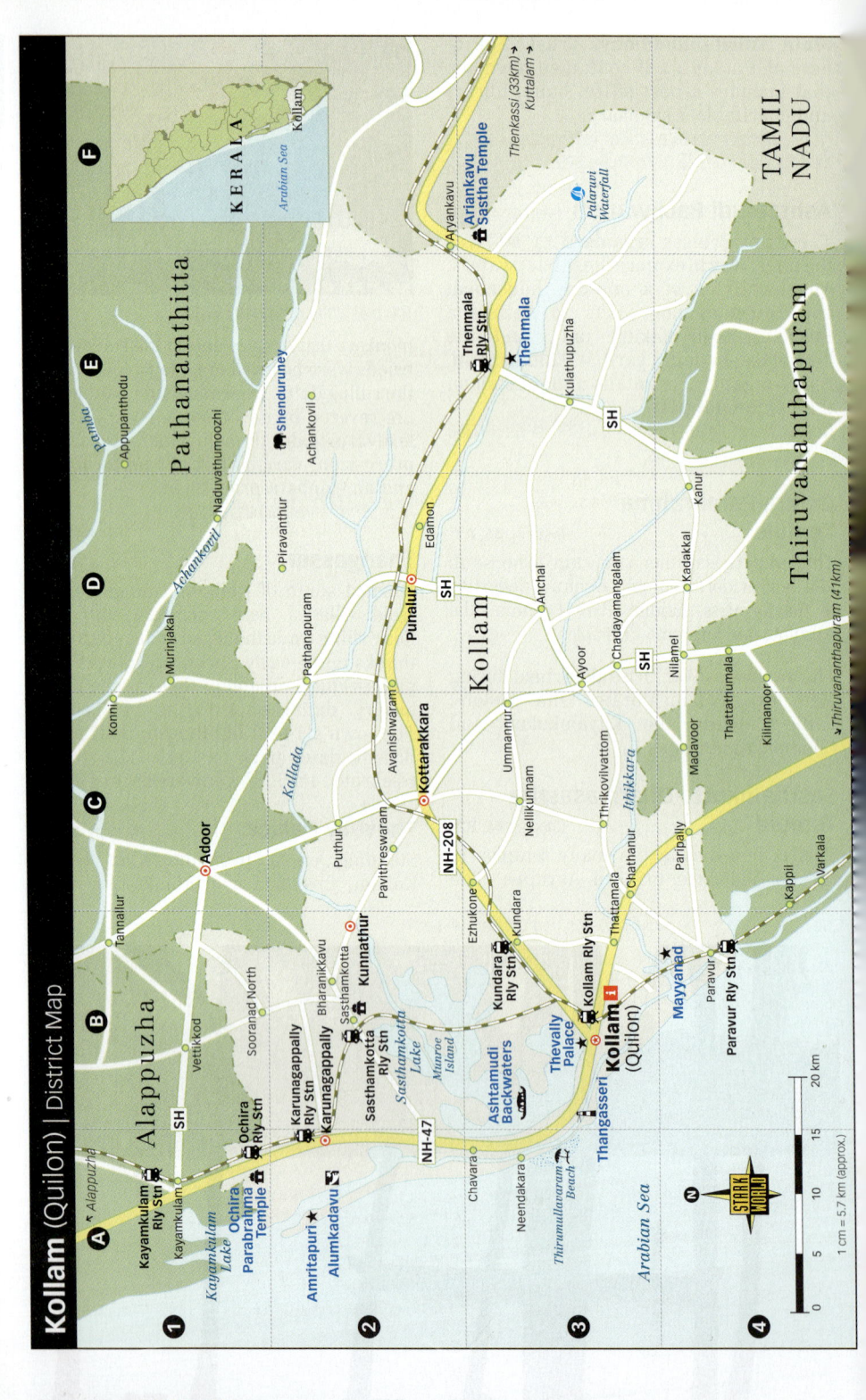

46 | KERALA MAPS & MORE

Houseboats

In Kerala, houseboats are known as *kettuvalloms*. Boats in a variety of shapes and sizes have traditionally been the chief mode of transport in the backwaters for men and material since olden days. Thatched roof covers over wooden hulls, 100 ft in length, provided protection from the elements. Over time, simple facilities were added to the boats used exclusively for travel. For the royalty, these boats even became comfortable living quarters. Later, tourism provided the necessary fillip in transforming the age-old *kettuvalloms* into veritable floating cottages with all the modern amenities. A day's trip for a family with lunch and snacks would cost about Rs 3,000.

DON'T MISS

» Houseboat cruise
Spend a couple of days on a houseboat to experience the backwaters at their pristine best. The private and DTPC houseboat cruises to backwater villages are a must-do.

SIGHTS AND ATTRACTIONS	Grid
Alumkadavu (boat building)	A2
Amritapuri (Matha Amritanandamayi Math)	A2
Ariankavu Sastha Temple	F3
Ashtamudi Backwaters	B3
Mayyanad	B4
Munroe Island	B2
Ochira Parabrahma Temple	A1
Sasthamkotta Temple	B2
Shenduruney Wildlife Sanctuary	E2
Thangasseri (light house)	B3
Thenmala (ecotourism centre)	E3
Thevally Palace	B3

WATERFALLS AND DAMS
Palaruvi Waterfall.................F3

BEACHES AND LAKES
Sasthamkotta Fresh Water Lake........A3
Thirumullavaram Beach................A3

Ashtamudi Lake and is best viewed from the lake itself. Built during the reign of Gauri Parvathi Bai, between 1811 and 1819, it was the residence of the erstwhile Maharaja during his visits to Kollam to meet the British Resident.

Adventure Park (Map pg **46**, B3)

Located in the midst of the backwaters of Ashramam, this village has an adventure park, boating club, children's traffic park and a Yatri Nivas, all in its sprawling campus. The stately 200-year-old residence, once used by Lord Munroe, is now a government guest house. The **Paaramparya Museum** in the premises is also worth a look. On display are paintings from different parts of the country.

☏ *94470 65489*

Munroe Island (Map pg **46**, B2)

This green, palm-covered little island is tucked away in the backwaters of Kollam. The **Stone Age tools and megaliths** discovered here prove the island's antiquity. Formed by the backwaters of the Ashtamudi Lake and the Kallada River, it has been named after Colonel Munroe, the British resident of the erstwhile Travancore State. He is credited with having integrated several backwater regions through the construction of canals.

Cruising along in a country-made craft, criss-crossing the mazelike canals, offers a glimpse of village life in all its pristine purity.

Alappuzha

(Map pg **49**, **A4**)

Its criss-crossing canals and once busy waterways inevitably evoke comparisons with Venice. A prosperous trading town of yesteryears, which exported coir products to different parts of the world, Alappuzha relinquished its commercial position to other towns, notably Kochi, in later years. Today, tourism has appeared as its new saviour. Old settlers have left behind architectural treasures – numerous old mansions and trading houses built in a unique style. These buildings, along with the quiet streets and winding canals, lend this quaint town its distinctive allure.

Muscular arms power slender wooden boats in the Nehru Trophy boat race

Situated at the south-western tip of India's longest lake, the Vembanad, Alappuzha lies sandwiched between the lake and the Arabian Sea – a sliver of land barely 4 km wide. It attracts tourists throughout the year for that singular experience of backwater cruising, especially in the Kuttanad region, a vast area of partly reclaimed land, covered in emerald green paddy fields and separated by dikes from waters that are actually a few feet higher.

Getting There

By Air
The nearest is Cochin International Airport, 90 km
☎ 0484–261 0115

By Rail
Alappuzha railway station (☎ 0477–225 3865) is well connected to Ernakulam in the north and Thiruvananthapuram in the south.

By Road
Alappuzha is on NH 47. Good road connectivity to all towns and cities by KSRTC and private buses. The KSRTC bus stand (☎ 0477–225 1518) is 5 km from the railway station.

FACT FILE

District: Alappuzha
STD code: 0477
When to go: August to March-end

For information contact
District Tourism Promotion Council
✉ Near Boat Jetty
☎ 0477–225 1796

Department of Tourism
✉ Boat Jetty Rd
☎ 0477–226 0722

SIGHTS AND ATTRACTIONS	Grid
Ambalappuzha (temple)	B4
Arthunkal (church)	A2
Chakkulathukavu (Bhagavathi Temple)	C5
Champakulam (church)	B4
Chavara Bhavan	B4
Cheppaud (church)	C5
Chettikulangara (Bhagavathi temple)	C5
Edathua (church)	B4
Haripad (temple)	B5
Karumadi Kuttan (Budha statue)	B4
Krishnapuram Palace Museum	C6
Mannarassala (Sree Nagaraja Temple)	B5
Pathiramanal Island	B3
R Block	B3
Thakazhi Museum and Smritimandapam	B5
Thanneermukkam Bund	B2

BEACHES AND LAKES
Alappuzha Beach	A4
Vembanad Lake	B3

48 | KERALA MAPS & MORE

Alappuzha (Alleppey) | District Map

BACKWATERS

Ernakulam
- Chottanikkara
- Arur
- Ezhupunna
- Olavipe Island
- Turavur
- Turavur Rly Stn
- NH-47
- Thalayolaparambu
- Vaikom
- Kuthattukulam
- Kuravilangad

Kottayam
- Pala
- Cherthala Rly Stn
- Cherthala
- Thanneermukkam Bund
- Champakkara
- Arthunkal
- SH
- Mannanam
- Ettumanur
- Mararikulam Rly Stn
- Mararikulam
- Pathiramanal Island
- Muhamma Boat Jetty
- Kumarakom Boat Jetty
- Alappuzha
- Poonkavu
- Vembanad Lake
- Kottayam
- Vijayapuram
- Meenachil
- Punnamada
- R Block
- Karukachal
- Karikkatur
- Alappuzha Beach
- Chavara Bhavan
- Kuttamangalam
- **Alappuzha (Alleppey)**
- Alappuzha Rly Stn
- Alappuzha Boat Jetty
- Chennamkari
- Nedumudy
- Changanacherry
- Perunna
- Champakulam
- SH
- Ambalapuzha Rly Stn
- Karumadi Kuttan
- Edathua Boat Jetty
- Thiruvalla
- Manimala
- Ambalappuzha
- Edathua
- Chakkulathukavu

Pathanamthitta
- Thakazhi Museum & Smritimandapam
- Thakazhi Boat Jetty
- Pamba
- Mannarassala
- Chengannur
- Kozhencherry
- Haripad
- Achankovil
- Mavelikkara Rly Stn
- Thrikkunnapuzha
- Haripad Rly Stn
- Cheppaud
- Mavelikkara
- **Pathanamthitta**
- Arattupuzha
- Chettikulangara
- Thonnallur
- Kayamkulam Rly Stn
- Kayamkulam
- SH
- Thekkekkara
- SH
- Krishnapuram Palace Museum
- Adoor

Arabian Sea
- Kayamkulam Lake

Kollam
- Kollam

KERALA (inset)
- Alappuzha
- Arabian Sea

N — STARK WORLD

0 5 10 15 20 km
1 cm = 5.6 km (approx.)

MAPS & MORE KERALA | 49

Dawn breaks over a houseboat in the Vembanad Lake

SIGHTS

Ambalappuzha Sree Krishna Temple
(Map pg **49**, **B4**)

The reigning deity of this temple is the infant Krishna. Paintings of the 10 incarnations of Lord Vishnu adorn the inner walls of the *chuttambalam* or circumambulatory. The annual festival in April draws thousands of devotees, who also gather here for a feast. The Pallipana ritual, held once in 12 years, witnesses **performances by sorcerers**. The temple is also renowned for its offering of *palpayasam*, a milk and rice pudding.

Kunjan Nambiar's *ottan thullal*, a satirical art form, was first performed here.
Note: Entry is restricted to Hindus.

Chakkulathukavu Bhagavathi Temple
(Map pg **49**, **C5**)

Sandwiched between the two rivers, Pamba and Manimala, and located on the border of Pathanamthitta and Alappuzha districts, this shrine is **open to people of all religions**. Goddess Vanadurga's (the presiding deity) affinity for women and children has made the temple particularly popular with women devotees.

St Mary's Church, Champakulam
(Map pg **49**, **B4**)

Located on the site at which St Thomas is believed to have built one of his seven churches, the shrine draws hundreds of devotees, especially during the annual feast in October. The feast of St Joseph in March is also an important event. Wooden statues of Christ, made nearby, are exported to various countries.

Chavara Bhavan
(Map pg **49**, **B4**)

Chavara Bhavan, 6 km from town and accessible only by boat, is situated in Kainakary, a small village in the backwaters of Alappuzha. It is the ancestral home of **Father Kuriakose Elias Chavara**, one among the three Malayali candidates under consideration for sainthood by Rome.

Bhagavathi Temple
(Map pg **49**, **C5**)

Located in Chettikulangara, it houses the largest stone lamp in the country – 11 ft high, with 13 tiers. The deity, an incarnation

St Mary's Church, Champakulam

of Bhadrakali, is supposed to possess **miraculous powers** and legends abound about favours conferred on devotees. The annual Kettukazhcha festival witnesses spectacular processions with bright effigies on decorated chariots. An all-night Kathakali performance marks the conclusion of the cultural events.

St George Orthodox Syrian Church (Map pg **49**, **C5**)

This Syrian church has been constructed partially with portions of an old 13th century church located at Haripad, 44 km north of Kollam. Its porches and porticos follow typical temple architecture. **Biblical frescoes** showing the art forms of the early medieval period adorn its walls.

Subrahmanya Temple (Map pg **49**, **B5**)

This temple dedicated to Sree Murugan (Subrahmanya) is renowned for its architectural splendour – the tall flag mast, the large temple tank, and the *koothambalam*, or theatre, with its exquisite wooden carvings on the ceiling.

Karumadi Kuttan (Map pg **49**, **B4**)

The deity of Karumadi Kuttan, which stands by the side of the public canal to the west of the Kamapuram temple, is a **black granite Buddha**, said to belong to the ninth or 10th century. The idol has now been installed in a smaller shrine to protect it. Kerala's Ay kings were patrons of Buddhism, which, however, is known to have declined in the State by the eighth century.

Krishnapuram Palace Museum (Map pg **49**, **C6**)

This palace was built during the reign of Maharaja Marthanda Varma. It is a miniature model of the Padmanabhapuram Palace, near Thiruvananthapuram. The spectacular 16-block building sprawls over an area of 1.87 acres. Now an archaeological museum, the restored two-storey palace houses paintings, antique furniture and sculpture. Burial urns, bronze artefacts, swords, ancient vessels, weights, cannon balls, models of umbrellas, and even a **Sanskrit Bible**, are some of the exhibits.
0479–244 1133

Mannarassala Snake Temple (Map pg **49**, **B5**)

Traditionally, Hindu *naga* (serpent) worshippers have always built their temples in serpent groves. Of these, Mannarassala is the largest with **30,000 images of snake gods**, and hundreds of snakes living around the temple. Childless women come here for blessings and return for a 'thanksgiving' ceremony when they beget a child. Gifts equalling the weight of the child are offered to the diety.

R Block (Map pg **49**, **B3**)

R Block is one of the best managed private farms situated on one of the reclaimed lands in the Kuttanad region. This process of land reclamation started about 100 years ago. At nearly 850 acres, the farm constitutes the largest reclaimed region in the area and is almost entirely covered in coconut, areca and banana plantations.
Note: A return boat trip from Alappuzha takes one and a half hours one way and would cost Rs 450.

Pathiramanal Island (Map pg **49**, **B3**)

The Raja of Travancore offered this palm-covered island in the Vembanad Lake on lease to the family of a man named Andrew Pereira, a Portuguese national and a naval officer, who married a local Catholic woman and settled here. When the lease expired in 1979, Pathiramanal was taken over by the government. Subsequently, families residing there were rehabilitated and the island was handed over to the Tourism Department. It is a one-hour boat ride away from Alappuzha.

Several feet below the sea level, the Kuttanad region is abundant in paddy fields

BACKWATERS

MAPS & MORE **KERALA** | 51

Kumarakom

(Map pg **56**, **B3**)

Getting There

By Air
The nearest is Cochin International Airport, 72 km
☎ 0484–261 0115.
Thiruvananthapuram International Airport is 170 km
☎ 0471–250 1424

By Rail
The nearest is Kottayam Junction, 15 km ☎ 0481–256 2933

By Road
The nearest KSRTC bus stand is at Kottayam (☎ 0481–256 2935). Kumarakom is well connected to most parts of the State.

Set against the backdrop of rich green paddy fields and still grey waters, Kumarakom was, for years, just another sleepy town, resplendent in scenic beauty. However, when Kerala became a popular tourist destination, Kumarakom's charms were soon unveiled. Today, plush resorts scattered around a large lake and delightful backwaters have transformed this once quiet settlement into a sought after destination – Sir Paul McCartney, the former Beatle, wrote in his hotel register, 'Truly, this is god's own country'.

Located 15 km west of Kottayam town, the picturesque village of Kumarakom is actually a cluster of small islands on the eastern banks of the Vembanad Lake. Sandwiched between a lake that looks more like the sea and a parallel network of backwaters, this bewitching water world forms part of the Kuttanad region. Although situated in a labyrinth of lush waterways, Kumarakom's advantage is that it can be **reached easily by road** from Kottayam, Kochi and Alappuzha.

Tourists throng Kumarakom to experience its gentle pace of life and stunning views of nature. The only places to 'visit' are the nearby Bird Sanctuary, the **Driftwood Museum** and the Pathiramanal Island.

A stalk of tender coconuts – classic Kerala

FACT FILE

District: Kottayam

STD code: 0481

When to go: August to February

For information contact
District Tourism Promotion Council Office
✉ Boat Jetty, Kodimatha, Kottayam
☎ 0481–256 0479

Department of Tourism District Office
✉ Nattakom Government Guest House, Kottayam
☎ 0481–234 2303

Braving the sun, a couple goes out fishing

Duck farming is popular all along the backwaters

SIGHTS

Driftwood Museum (Map pg 56, B3)

This museum was the brainchild of Raji Punnose, a teacher who worked in the Andaman and Nicobar Islands for 25 years. She started collecting pieces of driftwood washed ashore and spent hours pruning and giving shape to what had already been shaped by the sea.

Located at Chakranpadi, the museum has a stunning array of elegant driftwood sculpture. In its 'ferocity', a crocodile looks almost real. The flowers and buds collection is also worth a peek.

☎ 0481–251 7530, 94474 64296

Bird Sanctuary (Map pg 56, B3)

Spread across 14 acres in a former rubber plantation that was previously known as Baker's Estate, the Englishman who developed this area into a bird sanctuary would be glad to see the large number of delighted birdwatchers who gather here today.

At dawn and at sundown, the forests come alive with a cacophony of shrill calls and cries. Night herons, purple moorhen, Brahminy kites, teals, egrets, cormorants, darters and large Indian fruit bats have colonised these woods. There are also large populations of breeding darters, purple herons, little cormorants, Indian Shag, white ibis, local waterfowl and pond herons. Neighbouring areas such as Kaipuzha Muttu, Pathiramanal, Narakathara, Thollayiram Kayal and Poothanpandi Kayal are also excellent locations for spotting birds.

Note: An early morning trek is recommended for avid birdwatchers ⏰ 6 am to 6 pm.

Toddy Shops

Kallu shaap is ubiquitous in Kerala – signboards strung before shacks proclaim that toddy is available inside, and men can be seen weaving in and out of these shanties at all odd hours. Combining the mildly intoxicating spirit with snacks, usually spicy seafood, has been the tradition in Kerala for a long time.

Toddy tapping, in fact, has been an age-old rural vocation. Made from the sap of the coconut flower before it blooms, the sweetish liquid is allowed to ferment overnight in bottles or earthenware vessels to produce toddy.

Toddy is sold for around Rs 35 a litre.

Toddy and fish – an ideal combination

Midlands
Plantation Country

The midlands are known for their extensive spice plantations. Shown here is a cardamom plantation.

The midlands of Kerala, spanning three districts, have a varied topography and climate. Pathanamthitta harbours dense forests, whereas in genteel Kottayam, the topography and climate change sharply – from backwaters and plains to high ranges. Idukki is out-and-out hilly, with 97 per cent of its area covered in rugged mountains. Rivers, trekking trails, stunning views and wildlife make the midlands a haven for environmentalists. This region is also the nucleus of the literacy scene in Kerala, and home to many newspapers and periodicals.

The Meenachil River forms the lifeline of the midlands. Endowed with fertile soil, there has been intensive cultivation in the area, particularly of **cash crops**. Cashew, coconut, areca nut, tapioca, banana, mango, rice, ginger, pepper, cardamom, nutmeg, coffee, and various kinds of root vegetables grow extensively. While the weekly pepper and cardamom auctions at Kumily draw traders from all over, the vast rubber plantations have spawned a vibrant trade in raw rubber and its products.

Known as the heartland of Kerala – for its location as well as for its vital contributions to the economy of the State – the midlands may be quiet and laidback, but its people certainly know the importance of their region.

Highlights

The midlands consist of a mosaic of geographical features. Dense forests, humid backwaters, sweltering plains and cold high ranges make for an interesting landscape. While extensive plantations of rubber have fostered a thriving trading community, the region also harbours the nerve centre of Kerala's literary scene.

Getting There

By Air
The nearest is Cochin International Airport, 65 km
☏ 0484–261 0115

By Rail
Daily trains connect Kottayam railway station to all major cities
☏ 0481–256 2933

By Road
SH 1 connects Thiruvananthapuram and Angamaly and passes through Kottayam. NH 220 (KK Rd) connects to Madurai in Tamil Nadu. Kottayam's KSRTC bus stand has services from all major cities.
☏ 0481–256 2935

A granite cross at Valiyapalli

FACT FILE

District: Kottayam
STD code: 0481
When to go: August to February
For information contact
District Tourism Promotion Council Office
✉ Kodimatha, Kottayam
☏ 0481–256 0479

Kottayam

(Map pg **56**, **C3**)

MIDLANDS

Kottayam city is the district headquarters and an urban centre. However, by no means, can it be termed 'cosmopolitan', nor does it possess the bustle of a large city. As a local put it, 'the world seems to have bypassed Kottayam'. Chiefly known for its lakes, letters and latex, an undoubtedly unusual combination, Kottayam, in fact, is a land of many accomplishments.

Ever since **Benjamin Bailey** set up Kerala's first printing press in Kottayam, the district has been at the forefront of the publishing industry. Today, 80 per cent of the books published in the State come from here. Kottayam is also the nerve centre of the newspaper industry – five major dailies are published from here. Today, however, Kottayam is better known for the nearby attractions of the Vembanad Lake and the backwaters of Kumarakom.

The economic strength of the **large Christian community**, most of them owners of sprawling plantations, makes Kottayam the most prosperous town in Kerala. This is barely visible on the surface, though, as the town shuns pretensions and zealously clings to its age-old laidback ways.

SIGHTS

Valiyapalli
(Map pg **56**, **B3**)

'Valiyapalli' or 'big church' was built in 1550 by the descendants of the 72 families whose forefathers were the seven clans who migrated to India in 345 AD from Jerusalem. Built entirely of wood, the church was demolished in 1577, and a new one built of stone. It is famous for its interesting **woodcarvings**, **ancient Persian crosses, mural paintings and Syrian inscriptions**.

In 1579, a breakaway group set up another church, which came to be called 'Cheriyapalli' or 'small church'.
☏ 0481–256 3324

Cheriyapalli
(Map pg **56**, **B3**)

This is one of the few old churches that still exist in an almost original state. Built in 1579, extensive restoration work was carried out and completed in 1993, but without

MAPS & MORE **KERALA** | 55

Kottayam | District Map

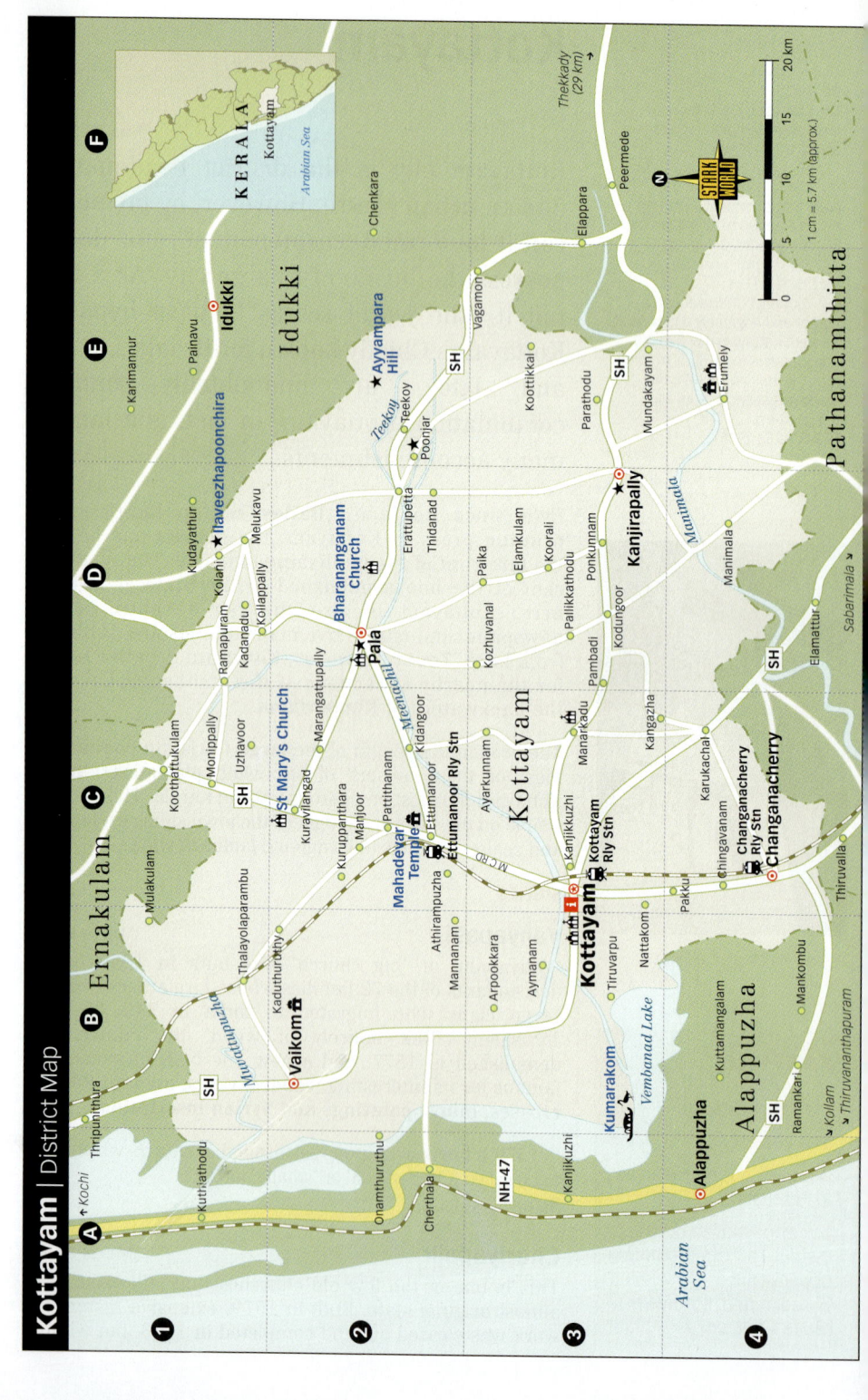

56 | KERALA MAPS & MORE

Thirunakkara Temple

changing architectural details. The façade is European, whereas the granite pillars lining the porch, added later, resemble those found in temples.

The **baptismal font** inside, carved out of a single granite stone, is said to be as old as the church itself. The sanctum sanctorum, called the *madbaha*, has a barrel vault built of carved and painted laterite stones.

☎ 0481–256 6744

Good Shepherd Church (Map pg **56**, **B3**)

Constructed in 1882 and renovated in 1964, this is the first church of the Diocese of Vijayapuram and was built in the Italian style. The annual feast of the church, located behind the civil station, is held every April.

Thirunakkara Temple (Map pg **56**, **B3**)

The highlight of the shrine, built by a Thekkumkoor king, is the low-roofed stage or *koothambalam*, one of the finest in the whole State. The carved wooden windows encircling the stage facilitate viewing of performances. Three festivals are celebrated here in October-November, June-July and March-April, of which the last is the most important. For the grand finale of Araatu, nine caparisoned elephants take part in a procession. **Folk arts** such as *mayilattam* (peacock dance) and *velakali* follow. A major attraction is the all-night Kathakali performance. A Hindu convention and an art festival also take place.

☎ 0481–258 3898

DON'T MISS

» **Thazhathangadi**
Once a thriving trading town, this peaceful village boasts of elaborate houses built in the traditional style by early Christian pepper merchants.

Letters, Latex and Lakes

The above form an integral part of life in the midlands. The early rulers of Kottayam were great patrons of learning. Little wonder then that the region evolved into the nucleus of the literary scene in Kerala. With Kottayam district alone accounting for the largest concentra-tion of rubber acreage in India, latex is undoubtedly an important product. And, sandwiched between the mountains and the sea, countless streams and major rivers flow through the region. Lakes are numerous, too.

Collecting sap from the rubber tree

SIGHTS AND ATTRACTIONS	Grid
Ayyampara Hill	E2
Bharananganam Church	D2
Erumely (temples, mosque)	E4
Ettumanoor Mahadevar Temple	C2
Ilaveezhapoonchira	D1
Kanjirapally (plantations)	D3
Kottayam (churches, mosque)	B3
Kumarakom (backwaters, bird sanctuary)	B3
Manarkadu Church	C3
Pala (plantations, churches)	D2
Poonjar Palace Complex	E2
St Mary's Church, Kuravilangad	C2
Vaikom Temple	B2

MAPS & MORE **KERALA** | 57

Pala

Getting There

By Air
The nearest is Cochin International Airport, about 96 km
☎ 0484–261 0115

By Rail
The nearest railhead is Ettumanoor, 16 km. Kottayam (☎ 0481–256 2933) is 27 km

By Road
SH 31 connects Kottayam to Pala through Ettumanoor. From Kochi, it is 80 km through Thripunithura, Thalayolaparampu and Kaduthuruthy.

(Map pg **56**, **D2**)

Situated on the banks of the Meenachil River, near the mountains, Pala is an archetypal small town, where almost everyone knows everybody else. The majority of the local population consists of Christians and with some of the oldest churches in the region situated here, much of the social activity revolves around the church. Pala is known for its huge plantations and much of its prosperity comes from rubber, the main cash crop.

The Meenachil River flows through the town and empties into the Arabian Sea miles later, providing access to the coast and spurring on a thriving spice trade – the spice market was established as early as 1736. '**Pala Pepper**', known for its superior quality, was popular in the international market. However, rubber later replaced pepper in importance. Pala is also the **nerve centre of Christianity** in Kerala – St Thomas himself is said to have set up the St George Church in Aruvithura.

The town is an ideal starting point for heading out to popular tourist destinations such as Munnar, Vagamon and Thekkady, as well as to pilgrim centres such as Sabarimala, Bharananganam and Mannanam.

St Mary's Forane Church

FACT FILE

District: Kottayam

STD code: 04822

When to go: August to January

For information contact
District Tourism Promotion Council Office
✉ Boat Jetty, Kodimatha, Kottayam
☎ 0481–256 0479

The rebuilt Portuguese style Valiyapalli

One of the two temple complexes housed inside the exquisite Poonjar Palace

SIGHTS

Shrine of our Lady of Immaculate Conception (Map pg **56**, **D2**)

A landmark structure, also called 'Jubilee Kappela', this shrine is constructed out of 14,444 granite stones and stands in the centre of town. A statue of Jesus Christ, 12.5 ft high, stands on top of the shrine.

Valiyapalli (Map pg **56**, **D2**)

Formally called, 'St Thomas Cathedral', this was built in 1002. Destroyed by Muslim invaders in the 17th century, it was rebuilt in the next century, adopting the Portuguese style of architecture.

📞 *04822–212 386*

St Mary's Church (Map pg **56**, **D2**)

St Mary's Church, located at Bharananganam, is an **important pilgrim centre** as the remains of the Blessed Sister Alphonsa, who died in 1946, are buried here. The podium used by the Pope when he beatified Sister Alphonsa in 1986 still stands.

📞 *04822–237 144* 🖥 *www.alphonsa.net*

Kayyoor Temple (Map pg **56**, **D2**)

Kayyoor is a Ghat region blanketed by lush hilly vegetation. There is a small temple atop the hill near Bharananganam **dedicated to the Pandavas**, where only ghee is used to light the votive lamps.

St George Church (Map pg **56**, **D2**)

This 120-ft-high structure in Erattupetta town has a **unique shape** resembling a cross. The annual feast held in April draws hundreds of people.

📞 *04822–272 113*

Poonjar Palace (Map pg **56**, **E2**)

Poonjar, near Erattupetta, was once the capital of the Poonjar royal family from 1155 to 1800. Located in a serene environment, surrounded by the Meenachil River on three sides, it is known for its exquisite architectural beauty.

📞 *04822–273 506, 274 221*

Ayyampara hills (Map pg **56**, **E2**)

Flat granite rock formations scattered over almost 30 acres of land offer fabulous views of coconut trees interspersed with rubber plantations in the valley below. The innumerable tributaries of the Meenachil River, originating from Illikkal Mala, shimmer in the distance.

Note: Take a detour near Teekoy Church on Erattupetta-Vagamon road.

St Mary's Forane Church (Map pg **56**, **C2**)

Built in 345 AD, this church is one of the oldest in Kerala, but has been rebuilt in 1960. A granite cross, 48 ft in height, and carved out of a single stone, is the highlight. The statue of Virgin Mary on the main altar is a rare blend of Romano-Portuguese art. The three massive church bells and the replica of the vessel used by Prophet Jonah are also must-sees.

📞 *04822–230 224*

Getting There

By Air
The nearest is Cochin International Airport, 130 km
☏ 0484–261 0115

By Rail
The nearest railhead is Kottayam, 39 km
☏ 0481–256 2933

By Road
Kanjirapally is on the Kottayam-Kumily road (NH 220). All buses from Kottayam KSRTC station (☏ 0481–256 2935) headed to Kumily/Erumely/Mundakkayam come to Kanjirapally.

FACT FILE

District: Kottayam
STD code: 04828
When to go: August to January
For information contact
District Tourism Promotion Council
✉ Near Boat Jetty, Kodimatha, Kottayam
☏ 0481–256 0479

St Dominic's Cathedral

Kanjirapally

(Map pg **56**, **D3**)

This tranquil little town in the foothills of the Western Ghats is often referred to as the gateway to the High Ranges. Once a hub of trading activities, Kanjirapally has now slipped into comparative quietude. But the abundance of rubber plantations still gives the town a degree of commercial importance. The numerous charming bungalows built by rich planters bestow upon it an old-world charm.

Agriculture now prevails over trade as the main source of income for the locals. The land, made fertile by the **Manimala River**, is a veritable planter's paradise. Apart from large rubber plantations, banana, tapioca, pepper, vanilla and ginger are some of the other important crops that support the town's economy.

The beautiful granite temple, Ganapathiyar Kovil, today in ruins, points to early Tamil influence. However, the Madurai Meenakshi Temple is now the most important Hindu shrine in town. The Shiva Temple in Chirakadavu and the Bhagavathi Temple in Cheruvalli are the two other popular shrines.

Apart from being a base camp of sorts for pilgrims setting off for Sabarimala, Kanjirapally is also an ideal take-off point for Thekkady, the Periyar Sanctuary, Peermede and Kumily.

SIGHTS

St Mary's Church (Map pg **56**, **D3**)
Locally known as 'Akkarapalli', St Mary's church was established in 1449 with the patronage of the Thekkumkoor rajas. A delightful stream flows close by, touching the courtyard of the church.
☏ *04828–204 586*

St Dominic's Cathedral (Map pg **56**, **D3**)
Built in 1826, St Dominic's Cathedral is noted for its architectural beauty. Both the old and the new church remained the parish churches for 18 years until 1842, when they were unified. The shrine was raised to the position of a forane church in 1919. Its reconstruction, begun in 1945, took nearly 16 years to complete. On March 17, 1977, it was elevated to the status of a cathedral.
☏ *04828–204 643, 202 343*

60 | KERALA MAPS & MORE

Ganapathiyar Kovil (Map pg **56**, **D3**)

Built by the Chetti community of Tamil Nadu, this 900-year-old structure is almost in ruins today, although the carvings and inscriptions on its granite pillars are still visible. Tamil inscriptions on walls and pillars tell the story of the **Pattunool Shetties**, the community known for weaving the textile known as *kanjirapally katcha*.

Note: On Kottayam-Kumily Road, opposite the Petta Government High School.

St Thomas Benedictine Abbey (Map pg **56**, **D3**)

The Benedictines are a Roman Catholic order with a network around the world. The St Thomas Benedictine Abbey has a church that displays a blend of Western and Indian cultural influences. The stone lamp at the entrance of the building, carved wooden doors, huge pillars at the altar, intricate floral motifs and domes are unusual. A **traditional Hindu jewel box** has been placed in the niche of a marble pillar, where the sacrament is kept and worshipped.

Note: It is 5 km from Kanjirapally on the Erattupetta road at Kappadu junction
📞 *04828–237 174, 235 346*

Malanadu Development Society (MDS) (Map pg **56**, **E3**)

This is an organisation that works for rural development and environmental sustainability. A **guided tour** through the 13-acre property takes you through the techniques of bee-keeping and honey processing, sericulture, oil extraction and milk processing. A shop sells MDS products.

Note: Prior intimation is required before a visit
📞 *04828–270 256, 270 456*

Milk being processed at MDS

Erumely (Map pg **56**, **E4**)

Erumely epitomises **religious harmony** – Hindu and Muslim shrines stand side by side. The loud chanting and the sound of conch shells from the two temples mingle with the muezzin's call to prayer from the minaret of the mosque located between the two. Erumely is a beehive of activity during the pilgrimage season, being an important destination for Sabarimala pilgrims.

IMPORTANT SHRINES IN ERUMELY

The many minarets of the Vavar Mosque

» **Vavar Mosque** Dedicated to Vavar, the Muslim friend and guide to Ayyappa. He is believed to have helped Ayyappa kill the demon in the form of a buffalo. Pilgrims proceeding to Sabarimala also worship at this mosque.

» **Kochambalam** Standing just opposite Vavar Mosque, there are two statues near its entrance, of Vavar Swamy and Kadutha Swamy. This is where the famous *petta thullal* – the ritual art form performed by pilgrims to Sabarimala – starts. As the name suggests (*kochu* means 'small'), it is a small temple, but is surrounded by vast grounds.

» **Valiyambalam** This is built in the traditional Kerala temple style and is located a kilometre from Kochambalam.

» **Puthenveedu** It is an old, thatched mud house, standing a few hundred metres from Kochambalam. Legend has it that an old woman who once lived here gave shelter and food to Lord Ayyappa for a night, and the god, in turn, presented her with the sword he had used to slay the buffalo demon, Mahisham. The sword is displayed in the hut.

MAPS & MORE **KERALA** | 61

Pathanamthitta

(Map pg **63**, **C3**)

This district may not possess sandy beaches, languid backwaters or misty mountains, but what it does have in plenty is unfettered nature nurtured by the three great rivers, Pamba, Achankovil and Manimala. These meander through an untamed land where wild elephants still roam free. Indeed, Pathanamthitta has a fierce splendour, which must be seen to be believed.

The district has three natural divisions – the lowlands, the midlands and the highlands. The highlands stretch through the Western Ghats and ease into the midlands in the centre. On the western side, close to Alappuzha, are the lowlands covered in extensive coconut plantations. A **landlocked area**, more than half of Pathanamthitta – nearly 1,500 sq km – is covered in forests. Timber is the mainstay of the economy, and wood-based industries abound.

The elephant training centre in Konni, the mammoth crowds that throng the Sabarimala shrine, the annual Christian convention near Kozhencherry, and the boat race at Aranmula that is held every year are noteworthy.

SIGHTS

Aranmula boat race
(Map pg **63**, **B2**)

The annual boat race is more of a regatta and is held in August, after Onam. It is the highpoint of the sleepy village of Aranmula. During the race, the village diety is invited to the scene through the devotional *vanchipaattu* song, sung by the crowd of hundred thousand, including oarsmen and singers.

Note: Aranmula is 9 km west of Chengannur on the Ernakulam-Kollam road.

Konni
(Map pg **63**, **C3**)

Chiefly an agricultural region, Konni is rich in cash crops and famous for its elephant rides. The **elephant training centre**, built in 1941, is one of the oldest in India.
☎ *0468–224 2233, Range Office* ☎ *0468–234 2005.*

Perumthenaruvi Falls
(Map pg **63**, **D1**)

The river Pamba plunges down a rocky path into a ravine about 100 ft below. This splendid natural waterfall is popular as a picnic spot.

Note: It is 36 km from Pathanamthitta.

Getting There

By Air
The nearest are Cochin International Airport ☎ 0484–261 0115) and Thiruvananthapuram International Airport ☎ 0471–250 1424) – both about 140 km away and accessible by rail and road.

By Rail
The nearest railway station is Thiruvalla, 25 km. Connects to all major towns and cities.

By Road
Connected to Thiruvananthapuram by the MC Rd. Frequent buses to Pamba, Kottayam, Alappuzha, Thiruvananthapuram, Kollam and Kochi from KSRTC bus stand on MC Rd
☎ 0468–222 2366

Aranmula Kannadi – a hand-polished metal mirror

SIGHTS AND ATTRACTIONS	Grid
Aranmula	B2
Chilanthiyambalam	C3
Gavi (trekking)	E1
Kaviyoor (temple)	B1
Konni (elephant care centre)	C3
Mannadi	B4
Maramon	B2
Niranam (church)	A2
Pandalam	B3
Sabarimala (pilgrim centre)	E2
Thiruvalla (temple)	A2
Vasthu Vidya Gurukulam (centre for traditional architecture)	B2
Vijnana Kalavedi (cultural centre)	B2
Waterfalls	
Perumthenaruvi Waterfall	D1

62 | KERALA MAPS & MORE

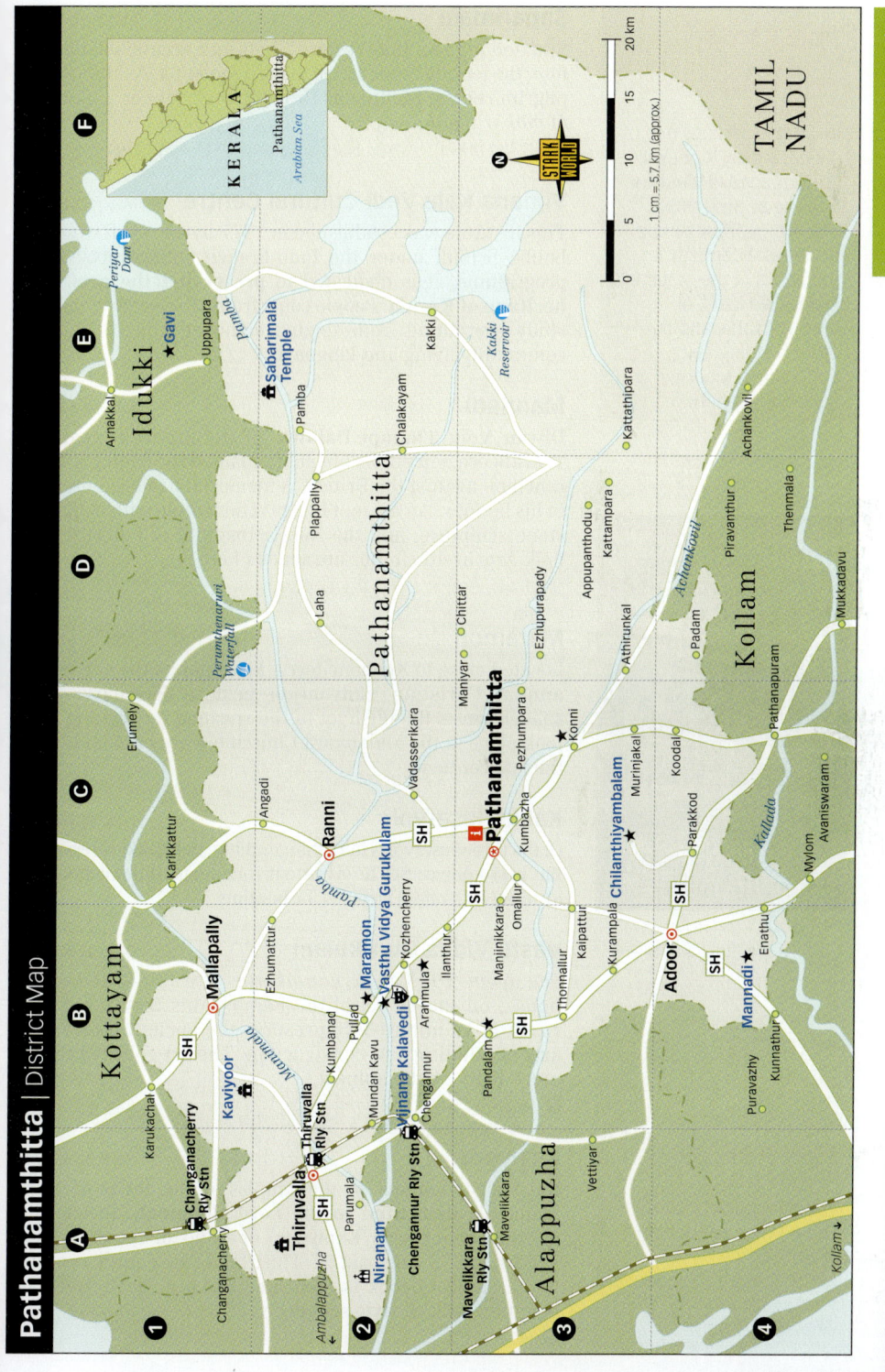

Pathanamthitta | District Map

DON'T MISS

» Sree Vallabha Temple, Thiruvalla
In what is perhaps one of a kind, a daily Kathakali performance is the ritual offering at this temple. The 400-year-old shrine occupies a complex on the banks of the Manimala River. Two idols, of Sree Vallabha, and the other residing deity, Sudarshana Moorthy, are consecrated here.

The largest Christian gathering in Asia – the Maramon Convention

FACT FILE

District: Kottayam

STD code: 0468

When to go: April to August

For information contact
Department of Tourism
District Office
✉ Collectorate Compound, Pathanamthitta
☏ 0468–222 9952

Sabarimala (Map pg **63**, **E2**)
Situated high on the Western Ghats and accessible only by foot, the temple is dedicated to Lord Ayyappa. An important pilgrim centre, multitudes throng the shrine for a glimpse of *makarajyothi*.
Note: The pilgrim season is from November to mid-January.

Vijnana Kala Vedi Cultural Centre (Map pg **63**, **B2**)
This institute was established in 1977 by a French woman, Louba Schild, under the Indo-French cultural exchange programme. It is dedicated to **preserving the arts and heritage of Kerala**. People come from all over the world to study everything from singing, dancing, and cooking to community living and language.

Mannadi (Map pg **63**, **B4**)
Diwan Velu Thampi Dalawa, of the erstwhile State of Travancore, ended his life at Mannadi after leading a brief rebellion against the British. A memorial has been erected in his honour. An ancient Bhagavathi temple with exquisite stone sculpture, and the Kerala Institute of Folklore and Folk Arts are the other attractions here.
Note: Mannadi is 13 km from Adoor.

Maramon (Map pg **63**, **B2**)
Located close to Kozhencherry, Maramon is the site of the **annual Christian convention** held in February. This convention is the offshoot of the spiritual awakening that took place in the Malankara Church towards the middle of the last century.

Kakki Reservoir (Map pg **63**, **E3**)
Of the three reservoirs in Pathanamthitta, the Kakki reservoir is the best known. Set in sylvan surroundings, this magnificent artificial lake offers facilities for **boating**.

Vastu Vidya Gurukulam (Map pg **63**, **B2**)
Set up in 1993 in a *naalukettu*, a traditional Kerala house, on the banks of the Pamba, this institute is the result of an initiative to preserve the ancient traditional arts of building and construction. The art gallery throws more light on the subject.
☏ 0468–231 9740 ⏰ 9 am to 4 pm

Kaviyoor (Map pg **63**, **B1**)
Kaviyoor is famous for the temples on the banks of River Manimala **dedicated to the Lord Hanuman**. In fact, its original name was 'Kapiyoor' or 'land of monkeys'. At Trikkakudi, 3 km east of Thiruvalla, an eighth century temple built of rock is dedicated to Lord Shiva and has beautiful Pallava style sculpture.
☏ 0468–231 9740

64 | KERALA MAPS & MORE

Kumily and Thekkady

Getting There

By Air
The nearest is Madurai Airport (Tamil Nadu), 140 km
☎ 0452-269 0433
Cochin International Airport is 190 km ☎ 0484-261 0115

By Rail
The nearest railhead is Theni, 60 km. Kottayam is 114 km.

By Road
Kumily is well connected by road to different tourist centres and major towns of Tamil Nadu. From Kumily's KSRTC stand, buses ply regularly to Kottayam, Kochi and Thiruvananthapuram.
☎ 04869-224 242

FACT FILE

District: Idukki

STD code: 04869

When to go: December to May

For information contact
District Tourist Information Office
✉ Thekkady Junction
☎ 04869-222 620

Eco Tourism Centre of Periyar Tiger Reserve
✉ Ambady Junction, Kumily
☎ 04869-224 571

Forest Information Centre
✉ Boat Landing, Periyar Tiger Reserve
☎ 04869-222 028

A bunch of peppercorns—abundant in the region

(Map pg **66, 71-C5**)

The first to promote environmental tourism in the State, Thekkady straddles both Tamil Nadu and Kerala. Together with the nearby plantation town of Kumily, it forms a convenient base to explore the surrounding Cardamom Hills. With its crisp, clean air, spice-scented plantations and undulating hills, the region continues to beckon the adventurous traveller.

Boating in the Periyar Lake at Thekkady

Kumily and Thekkady lie at the **foothills of the Western Ghats**. Kumily, a plantation town, is situated on the outskirts of the Periyar Sanctuary and drops down steeply to the plains of Tamil Nadu. An important centre for the spice trade, Kumily is also a bustling tourist destination. As compared to the languorous Thekkady, Kumily buzzes with activity. Some of the plantation bungalows have opened up to tourists and the spice plantation tours have become a popular attraction.

SIGHTS

Pandikuzhi
(Map pg **71, C4**)
Nestled between Chellarkovil and the Tamil Nadu border is Pandikuzhi, a 5 km drive from Kumily. The abundance of flowers and the nearby streams make it a trekker's delight and the favourite of photographers.

MAPS & MORE **KERALA** | 65

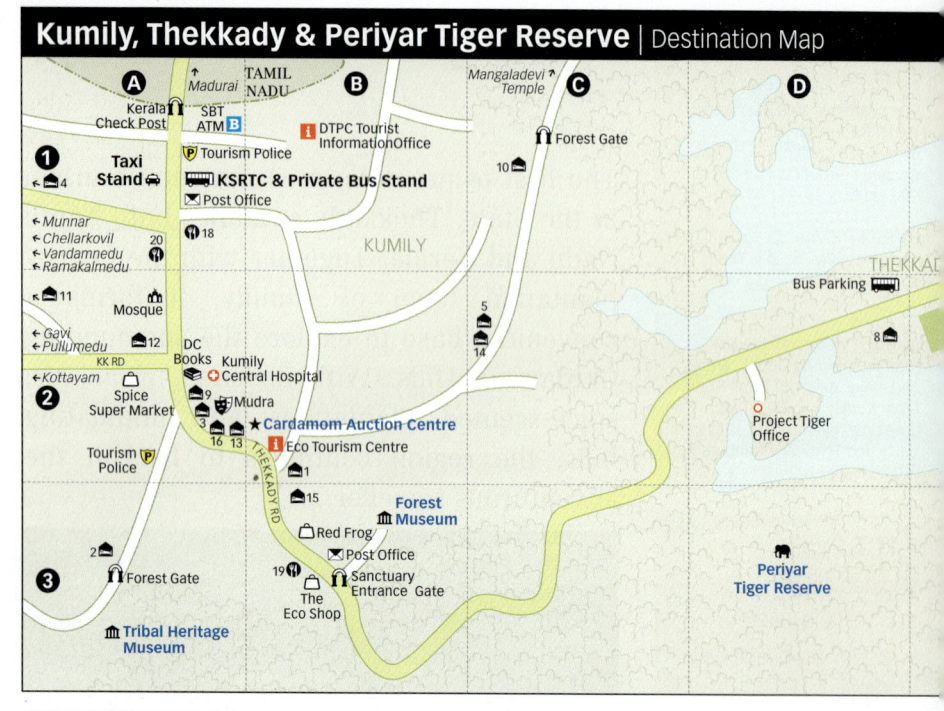

Kumily, Thekkady & Periyar Tiger Reserve | Destination Map

SIGHTS AND ATTRACTIONS	Grid
Boat landing	F1
Cardamom Auction Centre	B2
Forest Museum	B3
Periyar Tiger Reserve	D3
Tribal Heritage Museum	A3

WHERE TO STAY		
Ambadi	1	B2
Bamboo Grove	2	A3
Cardamom County	3	A2
Carmelia Haven	4	A1
Elephant Court	5	C2
KTDC Aranya Nivas	6	E1
KTDC Lake Palace	7	F1
KTDC Periyar House	8	D2
Michael's Inn	9	A2
Saj Jungle Village	10	C1
Shalimar Spice Garden	11	A2
SN International	12	A2
Spice Village	13	A2
Taj Garden Retreat	14	C2
Tree Top	15	B3
Wildernest	16	A2

WHERE TO EAT		
All Spices	(see 3)	A2
Café Periyarensis	17	E1
Cochin Bake House	18	A1
Coffee Inn & Restaurant	19	B3
Hotel Ambadi	(see 1)	B2
KTDC Aranya Nivas	(see 5)	E1
KTDC Lake Palace	(see 6)	F1
Saravana	20	A1
Spice Village	(see 13)	A2
Taj Garden Retreat	(see 14)	C2

LAKE	
Periyar Lake	E2

Tribal Heritage Museum
(Map pg **66**, **A3**)

The earliest inhabitants of the present-day Periyar Tiger Reserve were the indigenous **Mannans**. Until the 1940s, this tribe eked out a living by fishing in the lake and cultivating a few basic crops. As part of an ecotourism programme, a heritage museum was later built inside the original tribal settlement.

The museum displays numerous artefacts relating to traditional Mannan agricultural practices, marriage ceremonies, cultural events, dress, rituals and death ceremonies. Other displays include fishing gear, hunting weaponry, indigenous medicine and vessels, cereals, medicinal herbs and bamboo furniture.

The spice plantations draw eager visitors

AROUND KUMILY AND THEKKADY

Gavi (Map pg **71**, **C5**)

This is picturesque place is ideal for trekking, watching birds, outdoor camping and boating. The road from Kumily is 40 km long and snakes past hills and valleys, tropical forests, sprawling grasslands, cascading waterfalls and cardamom plantations. Chenthamara Kokka, a splendid vantage point, offers spectacular views of the deep ravine and the surrounding forests.

Chellarkovil (Map pg **71**, **C4**)

Fifteen kilometres from Kumily is Chellarkovil, a sleepy little hamlet, which offers a breathtaking view of the plains and cascading waterfalls. The village slopes down to the famous coconut groves of Kambam and the plains of Theni in neighbouring Tamil Nadu. A detour from here leads to Ramakalmedu, an enchanting retreat, which offers a bird's eye view of the picturesque villages of Bodi and Kambam on the eastern slopes of the Western Ghats.

Bamboo rafting on the Periyar Lake

The Periyar Model

The Periyar model is a successful ecotourism initiative on the part of the government to involve ex-poachers, villagers and women in conservation efforts. The Periyar Foundation, formed in 2005, takes care of the livelihood options of people involved in conservation.

DON'T MISS

» **Boating in Periyar**
Travel by boat on the Periyar Lake to spot the elephants and avifauna for which this reserve is well known. Boat cruises at sunrise and sunset are particularly recommended.

MAIN TREKKING ROUTES AROUND THEKKADY

» **Kurisumala** The 'mountain of the cross', a 2-km drive from Kumily, offers enchanting views.

» **Pullumedu** Accessible only by jeep, it lies 43 km from Thekkady. Part of it is the restricted forest zone, for which entry is restricted.

» **Nellikkampetty Area and Manakkavala** The Forest Department conducts daily treks from the boat landing station at Thekkady to the Nellikkampetty Area and Manakkavala, starting 7 am. Bookings through Wildlife Preservation Officer, Thekkady.

» **Ottakathalamedu** This is 5 km from Kumily.

» **Grampi** Near Vandiperiyar.

The Hills
Resplendent in green...

The picturesque tea plantations of Munnar against misty mountains and distant valleys

The rolling High Ranges of the Western Ghats, on the eastern border of Kerala, have always protected it from mainland invaders. The hills also play an important role in determining the climate of the State – they intercept the thick clouds rolling in from the Arabian Sea at the onset of every rainy season. The resulting precipitation ensures copious rainfall from June well into October – the *edavapathy*, and again, from November to February – the *thulavarsham*. The beauty of these green hills is unique to Kerala.

Vast areas of the region are given over to **plantations of tea, coffee and spices**. Little wonder then, that the British built sprawling bungalows, cottages and churches that reminded them of good old England. Places such as Nelliyampathy, Peermede and Munnar are steeped in nostalgia with a history that harks back to the days of the Raj.

Peermede was once the favourite retreat of the Maharaja of Travancore, Munnar boasts of the country's highest tea plantation – at Kolukkumalai. Most of the old planters' bungalows have now been converted into resorts and hotels. The hilly region abounds in wildlife sanctuaries, rivers and valleys and is a popular destination for trekkers. This is especially true of the district of Wayanad, which offers a variety of **trekking trails**.

Highlights

Rich in plantations of pepper, cardamom, cloves, nutmeg and cinnamon, the hills of Kerala are clothed in green all through the year. The government has played a significant role in developing tourism in these parts. Well trained staff, with a thorough knowledge of ecology and the environment, have been employed here so that the natural environment of the area is not disturbed.

KERALA

Kasaragod
Kannur
Thirunelly★ ★Wayanad
Kalpetta★ ★Sulthan Bathery
Vythiri★
Kozhikode
Malappuram
Palakkad
Nelliyampathy★
Thrissur
Ernakulam ★Munnar
Idukki
★Idukki
Kottayam ★Peermede
★Vagamon
Alappuzha Pathanamthitta
Kollam
★Thenmala
★Ponmudi
Thiruvananthapuram

Thenmala

(Map pg **46**, **E3**)

Getting There

By Air
The nearest is Thiruvananthapuram International Airport, 75 km
☏ 0471–250 1424

By Rail
The nearest broad gauge station is Kollam (☏ 0475–274 4930), 73 km. From here, a metre gauge train takes two hours and 45 minutes to reach Thenmala.

By Road
It is a two-hour drive from both Thiruvananthapuram and Kollam. Regular buses ply to Thenmala from Kollam, Kottarakkara, as well as Punalur.

Kerala clove

FACT FILE

District: Kollam

STD code: 0475

When to go: August to February

For information contact
Thenmala Ecotourism Promotion Society
✉ Thenmala Dam Junction, Thenmala 691 308
☏ 0475–234 4800

District Tourism Promotion Council
✉ Near KSRTC bus stand, Kollam
☏ 0474–274 5625
🖷 0474–275 0170

Thenmala literally means, 'honey hills'. Honey from these hills was sought after because it was mistakenly believed to have medicinal properties. However, today the region is better known for its eco-conservation efforts. As India's first planned ecotourism destination, Thenmala is the nerve-centre of 10 satellite ecotourism attractions scattered across the hills of Thiruvananthapuram, Kollam and Pathanamthitta.

Thenmala Ecotourism Promotion Society or **TEPS** is responsible for spreading eco-awareness and ensuring that the eco-system of the region is left undisturbed. The well-trained staff of the TEPS brief visitors on how best to explore the region, but also guide them on appropriate behaviour. The organisation has also taken under its wings the nearby Shenduruney Wildlife Sanctuary.

The Palaruvi falls, riverfront leisure zones, rock shelters and a deer rehabilitation centre are some of the attractions in Thenmala. Located 500 m above the sea level, in the foothills of the southern Western Ghats, Thenmala's diverse flora and fauna and vast tracts of forests attract adventure seekers, naturalists and conservationists.

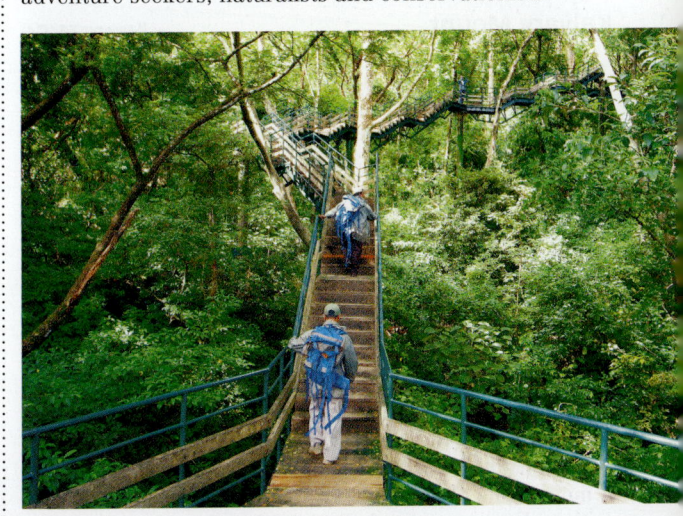

A wooden skyway winds upwards at Thenmala

Idukki

(Map pg **71**, **B3**)

The largest district in Kerala, Idukki covers nearly 13 per cent of the State's total area, 97 per cent of which is covered in rugged mountains and dense forests. Three large rivers, numerous trekking trails, stunning views and a diverse wildlife make it an outdoor enthusiast's delight. This pristine hideaway has successfully retained its charm – sans tourist hysteria.

Idukki has a predominantly tribal population with 200 tribal settlements scattered all over the district in remote hilly areas and dense forests. Base yourself at Cheruthoni or Kulamavu to explore the three great dams on the Periyar and other tourist attractions such as Nadukani Viewpoint, the Idukki Wildlife Sanctuary and the mesmerising Thommankuthu waterfalls.

SIGHTS

Idukki Arch Dam
(Map pg **71**, **B4**)

The Periyar River flows through a gorge formed by two huge rocks called *kuravan* and *kurathi*. The magnificent parabolic structure of Asia's first arch dam spans the gorge. On one side stretches the placid reservoir, whereas on the other, the dam plunges deep into a forested valley.

Kalvary Mount
(Map pg **71**, **C4**)

Located 35 km from Thodupuzha, Kalvary Mount offers a stunning view of its scenic surroundings – the vast Idukki reservoir and the forested valleys. A wonderful place for trekking, visitors may, if they are fortunate, spot a herd of elephants. During Lent, pilgrims climb up the hillock in a procession, and on Good Friday, they carry crosses up the hill to the top.

Thommankuthu
(Map pg **71**, **A3**)

Thommankuthu is famous for its waterfall. These falls have been named after Thomban, a tribal leader who was washed away near a waterfall called 'Thombankuthu'. Later, the name changed to 'Thommankuthu'. The seven-step fall drops down a rock from a height of 1,500 m and is a popular picnic spot. At each step, there is a cascade with a pool below it. The 12-km trek to the top of the hill is a memorable experience. The less adventurous have the option of enjoying the shallow pools below.

Getting There

By Air
The nearest is Cochin International Airport, 110 km
☎ 0484–261 0113

By Rail
The nearest railhead is Ernakulam
☎ 0484–237 5431), 120 km.
Kottayam railway station
☎ 0481–256 2933), is 114 km.

By Road
Thodupuzha, which provides easy access to Idukki, is about 65 km east of Kochi. Munnar – 65 km, Thodupuzha – 55 km, Aluva – 110 km, and Ernakulam – 115 km.

FACT FILE

District: Idukki

STD code: 04862

When to go: September to March

For information contact
District Tourist Information Office
Civil Station, Painavu, Idukki
☎ 04862–232 248

SIGHTS AND ATTRACTIONS	Grid
Anamudi Peak	C1
Chellarkovilmedu (View Point)	C4
Chinnakkanal	C2
Chinnar Wildlife Sanctuary	C1
Grampi (View Point)	C5
Idukki Wildlife Sanctuary	B4
Kalvary Mount (Pilgrim Centre)	C4
Kolukkumalai (Tea Plantation)	C2
Lockhart Gap	C2
Mangala Devi Temple	D5
Marayoor	C1
Munnar (Hill Station)	C2
Nadukani (View Point)	B4
Pattumala Church	C5
Peermede (Hill Station)	B5
Periyar Tiger Reserve	C5
Rajamala (Eravikulam National Park)	B2
Ramakalmedu (View Point)	C4
Thattekkad Bird Sanctuary	A2
Thekkady	C5
Top Station (View Point)	C2
Vagamon (Hill Station)	B4

WATERFALLS AND DAMS	
Attukal Falls	C2
Bhoothathankettu Dam	A2
Cheeyappara Falls	B2
Cheruthoni Dam	B4
Idukki Arch Dam	B4
Kulamavu Dam	B4
Kundala Dam	C2
Mattupetty Dam	C2
Periyar Dam	C5
Thommankuthu Falls	A3
Valara Falls	B2

Idukki | District Map

Munnar | Destination Map

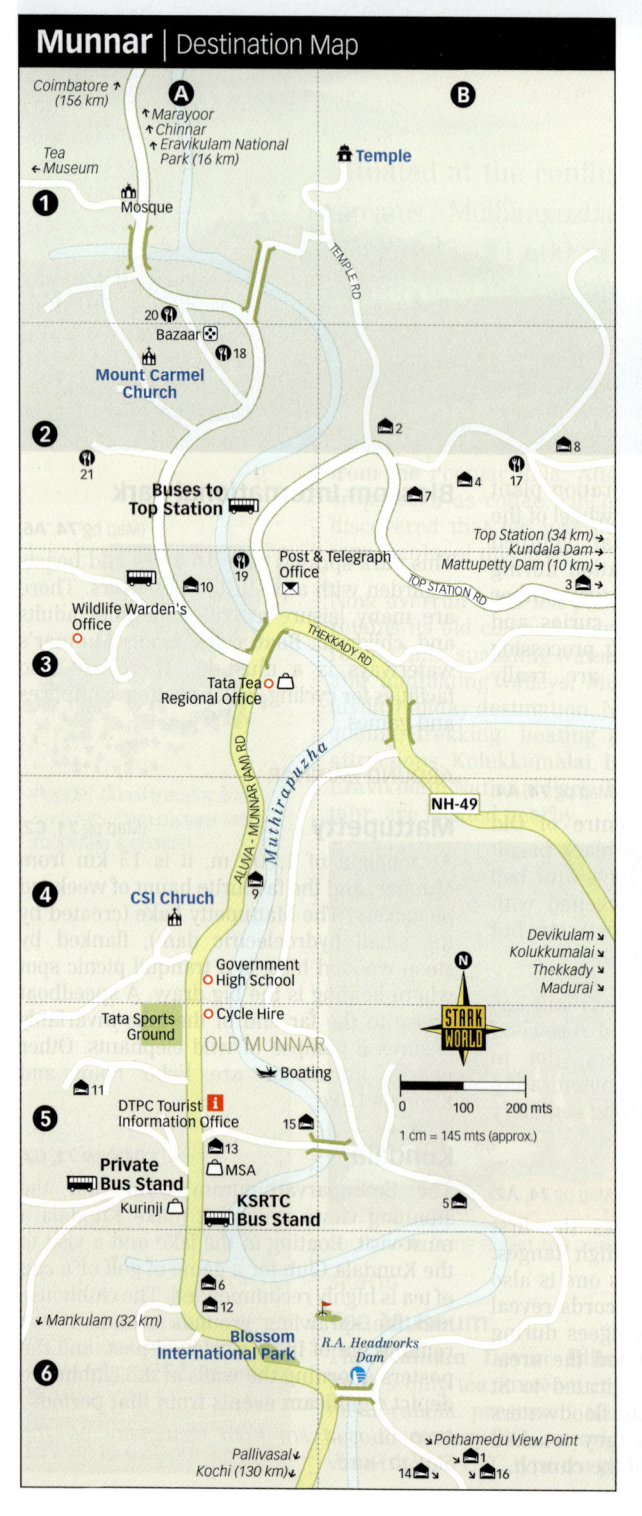

DON'T MISS

» Eravikulam National Park

Wedged between the picturesque Kannan Devan Hills and Anamudi, South India's highest peak, this 97-sq-km park is home to the endangered mountain goat, the Nilgiri tahr.

The Malabar cinnamon is second only to the Sri Lankan variety in aroma

SIGHTS AND ATTRACTIONS	Grid
Blossom International Park	A6
CSI Church	A4
Mount Carmel Church	A2
Temple	B1

WHERE TO STAY		
Copper Castle	1	B6
Edassery Eastend	2	B2
Elysium Gardens	3	B3
Government Guest House	4	B2
High Range Club	5	B5
Hill View	6	A6
Issacs Residency	7	B2
KTDC Tea County	8	B2
Misha Tourist Home	9	A4
Munnar Inn	10	A3
Poopada Tourist Home	11	A5
Royal Retreat	12	A6
Sree Narayana Tourist Home	13	A5
Tall Trees	14	B5
Westwood	15	A5
Windermere Estate	16	B6

WHERE TO EAT		
Greens	(see 2)	B2
Gurus	17	B2
Hazarath	18	A2
KTDC Tea County	(see 8)	B2
Patel's Restaurant	19	A3
Rapsy Restaurant	20	A1
Royal Retreat	(see 12)	A6
Saravana Bhavan	21	A2
Silver Spoon	(see 10)	A3

WHERE TO SHOP		
Kurinji (Souvenir)		A5
MSA (Souvenir)		A5
Tata Tea Regional Office		A3

74 | KERALA MAPS & MORE

Top Station (Map pg **71**, **C2**)

Top Station derives its name from a ropeway that once connected it, the highest point, through Middle Station to Lower Station in the valley. It is also the highest point on the Munnar-Kodaikanal road and the 34-km drive through verdant tea plantations on the High Ranges, offering panoramic views of the countryside, is truly unforgettable. Inhabitants of a tiny hamlet on the Kerala-Tamil Nadu border, perched precariously on a ridge, are the only permanent inhabitants of Top Station. From the summit, the plains of Tamil Nadu and the edge of the Western Ghats are clearly visible.

Marayoor (Map pg **71**, **C1**)

This fenced patch of dense greenery amid hilly terrain holds the **only natural sandalwood forest in Kerala**. Marayoor not only grows the finest sandalwood in the world, but is also a famous archaeological site. The caves found here, home to tribals, are also considered holy as sages are said to have meditated here in the distant past. Hence, the name, 'Muniyaras'.

Devikulam Lake (Map pg **71**, **C2**)

The drive along the winding road to Devikulam is a real treat. The lake here is said to be the highest in the region and is ideal for trout fishing. According to local folklore, Sita is believed to have taken a dip in the pond close by. Revered as a holy place, a small temple has been built here in her honour. In the middle of the lake is an island with a fishing lodge.

Note: Take prior permission from the Tata Tea Regional Office, Munnar, before a visit.

Kolukkumalai (Map pg **71**, **C2**)

This is said to be the highest tea plantation in the country. Located in the upper reaches of Tamil Nadu's Theni district, it is close to the Kerala border with an elevation of 2,400 m. Kolukkumalai offers some splendid views of the sweltering plains of Tamil Nadu. The drive to the top along a narrow winding road past sprawling tea plantations is an adventure in itself.

A treacherous serpentine route, once used by estate workers to carry tea chests to the plains, is today a big hit with trekkers. A visit to the tea factory here is especially interesting, and offers an opportunity to savour the special flavour of the famous Kolukkumalai tea.

Note: Vehicle entry fee at Suryanelli tea estate checkpost is Rs 50, factory visit is Rs 100 per head.

Viewpoints

Stunning vistas are a plenty in Munnar. The Lockhart Gap, located on SH 19, offers a bird's eye-view of Bison Valley and the surrounding hills extending up to Thekkady. It is also an ideal place for rock climbing. The view from Pothamedu, 6 km from Munnar, is equally spectacular. It has an exotic ambience with lush mountains and plantations all around. Vehicles on NH 49, creeping up the hills appear like toy cars. From the Nyamakad Gap on the Munnar-Coimbatore Road, there are great views of the Thalayar Valley on one side and the Munnar Valley on the other.

Waterfalls of Munnar

Munnar and its surrounding environs abound in waterfalls that are especially spectacular just after the rains. Located 18 km from Munnar, on the way to Thekkady, the Power House waterfalls cascade down a steep rock. Attukal, located between Munnar and Pallivasal, is a feast for the eyes. It is also ideal for trekking. Nyayamakad is another fabulous location. The enchanting surroundings make this an excellent picnic spot and trekking point. The Valara and Cheeyappara falls, located close to the national highway on the Adimali-Munnar route, are also delightfullly scenic.

Dawn over Devikulam Lake

THE HILLS

MAPS & MORE **KERALA** | 75

Getting There

By Air
The nearest airport is Cochin International Airport, 150 km
☎ 0484–261 0115

By Rail
The nearest railhead is Kottayam, 75 km
☎ 0481–256 2933.

By Road
Thekkady – 35 km, Vagamon – 25 km, Kottayam – 75 km, Munnar – 140 km, and Madurai – 50 km. Kuttikkanam, Elappara and Pambanar are all close by.

Turmeric – an aromatic seasoning from the ginger family

FACT FILE

District: Idukki

STD code: 04869

When to go: September to May

For information contact
District Tourist Information
✉ Thekkady Junction, Kumily
☎ 04869–222 620

Peermede

(Map pg **71**, **B5**)

Sprawling estates of tea, coffee, cardamom, rubber and eucalyptus surround this charming hill station, once famous as the summer retreat of the Travancore kings. Peermede's history is also closely linked to that of the Sufi saint, Peer Mohammad, believed to be the first trader of spices in the region.

Natural grasslands, pine forests and a salubrious climate make Peermede an enchanting and picturesque destination. The **legacy of the Raj** can still be seen in colonial buildings such as Ashley, Henwoods, and Greenwoods.

SIGHTS

Eagle Rock or Parunthumpara (Map pg **71**, **C5**)
Eagle Rock is actually a large, nearly circular piece of rock spread across half a kilometre. From its height, it offers a panoramic view of the surrounding countryside – rocky plains, lush hillsides and verdant forests.

CSI Church (St George's Church) (Map pg **71**, **B5**)
This was built in 1867 and is believed to be the first church of the High Ranges. It is situated on a 17-acre land in Pallikkunnu, surrounded by groves of cypress and pine trees. Embellished with decorative arches and carved teakwood beams, it is an **architectural marvel**.

Thrisangu Hills (Map pg **71**, **B5**)
Fiery sunsets and superb views beckon nature lovers to these hills, just half a kilometre from Kuttikkanam junction.

Summer Palace (Map pg **71**, **B5**)
The huge but now dilapidated palace where the maharajas of Travancore once spent their summers is surrounded by lush greenery. The smoke-stained hearths, endless corridors, underground passages, durbar halls, stables and prison cells recall the grandeur and glory of a bygone era.

Panchalimedu (Map pg **71**, **B5**)
The ancient granite edicts found on these hills near the Mundakayam Valley link this region to the great epic, the *Mahabharata*. During their exile, the five Pandava brothers are believed to have spent some time here. The name, 'Panchalimedu' itself is derived from 'Panchali', another name for Draupadi, the wife of the Pandavas.

Getting There

By Air
The nearest is Cochin International Airport, 120 km
☏ 0484–261 0115

By Rail
The nearest railhead is Kottayam, 64 km
☏ 0481–256 2933

By Road
The NH 49 to Thripunithura (Kochi) and SH 15 to Ettumanoor through Thalayolaparambu both lead to Vagamon. From Madurai it is 243 km through Kumily, Peermede and Elappara.

Vagamon

(Map pg **71**, **B4**)

Pristine forests, exotic flora and fauna and verdant meadows characterise Vagamon, a location straight out of a tourism brochure. Located 1,100 m above sea level on the western fringe of Idukki, and bordering Kottayam, the Vagamon mountain range was cleared by the early planters for the cultivation of tea and coffee.

Vagamon first witnessed changes in 1926 when Walter Duncan and Company set up their tea plantations in a massive 534-acre plot of land. A decade later, Christian missionaries set up the Kurisumala Ashram, which transformed the region into a **spiritual nerve centre**, popular even today.

The terrain differs from thickly wooded areas or grassy plains to the ruggedly mountainous. While pine trees cover large tracts, tea plantations are less in number compared to other hill stations such as Munnar. Indeed, Vagamon's charm lies in the relaxed ambience that makes it an ideal getaway.

SIGHTS

Kurisumala
(Map pg **71**, **B4**)

Located 5 km from Vagamon, is Kurisumala, an important Christian pilgrim centre, with a church atop a hill. There are 14 crosses along the path leading to the church, which commands stunning views of the surrounding countryside.

Devotees trek to Kurisumala

Kurisumala Ashram
(Map pg **71**, **B4**)

This Catholic monastery, which strives to combine Indian religiosity with Christian spirituality, has been attracting monks from around the world for close to four decades. Abbot Francis Acharya, a Belgian, and Fr Bede Griffiths, an Englishman, established this Cistercian abbey in 1958.
☏ 04822–289 277

FACT FILE

District: Idukki

STD code: 04869

When to go: August to May

For information contact
District Tourist Information
✉ Thekkady Junction, Kumily
☏ 04869–222 620

Murugan Para
(Map pg **71**, **B4**)

On the eastern side of Kurisumala is Murugan Para, a rock-cut temple dedicated to Lord Murugan that attracts a large number of worshippers.

Pine Forests
(Map pg **71**, **B4**)

This valley in Kolahalamedu, with its groves of pine trees, is a protected area. There are boards cautioning tourists to keep from littering the forest.

MAPS & MORE **KERALA** | 77

Getting There

By Air
The nearest airport is Cochin International Airport, 180 km
☎ 0484–261 0115
The airport in Coimbatore is 150 km
☎ 0422–257 3396

By Rail
The nearest railhead is Palakkad, 60 km.
☎ 0491–253 2156

By Road
From Kochi, Palakkad lies on NH 47 from Thrissur. From Palakkad, take the road through Koduvayur to Nenmara. The nearest KSRTC bus stand is in Palakkad
☎ 0491–252 7298

FACT FILE

District: Palakkad
STD code: 04923
When to go: September to January
For information contact
District Tourist Information Office
✉ West Fort Rd, Palakkad
☎ 0491–253 8996

Anthurium farms

Nelliyampathy

(Map pg **88**, **E5**)

Situated south of the Palakkad Gap, Nelliyampathy has all the attractions of a typical hill station – coffee, tea, and cardamom plantations, a pleasant climate, sublime scenery and an abundance of flora and fauna. Locally called 'poor man's Ooty', it offers the inhabitants of Palakkad an escape from the sweltering summer heat of the plains.

Nelliyampathy is close to the **wildlife sanctuaries** of Parambikulam, Anamalai and Peechi-Vazhani. The Nelliyampathy Range, once owned by the maharajas of Kollengode and Kochi, is now part of the Nenmara Forest Division. It consists of a chain of ridges separated by valleys that abound in evergreen and semi-evergreen forests, teeming with wildlife.

SIGHTS

Pothundy
(Map pg **88**, **D5**)

A picturesque reservoir, it lies on the way to Nelliyampathy, close to the scenic village of Nenmara, and is built across two tributaries of the Ayalar River – the Meenachadypuzha and the Padipuzha.

Seetharkundu
(Map pg **88**, **E5**)

Located within the Karuna plantations, Seetharkundu attracts visitors as much for the drive from Nelliyampathy as for the place itself. The drive offers a fabulous view of the plains, as far as Palakkad town and its surrounding countryside. Besides the waterfalls, there is a gnarled tree here, a major attraction. Legend has it that Rama, Sita and Lakshman once lived here, hence the name.

Mampara Grasslands
(Map pg **88**, **E5**)

These sprawling grasslands can be reached only through a treacherous road, but it is well worth the effort for the spectacular views of the **Palakkad range** – verdant slopes, thick forests and a patchwork of lush paddy fields.

Orange and Vegetable Farm
(Map pg **88**, **E5**)

Set up by the rulers of the erstwhile State of Cochin in 1943 to provide food for British troops and resolve a crisis that arose in the land during the time, this once thriving farm has now been revived and 237 acres of land re-planted with orange trees. The fruit preservation unit, located at Pulayanpara, where guavas and passion fruit are used to make delicious jams, preserves and squash, is open to visitors.

78 | KERALA MAPS & MORE

Getting There

By Air
The nearest to Kalpetta is Calicut International Airport at Karipur, Kozhikode, 88 km
☎ 0483–271 1314

By Rail
The nearest station is at Kozhikode, 63 km
☎ 0495–270 1234

By Road
Wayanad is on NH 212 that connects Kozhikode to Mysore. Buses from Kozhikode bus stand go through Vythiri to the nearest KSRTC stand in Kalpetta.

One of the many waterfalls in Wayanad

FACT FILE

District: Wayanad
STD code: 04936
When to go: November to March

For information contact
District Tourism Promotion Council
✉ Civil Station, Kalpetta North, Wayanad
☎ 04936–202 134

Wayanad

(Map pg **80**)

Wind-blown and lashed by rain, Wayanad lies across 2,126 sq km of the lofty Western Ghats and has been recognised as a bio-diverse region. Located on the southern tip of the Deccan Plateau, at an altitude ranging from 700 to 2,100 m above sea level, Wayanad encompasses sub-tropical savannah, thickly wooded hills and evergreen forests. While verdant spice plantations cover the hills, the valleys in the area consist of gently rolling paddy fields.

A land where the rain, rocks and trees reign supreme, Wayanad's history is as striking as its terrain. Historians believe that organised human life existed here from as early as 4,000 BC when Mesolithic culture first began in Kerala. The caves and rock carvings of Ambukuthimala provide proof of this. Roads winding up rugged hillsides, a legacy of the British, are the only mode of transport in the region. Pepper, cardamom and ginger grow extensively, surrounded by vast plantations of tea and coffee.

Vythiri (Map pg **80**, **C4**)

Vythiri stands as a gateway to Wayanad, to the realm of gurgling streams, hills and valleys. Lakes, gorges and ravines, verdant hills that nudge distant clouds, dreamy dawns and misty evenings are standard fare.

This region offers a true taste of Wayanad. The charming Pookot Lake is only a kilometre away, towards Lakkidi. The tallest summit in the district, Chembra peak, 6,890 ft above sea level, is nearest from Vythiri. Waterfalls, at Kanthampara and Sentinel Rock, lie to the south. A number of resorts, nestled in sylvan surroundings, add to the attraction of the destination.

SIGHTS

Lakkidi's Chain Tree (Map pg **80**, **C4**)

Apart from the stunning views of the surrounding plains, Lakkidi's other claim to fame is the chain tree. Local lore has it that when a British engineer was unsuccessful in his

THE HILLS

MAPS & MORE **KERALA** | 79

Wayanad | District Map

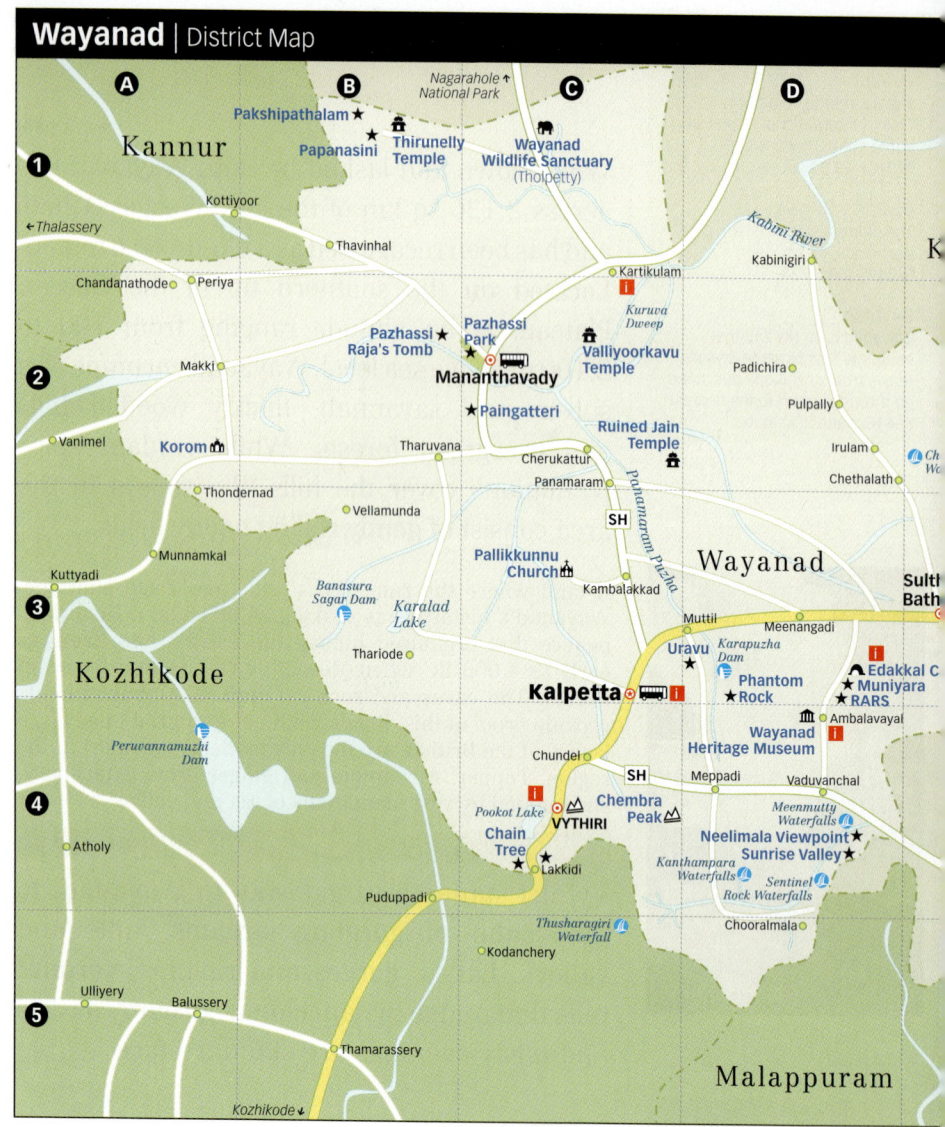

SIGHTS AND ATTRACTIONS	Grid
Chain Tree	C4
Chembra Peak	C4
Edakkal Caves	D3
Jain Temple	E3
Korom Mosque	A2
Kuruva Dweep (Island)	C2
Lakkidi	C4
Muniyara (Ancient Burial Vaults)	D3
Neelimala Viewpoint	D4
Paingatteri Gramam (Agraharam)	C2
Pakshipathalam	B1
Pallikkunnu Church	C3
Papanasini (Mountain Spring)	B1
Pazhassi Park	C2
Pazhassi Raja's Tomb	B2
Phantom Rock	D3
RARS (Regional Agricultural Research Station)	D3
Ruined Jain Temple	C2
Sunrise Valley	D4
Thirunelly Temple	B1
Uravu	D3
Valliyoorkavu Temple	C2
Vythiri (Hill Station)	C4
Wayanad Heritage Museum	D4
Wayanad Wildlife Sanctuary	E3
Wayanad Wildlife Sanctuary	C1

BEACHES AND LAKES

Karalad Lake	B3
Pookot Lake	C4

WATERFALLS AND DAMS

Banasura Sagar Dam	B3
Chethalayam Waterfall	E2
Kanthampara Waterfalls	D4
Meenmutty Waterfalls	D4
Sentinel Rock Waterfalls	D4

Ginger, used extensively in the food of Kerala

80 | KERALA MAPS & MORE

efforts to find a passage through the dense forests of Wayanad, a young tribal called Karinthandan guided him. Unwilling to share credit for the discovery, the engineer killed the native. Soon, Karinthandan's troubled spirit began haunting travellers on the new route. To pacify the vengeful soul, a priest chained the spirit to a tree. Only then did the haunting cease. A heavy chain anchored to the ground and placed around the stout branches seems to lend credence to the story.

Pookot Lake (Map pg **80**, **C4**)

This large lake is fringed by low wooded hills. Horses and horse carts trot along the 1.5-km pathway, passing around the lake. A curio shop next to the ticket counter sells bamboo and wooden artefacts and hill produce such as spices, tea and honey. Then there is the boat club where pedal and rowboats await visitors.

Note: It is 3 km from Vythiri and 15 km from Kalpetta

Soochipara and Kanthampara Falls (Map pg **80**, **D4**)

From Vythiri, the drive to these falls, considered one of the most beautiful in the district, is delightful. A winding road through verdant tea country, and then a narrow trail through rugged terrain lead to the falls in a dense forest. The three-pronged waters hit the sharp spikes of granite at the base, hence the name, 'Soochipara', or 'needle rocks'.

Note: It is about 20 km from Vythiri, and 23 km from Kalpetta.

Meenmutty Falls (Map pg **80**, **D4**)

Meenmutty Falls, a 300-m long cascade of water, is the largest and most spectacular waterfall in the whole of Wayanad. The drive from Vythiri itself is charming – all woods, verdant hillsides and rolling plantations. It will also take you past charming villages such as Chundel, Meppadi and Vaduvanchal.

The name 'Wayanad' is derived from Vayal Nadu, meaning 'land of paddy fields'

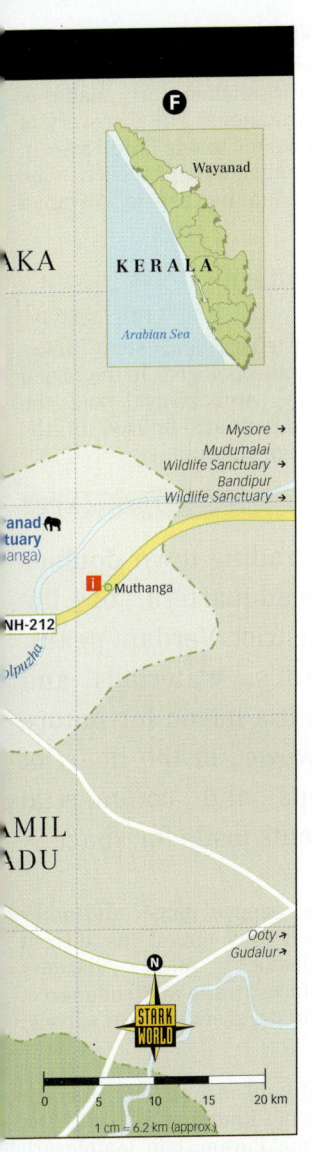

DON'T MISS

» **Spice Tour** A tour through acres of spice plantations spread across the hills is a must-do

» **Trekking** With its hills, valleys and water falls, Wayanad is the most popular trekking destination in Kerala.

Sulthan Bathery (Map pg **80**, **E3**)

Pre-historic caves, luxuriant vegetation, undulating hills, meandering rivers, and jungle trails invite you to explore the peaceful hill town of Sulthan Bathery.

'Bathery' is a corruption of the word, 'battery', and the name has stuck ever since Tipu Sultan, the town's one-time ruler, dumped his ammunition in the old Jain temple here. Known as 'Ganapathivattam' until then, the Sultan left another enduring legacy of his exploits in the town of Sulthan Bathery.

SIGHTS

Jain Temple (Map pg **80**, **E3**)
This 13th century temple, built in the architectural style of the reigning Vijayanagar dynasty, has had a rather chequered past – it served as a shrine, then as a centre of commercial trade, and finally, as the ammunition store or battery for Tipu Sultan's army.

The Edakkal Caves

Edakkal Caves (Map pg **80**, **D3**)

Located 12 km from Sulthan Bathery, these prehistoric shelters are made of natural rock formations. The discovery of the caves is attributed to one Fred Fawcett, the then Superintendent of Police, who had come on a hunting trip to Wayanad in 1890.

Wayanad Heritage Museum (Map pg **80**, **D4**)

Innumerable artefacts and stone relics discovered by anthropologists in the region around Bathery, Ambalavayal and the forests of Wayanad are housed in the Wayanad Heritage Museum.

Kalpetta (Map pg **80**, **C3**)

This small trading town doubles as the headquarters of the Wayanad district. Verdant peaks, trekking trails, waterfalls and lakes make it a haven for nature lovers. However, in the heart of town, shops and commercial establishments jostle for space.

Coffee, banana, pepper, ginger and other spices find their way out of the district through Kalpetta's many bazaars. Government offices, trade and commerce, and of late, tourists, give this town a lively, purposeful air.

A stronghold of Jainism for a long time, the glass temple of Kottamunda and the Anantha Krishna Puram Jain temple are reminders of this early heritage.

SIGHTS

Chembra Peak (Map pg **80**, **C4**)
At 2,100 m, this peak is the highest in Wayanad. The summit offers spectacular views of the surrounding hills, rocks and valleys. Despite a tricky ascent, the peak draws trekking enthusiasts in hordes.

Note: Trekkers can hire tents, sleeping bags and other gear from the District Tourism Promotion Council (DTPC).

Karalad Lake (Map pg **80**, **B3**)

A huge lake, spread across 7 acres and surrounded by dense bamboo groves, it is ideal for a peaceful, quiet break. Adjoining hills provide great trekking options. The Banasura Sagar Dam is only about 3 km to the north from the Karalad Lake.

Location: In Thariode, 16 km from Kalpetta.
Boating timings: 9 am to 6 pm.

Mananthavady (Map pg **80**, **C2**)

This township, despite its bustle, is surrounded by peaceful wilderness. Rather isolated from the other towns located on NH 212, Mananthavady has its own distinctive allure.

Mananthavady is the base for Pakshipathalam, a boulder-strewn area in the forests of the Bramhagiri hills, ideal for trekking and watching birds. The enchanting Kuruva Dweep Island and the Tholpetty Wildlife Sanctuary are close by.

This town has close links to the history of Wayanad as well. The Pazhassi tomb, a kilometre from Mananthavady, marks the place where the body of the fiery warrior, the Pazhassi Raja, was cremated after his defeat at the hands of the British.

SIGHTS

Thirunelly Temple (Map pg **80**, **B1**)

Thirunelly Temple, literally, 'the temple with the sacred gooseberry (*nelli*) tree', is located in a valley surrounded by the south Bramhagiri peaks. Myth relates this shrine to the Hindu gods, Brahma and Vishnu. The surrounding peaks are a trekker's delight.

📞 *04935–210 201*

Pakshipathalam (Map pg **80**, **B1**)

During their wanderings, saints and god men are believed to have taken shelter in the numerous caves and rocky hillocks strewn across this area. However, today Pakshipathalam is the haven for a large avian colony – mainly around the natural rock caves. It draws avid trekkers and birdwatchers during the summer months.

📞 *04935–240 233, 04936–202 134*

Thrissileri Temple (Map pg **80**, **C1**)

This architecturally pleasing Shiva Temple, with its antiquity shrouded in the distant past, is so inextricably linked to the Thirunelly Temple that the performance of rites at the latter shrine remains incomplete until it is followed by offerings at Thrissileri.

Pazhassi Museum (Map pg **80**, **C2**)

When Tipu Sultan ceded Malabar to the British, the Pazhassi Raja, scion of the Kottayam royal family, was the first to revolt. Forced to flee into the jungles of Wayanad, he engaged the British in guerrilla warfare. Finally defeated in the jungles of Mavilamthode near Pulpally, a tomb marks the spot where he was cremated. The small structure nearby houses a collection of memorabilia.

Nearly half of Kerala's tribal population of 400,000 live in Wayanad

Kuruva Dweep (Map pg **80**, **C2**)

Two streams, the Panamaram, originating from Lakkidi, and the Mananthavady rivulet, originating from the Thondaramudi peak, wind around a 950-acre wooded island nestled amidst sylvan surroundings called Karuva Dweep. DTPC operates bamboo-raft rides from Pulpally. The heavily wooded environs provide a home to a variety of birds and butterflies.

River Nila
The Artery of Life...

Highlights

The River Nila has its source in the humble Thrimurthy hills in Tamil Nadu. Flowing west through central Kerala, this mighty river empties itself into the Arabian Sea at Ponnani. On the way, it flows through three districts – Palakkad, Thrissur and Malappuram. The river also has an extensive catchment area and a web of tributaries that range from minor streams to gushing rivers.

Mohiniattam – a classical dance form of Kerala

River Nila stands for different things to different people – the fount of inspiration for poets and writers, the wellspring of cultural ethos, rousing the artistic and the aesthetic, a winning location for enthusiastic movie directors, a waterway for people and goods, a sand goldmine for avaricious traders... and so the list goes on. A source of life and livelihood for those living along its basin, it is the longest river in Kerala and has given birth to an ancient river civilisation. Nila has also had a profound influence on the State's classical and folk traditions, its religious and social life, its festivals and literature. It is the common thread that binds together traditions and cultures with the lives of people. But most significantly perhaps, the river has left its indelible mark on peoples' psyches as the symbol of all that is immutable in nature – noble and inviolate.

The river basin receives an annual rainfall of 2,300 mm, most of it during the monsoons. As rains peak during the soggy June to August season, the rain water rushes through the estuary at Ponnani before slamming into the sea.

Kalarippayattu performers bring alive the festivities of the ancient royal festival of Mamankam on the banks of the Nila

Wide swathes of ochre spread for miles before disappearing into the blue-green ocean. But once the rains depart, the river is no longer as alive and exuberant, a fact that continues to be a cause of concern for some time now. Officially known as 'Bharathapuzha', as it passes through the holy Bharatha kandham near Thiruvilwamala, this river is simply called 'Nila' by those who know her intimately.

Nurturing both the agricultural and cultural life along its banks, River Nila has inspired the literary luminaries, Thunchath Ezhuthachan and Kunjan Nambiar. Jnanpeeth award winner, MT Vasudevan Nair, has also written paeans to Nila. Vallathol too, has written many poems about the greatness of the river. G Sankara Kurup, Vyloppilli, P Kunhi Raman Nair, Olappamanna, Edassery and Balamani Amma are among the artistes inspired by Bharathapuzha. Great astronomers such as Thalakulath Bhattathiri and holy men such as Pakkanar and Naranath Bhranthan have also drawn inspiration from the river.

Acclaimed institutions such as the literature park, Thunchan Parambu, a draw for the intellectually inclined, have sprung up along the river banks. The place where the father of Malayalam literature, Thunchath Ezhuthachan, had spent the better part of his life scripting texts now hosts a centre for literary pursuits. The poet Vallathol Narayana Menon, set up the premier institute, Kalamandalam, in Cheruthuruthy. It is a centre for learning Kerala's performance arts – dance forms such as Kathakali, *mohiniattam* and *thullal* – as well as the traditional percussion instruments.

Playing the Mizhavu, a copper urn with sheepskin covering its mouth

River Nila (Bharathapuzha) | Circuit Map

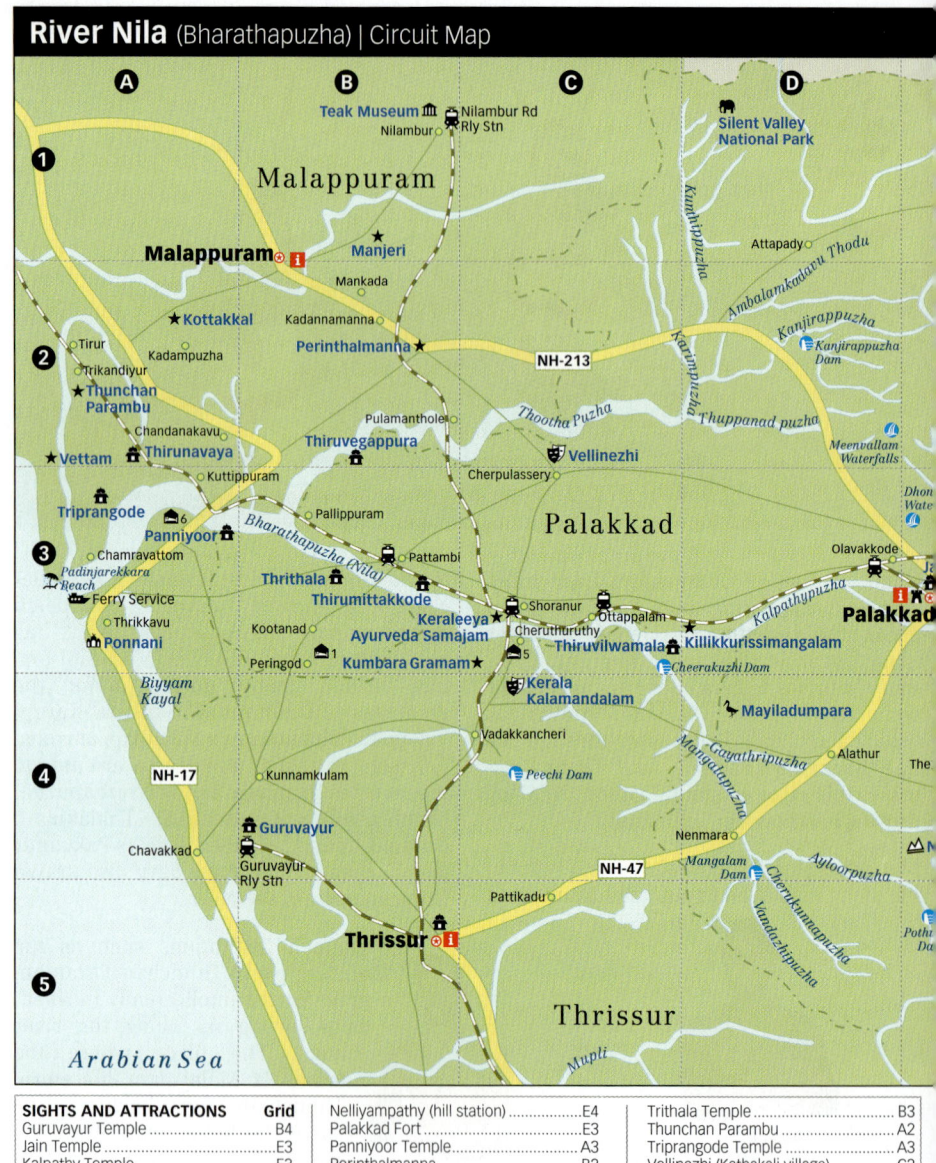

SIGHTS AND ATTRACTIONS	Grid
Guruvayur Temple	B4
Jain Temple	E3
Kalpathy Temple	E3
Kerala Kalamandalam (centre for the arts)	C4
Keraleeya Ayurveda Samajam	C3
Killikkurissimangalam	D3
Kottakkal (Arya Vaidya Sala)	A2
Kumbara Gramam (potters village)	C3
Manjeri	B1
Mayiladumpara (peacock sanctuary)	D4
Nelliyampathy (hill station)	E4
Palakkad Fort	E3
Panniyoor Temple	A3
Perinthalmanna	B2
Ponnani	A3
Seetharkundu (view point)	E5
Silent Valley National Park	D1
Thirumittakkode Temple	B3
Thirunavaya Temple	A2
Thiruvalathoor Temple	E3
Thiruvegappura Temple	B2
Thiruvilwamala Temple	C3
Trithala Temple	B3
Thunchan Parambu	A2
Triprangode Temple	A3
Vellinezhi (Kathakali village)	C2
Vettam (coconut segregation plant)	A2

BEACHES AND LAKES

Biyyam Kayal (lake)	A4
Padinjarekkara Beach	A3

WATERFALLS AND DAMS

Dhoni Waterfalls	E3

In the domain of ragas and rhythms, Kerala has a unique position – the State is rich in a variety of musical instruments.

Elathalam

Udukku

Conch

86 | KERALA MAPS & MORE

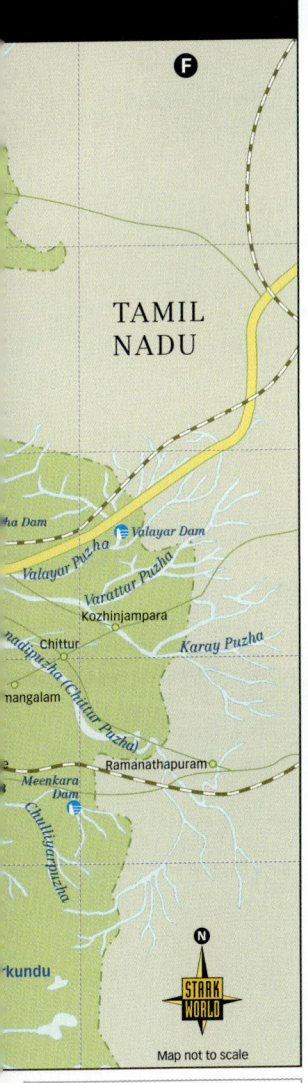

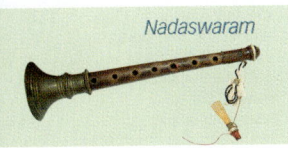

Kerala Kalamandalam (Map pg 86, C4)

The famous poet, Vallathol Narayana Menon, is credited with the setting up of this premier institute in 1930 to nurture the growth of Kerala's traditional dance forms. Initially located within the stately home of a feudal lord, it later shifted to the banks of the Nila at Cheruthuruthy. In addition to Kathakali, other dance forms such as *mohiniattam*, *koodiyattam* and *thullal* are also taught here. The courses taught in music include vocal classical and the *panchavadyam*, involving an ensemble of percussion instruments. The selected students undergo a rigorous training in their chosen art form, starting from the wee hours of the morning and stretching into the late afternoon.

It was in the late 1950s that the institute moved to its present location on a 30-acre plot of land, 1.5 km away at Vettikattiri. With the growing popularity of the centre, a grand theatre for the performing arts, called 'Koothambalam' was completed in 1977. 'A day with the masters', a half-day guided tour, is a major draw. An audio-visual presentation gives an overview of the institute.

📞 04884–262 418, 262 562
@ info@kalamandalam.com
🌐 www.kalamandalam.com

RIVER NILA

Meenvallam Waterfalls D2
Malampuzha Dam E3
Peechi Dam C4
Pothundy Dam E5

WHERE TO STAY
Ayurvedamana B3 1
Kairali E3 2
Kalari Kovilakom E4 3
Kandath Tharavad E4 4
River Retreat C3 5
The Riverside Retreat A3 6

Nadaswaram

A Kathakali artiste in the Hanuman vesham

MAPS & MORE **KERALA** | 87

Palakkad (Palghat) | District Map

SIGHTS AND ATTRACTIONS	Grid
Attapady Valley	C1
Fantasy Park (amusement park)	D3
Jain Temple	D3
Kalpathy Temple	D3
Lakkidi (Kunjan Nambiar Memorial)	C3
Mampara (viewpoint)	E5
Mayiladumpara (peacock sanctuary)	C4
Nelliyampathy (hill station)	E5
Palakkad Fort	D4
Parambikulam Wildlife Sanctuary	E6
Ramassery (idlis)	E4
Seetharkundu (view point)	E5
Shiva Temple (Thrithala)	A3
Silent Valley National Park	C2
Thiruvalathoor (Bhagavathi Temple)	E4

Palakkad

(Map pg **88**, **D3**)

For years, Palakkad has been the gateway to Kerala. It has provided access to the coast for conquerors and traders from the hinterland through what is known as the 'Palakkad Gap', a 40-km break in an otherwise unbroken wall of high mountains. Understandably, the region is a melting pot of cultures and cuisines, arts and music, and is known for its truly eclectic spirit.

The moat around Tipu's Fort

A largely **agrarian society** in which people continue to follow in the footsteps of their forefathers, Palakkad's reputation as the granary of the state is borne out by its undulating paddy fields which stretch for miles. Silent Valley, Kerala's most famous forest, is located in Palakkad and remains largely untouched, making an eloquent case for the preservation of nature in its purest form.

SIGHTS

Tipu's Fort
(Map pg **88**, **D4**)

Located in the heart of present-day Palakkad, this rather well preserved fort was built by Hyder Ali in 1766 ostensibly to facilitate communication between both sides of the Western Ghats. In reality however, Hyder Ali and his son, Tipu, wished to establish their suzerainty over Kerala.

The fort changed hands when the British captured it, after an 11-day siege, in 1784. Although it was later taken by the troops of the Kozhikode Zamorin, it was recaptured by

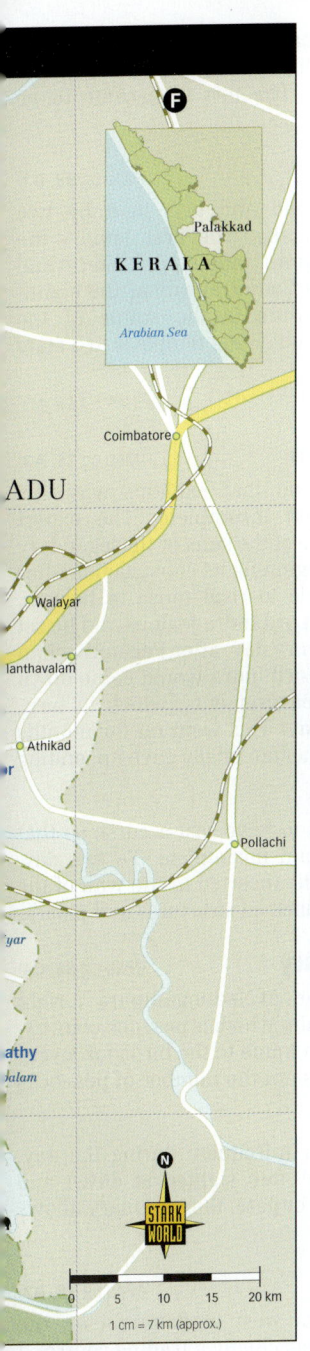

WATERFALLS AND DAMS	
Dhoni Waterfalls	D3
Malampuzha Dam	D3
Meenvallam Waterfall	D3
Pothundy Dam	D5
Vazhani Dam	B4

Getting There

By Air
The nearest airport is at Coimbatore, 60 km
☎ 0422–259 1905

By Rail
The nearest railhead is Palakkad station, well connected to all cities
☎ 0491–253 2156

By Road
Palakkad is on NH 47 that links Salem to Kanyakumari through Coimbatore. The KSRTC station is on Shoranur Rd and has buses to all major towns in the State
☎ 0491–252 7298

FACT FILE

District: Palakkad

STD code: 0491

When to go: August to February

For information contact
District Tourism Promotion Council
✉ West Fort Rd,
Palakkad 678 001
☎ 0491–253 8996
🖥 www.palakkadtourism.org

Poothan-thira-kali, a folk art form associated with the Nila

---

the British in 1790. Tipu Sultan, on the other hand, was not one to give up easily, but his repeated encounters with the British cost him his life. The fort then came to be known by his name.

Jain Temple
(Map pg **88**, **D3**)

This shrine is 1,500 years old and was built by two diamond traders from Karnataka. The first Jains – the Shettys, gave the temple its name, 'Jainamedu', a term still in use. The presiding deity is Chandraprabha, the eighth Thirthankara. A notable feature is the statue of the *kshetrapalan*, the guardian. Today, the temple is in a state of disrepair.

Note: Open for viewing at 5 pm when the daily pooja takes place.

Varahamoorthi Kshetram
(Map pg **86**, **A3**)

There is an interesting legend that explains why this ancient temple has been left incomplete. The expert carpenter, Perumthachan, one of the sons of the legendary Vararuchi, is credited with beginning its construction after being asked to build a temple to rival those in heaven. This, so the story goes, made Lord Indra jealous and he set about disrupting the work. Every day, after Perumthachan completed his day's labour, Lord Indra would come down and change some minute measurements, which in turn, would affect work the next day. This went on for months until an exasperated Perumthachan finally gave up, ending his career as a carpenter.

Perumthachan is also known to have cast a curse so that the work would forever remain incomplete. To this day, his measuring scale and axe lie inserted in the wall of the temple, which stands with unfinished structures and pillars.

Mayiladumpara Sanctuary
(Map pg **88**, **C4**)

About 25 km south of Palakkad, at Nedungathpara, a right turn leads into a wooded terrain, which is peacock country. This extensive forest has been home to the birds for a very long time. Tentative estimates put the number of peacocks at around 200.

Although sightings are rather infrequent during the day, locals say that peacocks are often sighted at dawn and dusk. Not bound by any fence or gate, the sanctuary allows free access.

Trithala
(Map pg **88**, **A3**)

Trithala, located about 8 km west of Pattambi on the Pattambi-Kuttipuram road, was chiefly a trading centre. It was also the *karma bhumi* of the children of Vararuchi, the famous sage. It is in this historical temple town that the sage Agnihotri conducted the 99 *yagnas* that made even Lord Indra envious. The Agnihotri *ilam* (ancestral house) attracts a lot of visitors.

Ponnani

(Map pg **92**, **B6**)

Ponnani is where the Nila finally ends her long, meandering journey and empties out into the Arabian Sea. Located on the edge of the land that juts out over the sea, and surrounded by the estuary to the north and the backwaters to the south, this scenic coastal town was once a famous seaport and formed part of the old Tirumanasseri, ruled by the Namboodiri feudal lords.

Today, Ponnani counts as one of the most important **fishing centres** along the Malappuram coast. High sea fishing operations are centred mainly around Ponnani and Parappanangadi, with nearly 350 mechanised boats plying from Ponnani alone. Although the shifting shoal in the port poses a danger to the uninitiated, native vessels are quite adept at avoiding it.

Islam has always had a strong presence in Ponnani, harking back to the times of the early Arab traders. The Juma Masjid is said to have been built in the mid-15th century by Zainuddin Ibn Bin Ahmed, a descendant of one of the theologians who came from Arabia and settled here. Some have even called Ponnani, a '**small Mecca**'.

The Padinjarekkara Beach, Juma Masjid and the Vallabhatta Kalari Academy are some of the interesting

The 600-year-old Juma Masjid is an important pilgrim centre

RIVER NILA

Getting There

By Air
The nearest is Calicut International Airport, 65 km
0483–271 1314

By Rail
The nearest station is Kuttipuram (0494–260 7900), a short distance away. Long distance trains ply from Kozhikode.

By Road
Ponnani is 17 km off NH 17 and two hours away from Kozhikode. Buses ply regularly, connecting the two towns.

The two-stringed Nanthuni is a cross between a guitar and a veena

FACT FILE

District: Malappuram

STD code: 0494

When to go: September to March

For information contact
DTPC Tourist Information Centre
✉ Malappuram
☎ 0483–273 1504

Public Relations Department, Collectorate
✉ Malappuram
☎ 0483–273 4387

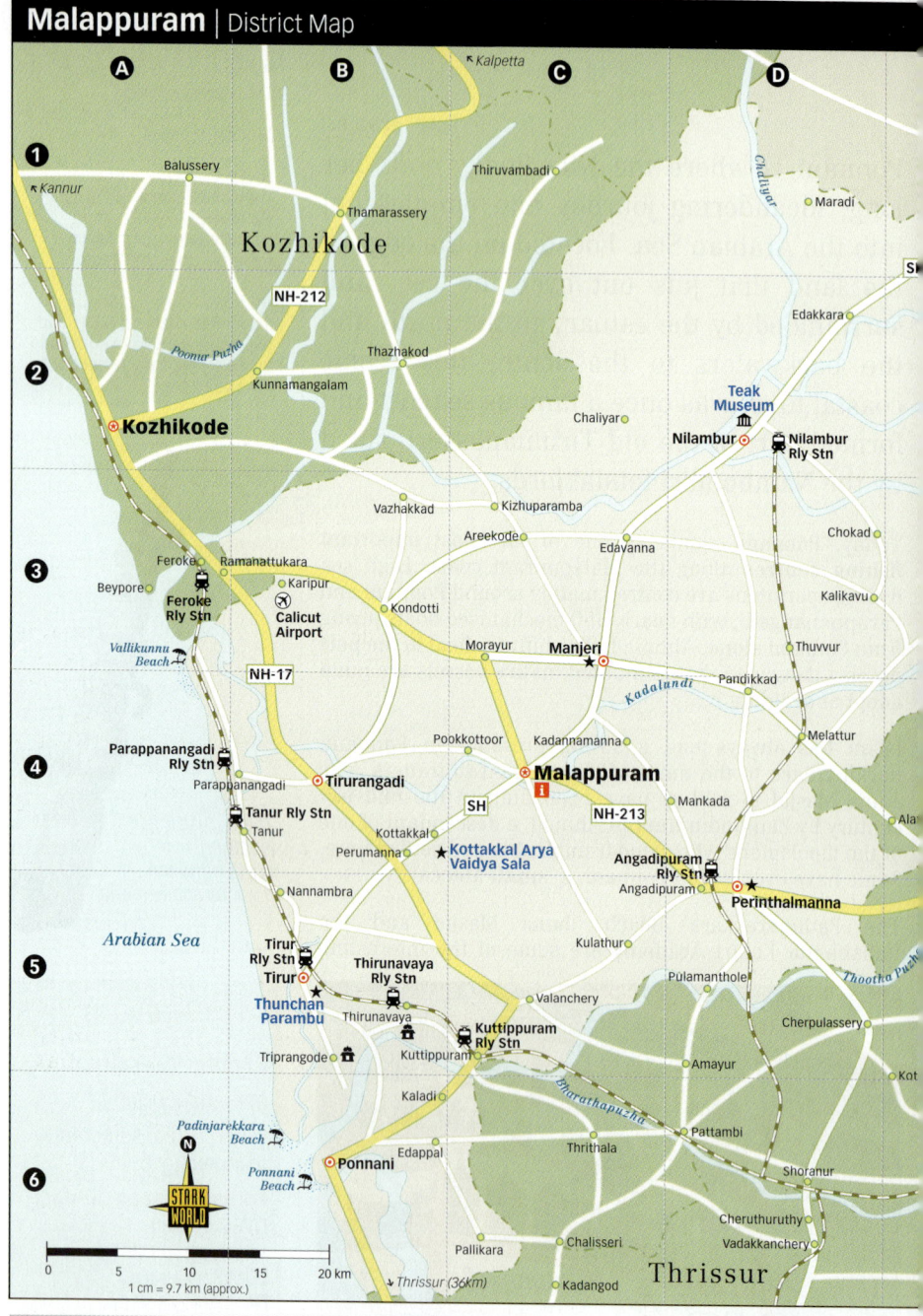

Malappuram | District Map

SIGHTS AND ATTRACTIONS	Grid
Kottakkal Arya Vaidya Sala	B4
Manjeri	C3
Nilambur (teak museum)	D2
Perinthalmanna	D5
Thirunavaya Temple	B5
Triprangode Temple	B5
Thunchan Parambu	B5

BEACHES

Padinjarekkara Beach	B6
Ponnani Beach	B6
Vallikunnu Beach	A3

Thimila

92 | KERALA MAPS & MORE

RIVER NILA

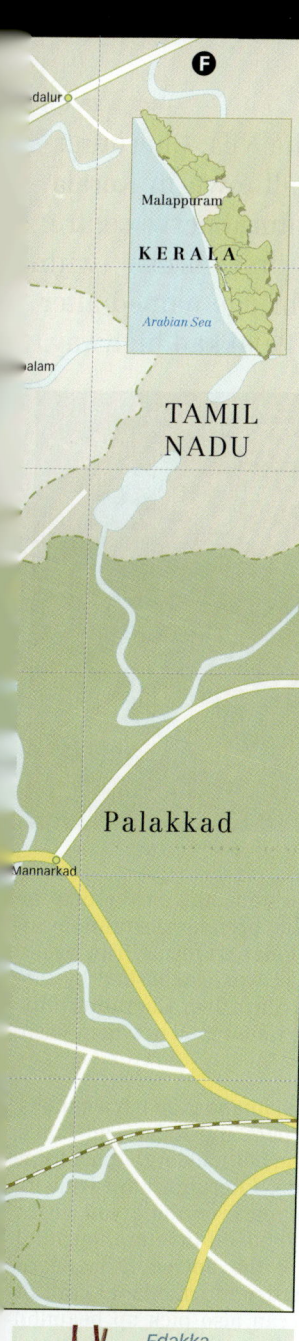

Elephants form an important part of Kerala's culture

local sights. The one-of-its-kind Teak Museum is located at Nilambur. Kuttippuram, Tirur, Thirunavaya, Manjeri, Kottakkal and Perinthalmanna are important towns located nearby along the banks of the Nila.

THINGS TO DO

River Rafting

The raft used is made of recyclable and eco-friendly material, fashioned out of wild bamboo and fastened with coir ropes. Supported by large truck tyre tubes, rafting in this vessel down the Thootha River is an experience not to be forgotten. Beginning at Perinthalmanna, the route proceeds along the three districts of Palakkad, Thrissur and Malappuram and follows the course of the river.

Note: Contact The Blue Yonder, Bangalore
📞 080–3290 6620 ✉ nila@theblueyonder.com

Boating in Tirur Puzha

A boat cruise down the river, starting from Ettrikadavu, and gliding down the backwaters to the estuary in Ponnani, where the river flows into the sea, is a singular experience. Besides the captivating scenery, you may encounter different species of migratory birds along the way and get a glimpse of the lives of the people living along the banks.

Note: Contact The Blue Yonder (see above).

Boating at Kootai

Close to the Tirur railway station is a boat jetty located on a tributary of the Nila, locally known as the Kanoli canal. Here, the block *panchayat* maintains facilities for boating – there are two-seaters, gondola-like shikaras, platform boats and speedboats that travel all the way up to Azhimugham, 19 km away. Although the water is turbulent during the monsoons, a trip down the canal is an enjoyable and exciting experience.

Note: Contact the Tirur Panchayat, Azhimugham Tourism Project
📞 92499 86767

MAPS & MORE KERALA | 93

Getting There

By Air
The nearest is Cochin International Airport, 78 km
☏ 0484–261 0115

By Rail
The nearest railhead is Shoranur Junction, 3 km ☏ 0466–222 2913

By Road
The town lies 31 km from Thrissur on the State highway connecting Thrissur and Shoranur. KSRTC buses are available from all over Kerala to Thrissur.

FACT FILE

District: Thrissur
STD code: 04884
When to go: September to March
For information contact
District Tourism Promotional Council
✉ Opposite Town Hall, Palace Road, Chembukkavu, Thrissur
☏ 0487–232 0800

Seethankanthullal – a slower version of the Ottanthullal

Cheruthuruthy

(Map pg **28**, **C1**)

Situated on the banks of the Nila, Cheruthuruthy is like any other small town in Kerala, except for its fame as a cultural nerve centre. The casual traveller's first brush with Cheruthuruthy is the toll bridge named after the town on the Thrissur-Palakkad highway.

Students at Kalamandalam

The establishment that put Cheruthuruthy on the map is the famous Kalamandalam, the premier institution in Kerala for training in the traditional art forms. The result of one man's vision, the institute was established by the poet, Vallathol Narayana Menon. Since then, Cheruthuruthy has played host to innumerable visitors, all of whom wish to see the institute.

Not far from the site of the old Kalamandalam is Vallathol's tomb. A portrait gallery of the poet and Kalamandalam's artistes is housed in a part of the old building. Apart from the magic of this great institute, Cheruthuruthy with its peaceful, rustic environs gives you everything you might want for a quiet, restful holiday. Spend time in thoughtful contemplation on the banks of the ancient Nila, learn something new about the wizardry of traditional craft at the potter's colony where you can also pick up beautiful souvenirs and mementoes for those back home, or treat yourself at the well-equipped ayurvedic hospital and research centre, situated close to River Nila. The railway town of Shoranur lies just across the river.

Kerala. Like never before

STARK WORLD

Kerala

Stark World - Kerala takes you into God's Own Country, in all its unseen splendour. With exhaustive and in-depth information on unexplored experiences - where to stay, what to see, and maps that help you plan your travel. Over 1000 stunning visuals that bring to life the magic of Kerala. Cities. Backwaters. Midlands. Hills. The Nila. All in a book.

www.starkworld.net

Coastal Circuit
Enduring allure...

The crescent-shaped beaches of Kovalam are international tourist destinations

The 550-km coastline on India's south-western corner, covering the length of Kerala, is characterised by unique geographical features. Enriched by the age-old traditions and customs of its people, the coastal area has fascinated visitors since ancient times.

The topography of Kerala's coastal region, with its large, sandy beaches, is distinctive. However, as we move inland, it changes abruptly. Towards the north, in places such as Bekal, Thalassery and Kannur, the headlands rise above the shore from the fringe of the beaches. With a panoramic view of the surroundings, these highlands are dotted with forts built by the early colonial rulers – the Dutch, the Portuguese and the British.

Malabar Coast

From Kozhikode, once the hub of the Malabar Coast, there is a marked change in topography. Flat land replaces the promontories and hills. However, one overriding feature of the coastline is the ubiquitous coconut tree. Dense groves of coconut line the coast and extend into the interiors of the State. Indeed, these tall, slender trees, which not only lend their name to the State, but also provide a source of livelihood for its people, constitute the most widespread vegetation of the coastal area.

Kerala's history is inextricably linked to its long coastline. Long associated with the legends of buccaneer seafarers, traders and colonialists, today it is a haven for beach buffs and jet-setting tourists.

Highlights

The coastal circuit offers a variety of options to the traveller, and draws tourists from all over the world. From the southernmost resort of Poovar, a tranquil getaway, and the bustle of Kovalam, an international tourist destination, to Kochi, with its quaint mix of antiquity and commercial activity, this region has something for everyone.

Kovalam

(Map pg **15-C4, 98**)

Three crescent-shaped beaches, separated by rocky outcroppings, constitute the chief attraction of this coastal town. Backed by the palm-covered steep headlands, the beaches are lined with a host of shops that offer all kinds of goods and services, creating an unmistakably resort-like atmosphere.

Shallow waters, stretching hundreds of metres, are ideal for swimming. The vast expanse of shimmering sea, sandy coves, rocky outcroppings over the water, exuberant surf and brilliant sunshine impart an unreal quality to this popular tourist spot.

SIGHTS

Lighthouse
(Map pg **98, A5**)

The 35-m lighthouse stands atop the Kurumkal hillock, jutting out on to the sea. For a nominal fee, visitors can climb the spiralling staircase inside to the top of the red and white tower. The palm-covered hillock offers a spectacular view of its surroundings.

Note: Beach chairs, umbrellas and surfboards can be hired at pre-fixed rates of Rs 50 a day.

Backwater Cruise
(Map pg **98, A1**)

Twelve kilometres from Kovalam, the Karamana River crosses the highway at Thiruvallom. This is an idyllic spot, offering a delightful view of the backwaters. A boat club offers a variety of cruises from canoe rides and kayaking to jaunts in *kettuvalloms*. Day tours to the nearby Pozhikara and Edayar islands and homestays at Idayar homes can also be arranged.

Vellayani Lake
(Map pg **98, B1**)

One of the few freshwater lakes in Kerala, this pristine water body is a must-see. Accessible by boat from Kovalam, 7 km away, the lake draws huge crowds during the Onam boat races.

Valiyathura Pier
(Map pg **98, B1**)

This 214-m long pier at Vallakkadavu offers magnificent views of the coast. However, because it is constantly pounded by the sea, the pier today has been reduced to a mere shadow of its busy former self. Fishermen fling their

---

Getting There

By Air
The nearest is Thiruvananthapuram International Airport, 13 km
☎ 0471–250 1424

By Rail
The nearest railhead is Trivandrum Central, 14 km
☎ 0471–232 1568

By Road
Buses ply to Kovalam, at half-hourly intervals throughout the day from the Thampanoor bus stand in Thiruvananthapuram.

The Lighthouse Beach

FACT FILE

District: Thiruvananthapuram

STD code: 0471

When to go: October to February

For information contact
Tourist Facilitation Centre, Department of Tourism
☎ 0471–248 0085

District Tourism Promotion Council
✉ Opposite Raj Bhavan, Kowdiar PO, Vellayambalam
☎ 0471–231 5397

COASTAL CIRCUIT

Kovalam | Destination Map

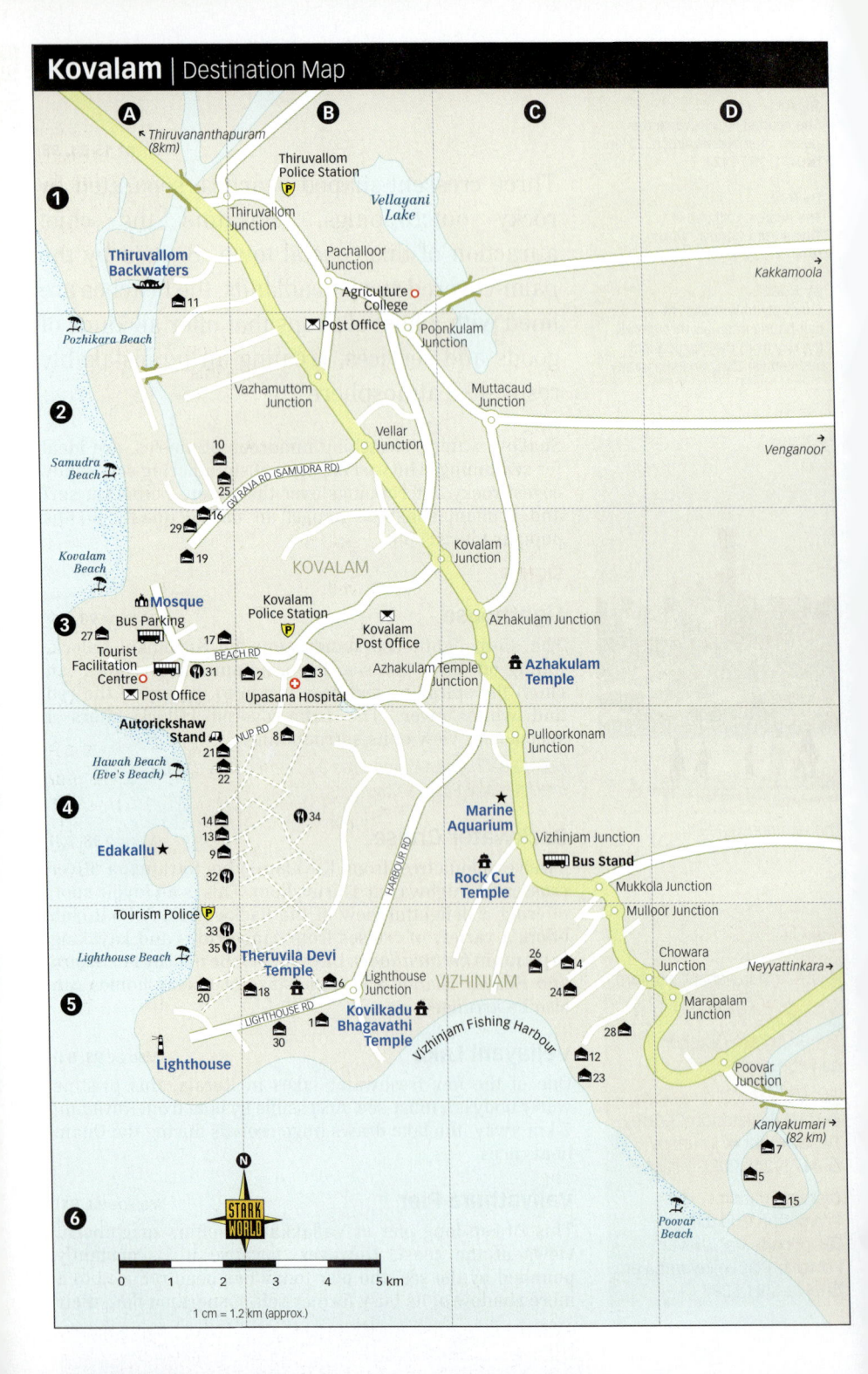

DON'T MISS

» **Cycling by the Sea**
Go cycling along the coast, skirting Lighthouse Road, for a truly magnificent view of the sea.

SIGHTS AND ATTRACTIONS	Grid
Azhakulam Temple	C3
Edakallu (sunset viewingpoint)	A4
Kovilkadu Bhagavathi Temple	B5
Lighthouse	A5
Marine Aquarium	C4
Mosque	A3
Rock Cut Temple	C4
Theruvila Devi Temple	B5
Thiruvallom Backwaters	A1

WHERE TO STAY		
Abad Palm Shore	1	B5
Beach Castle	2	B3
Best Western Swagath Holiday Resort	3	B3
Coconut Bay Beach Resort	4	C5
Estuary Island	5	D6
Golden Sands Beach Resort	6	B5
Isola Di Cocco	7	D6
Jasmine Palace	8	B4
Jeevan Ayurvedic House	9	A4
Kadaloram Beach Resort	10	A2
Lagoona Davina	11	A1
Manaltheeram	12	C5
Neelakanta	13	A4
Pappukutty Beach Resort	14	A4
Poovar Island Resort	15	D6
Puja Mahal	16	A3
Raja	17	A3
Sagara Beach Resorts	18	B5
Samudra KTDC	19	A3
Sea Flower	20	A5
Sea Rock	21	A4
Sea Face	22	A4
Somatheeram	23	C5
Surya Samudra	24	C5
Taj Green Cove	25	A2
Thapovan	26	C5
The Leela Kovalam	27	A3
Travancore Heritage	28	C5
Uday Samudra	29	A3
Varma's Beach Resort	30	B5

WHERE TO EAT		
Ashok Family Restaurant	31	A3
Café De La Mer	(see 9)	A4
Fusion	32	A4
German Bakery	33	A5
Lonely Planet	34	B4
Pizzeria	35	A5

BEACHES AND LAKES	
Hawah Beach (Eve's Beach)	A4
Kovalam Beach	A3
Lighthouse Beach	A5
Poovar Beach	D6
Pozhikara Beach	A2
Samudra Beach	A2
Vellayani Lake	B1

catamarans into the sea, jump in after them, and swim to the boats. Crowds gather just to watch this improptu show.

Vizhinjam (Map pg 98, C5)

Located 17 km from Thiruvananthapuram, close to Kovalam, is this historic spot – the ninth-century capital of the Ay kings. Today, it is a quiet village, with only its relics, such as the cave temple, linking it to the past. The fishing harbour becomes a beehive of activity at dawn. The bay makes a pretty picture.

The Cave temple (Map pg 98, C4)

A huge granite boulder has an opening, now blocked, said to lead to an underground cave. A half-finished bas-relief of Shiva appears on the stone and an idol of Saraswati sits at the mouth of the cave. Frequented by both Hindus and Muslims, it is now a protected monument under the ASI.

Chowara (Map pg 98, C5)

Chowara, a tiny fishing village 8 km south of Kovalam, boasts broad sandy beaches minus the crowds. Uncluttered and pristine, the beach attracts solitude-seeking beach-combers rather than revellers and beach buffs.

Chowara's location and serenity have also made it home to ayurvedic and heritage resorts. Of the three resorts located here, two attract tourists seeking ayurvedic treatments, whereas the third is known more for its lovely architecture.

Poovar (Map pg 98, D6)

Two kilometres south of Kovalam is another peaceful but stunningly beautiful beach, Poovar. Situated close to the Neyyar River estuary, Poovar was a trading port in its early days. Today, it is recognised as a tourist destination, mainly due to the many resorts in the area such as the Poovar Island Resort, Isola di Cocco and the Estuary Island Resort.

Largely unexplored and unspoilt, the island of Poovar has developed into an up-market tourist destination. Enveloped by serene backwaters and at places, separated from the sea only by narrow sand banks, Poovar, with its virgin beaches, is very popular with tourists.

The bustling Vizhinjam fishing harbour

Varkala

(Map pg **15-A2, 101**)

About 45 km north of Thiruvananthapuram, Varkala has a laidback, relaxed atmosphere and a rather compact beach that does not take too long to explore.

The beach at Varkala has no shops or restaurants. Most of the hotels and eateries are spread across the two cliffs north and south of the spacious cove that forms the famous **Papanasam Beach**. The wide plateau atop the steep laterite cliffs also offers a wonderful view of the sea. A dip in these waters is believed to wash away sins (*papam*). Priests at the Janardhana Temple, 2,000 years old, offer help with ritual pooja. The remains of Sree Narayana Guru, the well known social reformer and saint, are interred at Sivagiri Mutt at the eastern edge of town.

European backpackers and tourists with a lower budget who find the low tariffs and cost of food a big bonus, form the bulk of the tourist population to Varkala.

SIGHTS

Sivagiri Mutt (Map pg **15, A2**)

Located 3 km away on the eastern edge of town, is the ashram that was the final resting place of Kerala's famous saint and social reformer, Sree Narayana Guru. This *mutt*, with its distinctive multi-tiered white turret, is believed to be sacred. Lower down, is Sree Narayana Guru's old residence, which now displays some of his personal belongings. Nearby is the Sharda Temple, dedicated to Saraswati, whose idol was installed by the guru himself.

Papanasam Beach and the south cliff

Getting There

By Air
The nearest is Thiruvananthapuram International Airport, 55 km
☎ 0471–250 1424

By Rail
Varkala has its own railway station. Take a train for Kollam or Kochi from Thiruvananthapuram. Check beforehand if the train stops at Varkala.

By Road
Varkala is connected to Kollam (nearer), Ernakulam and Thiruvananthapuram.

SIGHTS AND ATTRACTIONS — Grid
- Durga Temple C2
- Hanuman Temple E4
- Janardhana Temple E4
- Springs C3

WHERE TO STAY
- Eden Garden .... 1 .... D4
- Ever Green .... 2 .... B1
- Golden Beach Resort .... 3 .... C4
- Govt. Guest House .... 4 .... E3
- Green Palace .... 5 .... B2
- Hill Palace .... 6 .... B2
- Hill-Top .... 7 .... B2
- Krishnatheeram .... 8 .... B1
- Le Mangalath .... 9 .... B1
- Nikhil Beach Resort .... 10 .... E4
- Palm Ayurvedic Beach Resort ... 11 .... C3
- Panchavadi Beach Resort .... 12 .... D4
- Preeth Beach Resort .... 13 .... C2
- Raja Park .... 14 .... C2
- Santaclaus - All Season's Village .... 15 .... B2
- Sea Breeze .... 16 .... B1
- Sea Pearl Chalets .... 17 .... C4
- SS Beach Resort .... 18 .... C3
- Taj Garden Retreat .... 19 .... E3
- Thiruvambadi Beach Retreat .... 20 .... B1
- Varkala Marine Palace .... 21 .... C4

WHERE TO EAT
- Cape Comorin .... (see 19) E3
- Kadaloram No.1 .... 22 .... C2
- Mamma Chompos .... 23 .... B2
- Oottupura (Veg) .... 24 .... C3
- Sea Rock .... 25 .... C3
- Sunset .... 26 .... C2
- Trattoria .... 27 .... B2

BEACHES AND LAKES
- Black Beach A1
- Papanasam Beach B3

Varkala | Destination Map

COASTAL CIRCUIT

Locations marked on map:

- Black Beach
- Odayam Beach
- Kollam
- Kappil Beach
- Thiruvamagadi Rd
- North Cliff
- Papanasam Beach
- Kurakanni Junction
- Durga Temple
- Varkala Cultural Centre
- Autorikshaw & Taxi Stand
- Tourism Police
- Springs Helipad
- Govt. Nature Cure Hospital
- Kochuvila Junction
- Tourist Amenity Center
- Cliff Rd
- South Cliff
- Beach Rd
- Tourism Police
- Hanuman Temple
- Tank
- Janardhana Temple
- Post Office
- Temple Junction
- Thiruvananthapuram (42km) →
- Sivagiri Mutt (3km) →
- Railway Stn (2km) →
- Arabian Sea

1 cm = 230 mtts (approx.)
0 | 0.25 | 0.5 | 0.75 | 1 km

STARK WORLD

MAPS & MORE KERALA | 101

DON'T MISS

» Coir Making
In the backwaters surrounding the Nedunganda village that overlooks the Ponnumthuruthu Island, coir making is an important vocation.

Sivagiri Mutt, a religious nerve centre

FACT FILE

District: Thiruvananthapuram
STD code: 0471
When to go: October to March
For information contact
Tourist Information Centre
✉ Railway Station
☎ 0470–260 2126

Janardhana Temple (Map pg **101**, **E4**)

Believed to be nearly 2,000 years old, and devoted to **Lord Vishnu**, this shrine stands at the entrance to the beach road. A flight of broad steps lead to the temple grounds past a high entrance arch. Clusters of brightly painted idols of Shiva, Hanuman and others are arranged around the sanctorum. Lighted wicks burn from oil trays cut into tall granite posts, while heavy brass bells strung from ceilings and poles gleam in the sunlight. The main temple bell, presented by the Dutch captain of a sailing ship, is believed to date back to the middle of the 17th century.

Ponnumthuruthu Island (Map pg **15**, **A2**)

This is a delightful island, located 20 km away, surrounded by the Anjengo backwaters. Approachable by boat from the makeshift jetty at the nearby Nedunganda village, the island is uninhabited, save for a 100-year-old Shiva-Parvati temple. Exposed to the vagaries of nature and time, it was in a state of disrepair until most of it was rebuilt about 10 years ago. The entire island is temple property.

Anjengo Fort (Map pg **15**, **A2**)

Built in 1695 by the Portuguese, this fort stands on a strip of land called 'Anjengo', sandwiched between the sea and the backwaters. Used originally as a depot to store merchandise, the British, under Captain Keeling, converted it into a fort. It does not have the formidable look of other forts in Kerala though, being more of an enclosed bastion with a bulwark of high laterite walls and lookout points. There are many tombstones at Anjengo, the earliest one dating back to 1704, with inscriptions offering a glimpse into the past.

Lighthouse (Map pg **15**, **A2**)

The lighthouse here is 130 ft tall. The ruins of one of the earliest factories set up by the British East India Company, built in 1684, can also be found at Anjengo. The 15-km route from Varkala winds past charming coastal villages and the beautiful Chilakoor Beach, which offers glorious views of the sunset.

Kappil Beach and Backwaters (Map pg **15**, **A2**)

A confluence of the sea and the Kappil River, the tongues of backwaters, the extensive estuary, and the magical interplay of land and water all add up to make this an idyllic spot. The small palm-covered islets within the estuary further enhance its charms. The coastal road passing through this area practically holds the sea and the estuary apart for a long stretch, offering delightful views of the waters on either side. There are no tourists, vendors or shops, and absolutely no traffic whatsoever. Lacking all tourist amenities, except for boating, Kappil in fact, seems to be a closely guarded secret.

Kannur

(Map pg **104**)

Getting There

By Air
The nearest is Calicut International Airport, Karipur, 114 km
☏ 0483–271 1314

By Rail
Kannur railway station is well connected to all major cities in the State and other important ones in the country
☏ 0497–270 5555

By Road
NH 17 connects Kannur to Kozhikode (86 km), Mangalore (138 km), and Kasaragod (89 km). Regular buses ply from Kannur's KSRTC bus stand.

FACT FILE

District: Kannur
STD code: 0497
When to go: May to February

For information contact
District Tourist Information Office
✉ Near Collector's Office, DTPC complex, Kannur
☏ 0497–270 6336

DTPC Tourist Information Centre
✉ Railway station
☏ 0497–270 3121
🌐 www.kannurtourism.org

Identified as the ancient port town of Naura, which was known even to the early Greeks and Romans, Kannur, in northern Malabar, has been famous for its exports to the outside world from very early times. Over time, it also came to be known for its quality timber. Today, the town's rich history lives on through its ancient forts, old shrines, and many venerable institutions.

While spices, coir, wood and sandalwood were exported from Kannur, traders from places as far flung as Sumatra and Arabia brought to the town varied merchandise –

Theyyam, the popular ritualistic dance form of northern Kerala

sugar, opium, dry fruits, silk, camphor, and even horses. Indeed, the celebrated Venetian traveller, Marco Polo, referred to the town as **a great emporium of spice trade**.

Kannur has some beautiful sandy beaches, the longest of which is the Payyambalam. This beach is quiet and peaceful, perhaps because there is a Hindu burial ground nearby, where the remains of people such as EK Nayanar and AK Gopalan, the famous Communist party leaders of Kerala, are interred. The Kannur cantonment, established in 1938, is the only one in the State.

The **Trichambaram Vishnu Temple** at Taliparambu, 20 km from town, is a fine example of medieval temple architecture. Kannur is also known for its handloom, *beedi*, fisheries and plywood industries.

The Rajarajeshwara Temple

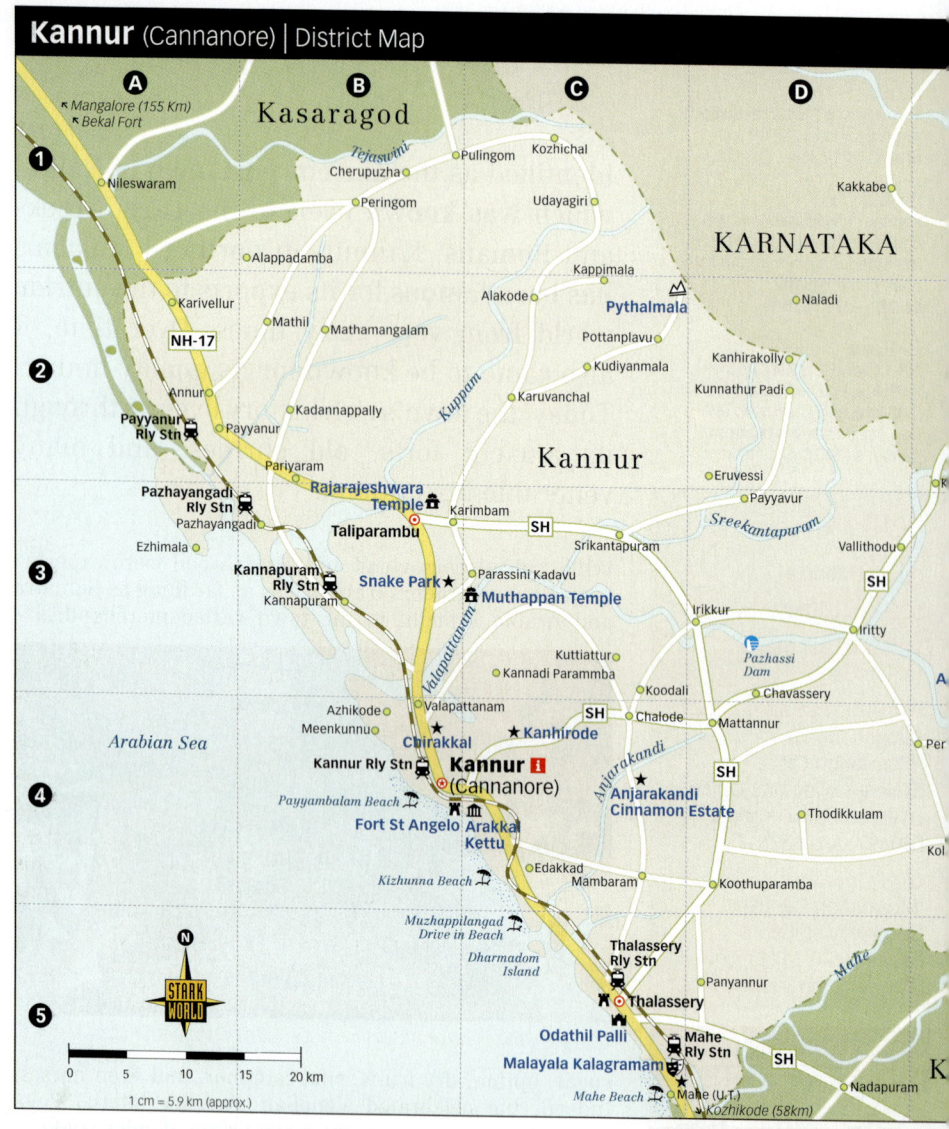

Kannur (Cannanore) | District Map

SIGHTS AND ATTRACTIONS	Grid
Anjarakandi Cinnamon Estate	C4
Arakkal Kettu	C4
Aralam Wildlife Sanctuary	E3
Chirakkal (Folklore Museum)	B4
Dharmadom Island	C5
Fort St Angelo	B4
Kanhirode (weaving centre)	C4
Kottiyoor Reserve Forest	F4
Kottiyoor Shiva Temple	F4
Malayala Kalagramam (centre for arts)	C5
Mahe (Union Territory)	C5
Muthappan Temple	C3
Odathil Palli	C5
Parassini Kadavu Snake Park	B3
Pythalmala (hill station)	C2
Rajarajeshwara Temple	B3
Thalassery Fort	C5

BEACHES

Kizhunna Beach	C4
Mahe Beach	C5
Muzhappilangad Drive in Beach	C5
Payyambalam Beach	B4

DAM

Pazhassi Dam	D3

DON'T MISS

» The Arakkal Kettu Museum

This old palace of the Arakkal dynasty has now been converted into a museum that houses the heirlooms and artefacts of the erstwhile rajas. It is located opposite Ayikara Mappila Bay, and is closed on Mondays.

SIGHTS

Fort St Angelo (Map pg **104**, **B4**)

In 1505, Dom Francesco de Almeida, the first Portuguese viceroy of India, built a fort here on a cliff overlooking the sea, with permission from the Raja. The fort was named 'St Angelo'. This triangular structure is surrounded on all three sides by the sea and has a moat running all along its landward side.

A row of cannons still stand, positioned seawards through portholes cut into the massive laterite walls. Ammunition dumps, stables, underground jails, secret tunnels to the sea, and an old, dilapidated chapel can also be seen.

Note: It is located after Cantonment, near the Government Hospital.

Payyambalam Beach (Map pg **104**, **B4**)

Just a stone's throw away from Fort St Angelo, is this long beach. At one end, laterite cliffs jut out into the sea with the Mascot Hotel perched atop. Close by is the beach park, with the unusual name of Baby Beach, beautifully landscaped and adorned with sculpture.

Just a few kilometres to the north, at Azhikode, is Meenkunnu Beach. Although few visitors come here, this palm-fringed expanse of clean, golden sands and white surf, thanks to the absence of laterite cliffs, offers a rather unique ambience.

Parassini Kadavu Temple (Map pg **104**, **C3**)

Built on the banks of the Vallapattanam River and situated 18 km northeast of Kannur, the Parassini Kadavu Temple is one of the most important shrines in the region. This three-tiered temple, painted a brilliant white, is locally

Festival time at the Kottiyoor Shiva temple

DON'T MISS

» Theyyam

Theyyam or *kaliyattam* is one of the most popular ritualistic dance forms of the region. It is a devotional form with a surrealistic representation of the divine. The performers are regarded as gods and devotees come forward to take their blessings.

COASTAL CIRCUIT

One of the many cannons at the Fort St Angelo

known as 'Parassini Madapura'. It is an important centre of the *muthappan* cult and the *theyyam*. Performances start early in the morning on all days, except when there is no moon or there is a dark moon. This celebrated shrine follows the unusual custom of offering dried fish and toddy to the deity. It is **open to people of all religions**.

Rajarajeshwara Temple (Map pg **104**, **B3**)

This Shiva temple is one of the holiest in these parts and the *linga* is believed to be thousands of years old. The temple follows an unusual custom – women are allowed inside only after eight in the evening as it is believed that Shiva is with Parvati at that time and will grant women devotees all that they desire.

Note: It is at Taliparambu, 25 km from Kannur.

Kerala Folklore Academy (Map pg **104**, **B4**)

Six kilometres north of Kannur, just off NH 17, is Chirakkal, the one-time capital of the Kolathiri rajas and an erstwhile centre for folk art and culture.

Kerala is home to many lesser known art forms, such as the dance forms, *marathukali* and *poorakali*, ballads such as *vadakkenpaattu* and *vedanpaattu*, and folk plays such as *godaveri*. There are also the mural paintings or *todikkalam*. In an effort to preserve this rich heritage, the 130-year-old abode of the Chirakkal family, the Chirakkal Kovilakom, was converted into a museum. Each dance or art form has a separate room devoted to it, where costumes, headgear, photographs and other such trappings are displayed. The Muslim dance forms, *oppana* and *arabana*, also find a place here. The library attached to the academy contains books on these subjects.

Kanhirode Weaving Co-operative (Map pg **104**, **C4**)

This is a co-operative where around 400 workers create high quality furnishing fabrics. Apart from producing exquisite bed linen, upholstery and curtain material, weavers working on huge looms produce fine shirts, colourful *lungis* and saris. Visitors can buy these from the attached retail outlet. The annual **Onam fair** at the Kannur police grounds is the best place for looking at and buying these handlooms.

☎ 0497–285 7259

Kottiyoor Shiva Temple (Map pg **104**, **F4**)

This shrine at Kottiyoor, also known as the **Varanasi of the South**, is an important pilgrim centre. There are actually two temples here – the Akkara and Ikkara Kottiyoor – located in a forested area on the banks of a river. During May-June every year, a 28-day festival that begins with the *neyyattam* and ends with the *thirukulasathu*, draws devotees from far and wide.

During the *neyyattam*, a sword with deep religious significance, kept in Muthirikavu in Tavinal village, is brought to the Ikkara Kottiyoor to mark the beginning of the celebrations. Ghee is poured on the sword as a mark of devotion. Another ritual performed during the festival is *elaneerattam*, the pouring of tender coconut water.

Note: It is located on the banks of the Bavalu River
🕒 *5 am to 10 am and 4 pm to 8 pm.*

Nileswaram

Getting There

By Air
The nearest is Bajpe Airport in Mangalore, 110 km
☎ 0824–225 2433.
Calicut International Airport, Karipur, is about 155 km
☎ 0483–271 1314

By Rail
Kasaragod station is well connected to most railway stations in Kerala and outside, 40 km
☎ 04994–230 200

By Road
Well connected to major towns in Kerala and neighbouring Karnataka. The coastal highway, NH 17, connecting Cape Comorin and Mumbai, runs through Kasaragod.

FACT FILE

District: Kasaragod
STD code: 0467
When to go: August to February
For information contact
✉ BRDC, Kappil
☎ 0467–227 2900

District Tourism Promotion Council
✉ Kasaragod
☎ 04994–256 450

The Valiyaparamba Backwaters, idyllic and serene

(Map pg **111, C4**)

Nileswaram is not quite a tourist hub, but its delightful backwaters, meandering rivers and tranquil beaches draw visitors. A quiet, peaceful little town, it is also known for some unique attractions, such as the forest that has been created out of nothing, and the family that holds sway over an entire village.

A palm-covered islet in the middle of a stretch of backwaters

Situated 40 km south of Kasaragod town in Hosdurg taluk, this town is very close to the Nileswar River. The bridge across the river roughly marks its northern boundary, and is followed by the town centre with a bus depot, auto stand, and a cluster of shops and hotels.

Delightful Backwaters

Roads lead westwards into a delightful stretch of backwaters. Just 2 km west is Kottapuram on the banks of the river. The rivers, Tejaswini and Nileswar, meet a short distance away before spilling jointly into the sea at Taikadappuram.

Ferryboats run at regular intervals from Kottapuram, providing basic transport to the numerous jetties on either side of the banks as bridges are few and far between. One of them, a long slender wooden structure, barely a couple of feet wide, connects Kottapuram to **Achan Thuruthu**, an islet across the river that houses 35 families amid dense green groves of palms and tropical foliage.

Alluring Beaches

The nearest beach is at **Thaikandapuram**, 5 km away. A small fishing harbour is located here, close to the estuary.

COASTAL CIRCUIT

MAPS & MORE **KERALA** | 107

Another beach at the mouth of the estuary at Azhithala is also worth a visit. Waves lashing the shore at high tide carve out large sections of the beach, literally altering its topography overnight.

SIGHTS

Ummichipoyil and Varikulam (Map pg 111, C4)

At Ummichipoyil, near Karinthalam Village on the banks of the Nileswaram River, blocks of laterite are said to have been hewn from a hill and used by the people of the Megalithic Age. There are a few tribal hamlets nearby, but today, the area is mostly covered with rubber plantations. The rock-cut caves, or Muniyaras, found here, **predate any other architectural structure found in Kerala**. These sepulchral monuments are at least 2,000 years old. The caves hold benches and beds, with intricately carved door frames and unique funerary offerings.

Ten kilometres from Kolathur village is Varikulam, where there are more such architectural structures overlooking the Chandragiri River. The attractions here include caves cut into the bedrock with benches inside, carved door frames with funerary offerings, and the majestic 'Umbrella Stones', or *kudakallu*.

Mahalingeshwara Temple (Map pg 111, B3)

Located on the edge of green paddy fields, this 13th century temple houses an idol of Shiva. A corniced laterite wall encircles the complex, and the roofs are covered in tiles. **Exquisite carvings** on wooden rafters depict scenes from the holy scripts. Colourful paintings of Ganapati and Saastha adorn the walls. During the annual pooja, Kathakali and theatrical performances are staged.

Valiyaparamba Backwaters (Map pg 111, C5)

Counted among the most delightful backwaters in Kerala, this large water body is fed by no less than five rivers and surrounded by lush green tongues of land. The place derives its name from Valiyaparamba Island, the longest in this region, stretching 24 km from Azhithala to Ezhimala.

Ferryboats ply from a jetty at Kottapuram up to Kowal Kadapuram in Valiyaparamba. Verdant islets lie scattered in the waters and charming little villages line the leafy banks. Bekal Houseboats, leased from BRDC, caters to business and corporate clients on larger houseboats, as well as to smaller groups and families for short or overnight cruises. They also arrange bonfire dinners on nearby islands, canoeing, visits to temples, forts and tribal villages, ayurvedic massages and homestays.

Cheruvathur Kota Palli (Map pg 111, C5)

Although 'Kota Palli' refers to a mosque within a fort, there is actually no fort here. Nevertheless, large laterite outcroppings on the top give this little shrine, located 5.5 km from Nileswaram, a fort-like appearance. A long flight of steps meanders up the hill.

Cheruvathur Kota Palli was built in memory of an Arab sage who died here. The masonry grave, nearly 15 ft long, and housed inside the small, thatched tomb, suggests that the sage belonged to the time of Malik Ibn Dinar. Devotees flock here with the belief that their hopes and wishes will be fulfilled.

Kottapuram Bridge, The longest walking bridge in Kerala

Getting There

By Air
The nearest is Bajpe Airport in Mangalore, 69 km
☏ 0824–225 2433. Calicut International Airport, Karipur, is about 200 km
☏ 0483–271 1314

By Rail
Kasaragod station is well connected to all stations in the State
☏ 04994–230 200

By Road
Well connected to major towns in Kerala and Karnataka. NH 17, connecting Cape Comorin and Mumbai, runs through Kasaragod.

The Ananthapura Temple

FACT FILE

District: Kasaragod
STD code: 0467
When to go: August to February
For information contact
District Tourism Promotion Council
✉ Kasaragod
☏ 04994–256 450
Bakel Resorts Development Corporation
✉ Near Bakel Fort
☏ 0467–227 2900
@ brdc@sancharnet.in

Kasaragod

(Map pg **111**)

Situated on the banks of the Payaswini River, Kasaragod's many monuments bring back the colourful days of the Kolathiri rajas. Home to the largest and most well preserved fort in the entire State and abode of the popular Malik Ibn Dinar Mosque, it can also boast of the only lake temple in Kerala.

The hinterland of this district is lush and green as it has 12 major and minor rivers coursing through it. The two rivers, Talapady and Trikaripur, actually demarcate the northern and southern boundaries of this busy town. The centre of Kasaragod bustles with business and trade – in **coir products, hides, skins and handloom**. There are many bustling restaurants, and glitzy shops with rows of electronic goods and perfumes, owned by those who have returned from the Gulf countries, peddle their ware between outlets hawking banana and jackfruit chips.

SIGHTS

Bekal Fort
(Map pg **111**, **B3**)

This 17th century edifice, one of the best maintained in all of Kerala, is situated nearly 40 m above the waves of the Arabian Sea that crash against its bastions. An observation tower in the centre and the walkway along the periphery, both offer **stupendous views of the ocean**. There are underground tunnels connecting the moat on its eastern side with the sea. A 1909 British-built guest house is now an outpost for the tourism police.

The Anjaneya Temple beside the gate has colourful stucco images of gods on its walls. Just outside is an old mosque with tall minarets and arched entrances, said to have been built by Tipu Sultan. The Pallikere Beach lies next to the fort. Other attractions include a Bekal hole aqua park and boat rides to the backwaters.

Note: 9 am to 5.30 pm.

Chandragiri Fort
(Map pg **111**, **B3**)

The village of Chandragiri, situated near the confluence of the Payaswini River and the Arabian Sea, is famous for the fort atop a small hill, overlooking the estuary. However, now only the ruins of this 17th century fort, built by Shivappa Nayak, are left standing. The views of the gently flowing river and the shimmering sea beyond are spectacular.

COASTAL CIRCUIT

MAPS & MORE **KERALA** | 109

One of the bastions of the Bekal Fort visible through a porthole

Anandashram (Map pg 111, B4)
Founded in 1931 by Swami Ramdas and Mother Krishnabai, visionaries who devoted their lives to spreading the message of universal love and service, this ashram is located in an **internationally known spiritual centre**. Prayer halls and visitor cottages are located within the large, shady compound.
☎ 0467–220 3036

Malik Ibn Dinar Mosque (Map pg 111, B2)
Malik Ibn Dinar was a missionary from Arabia who is credited with bringing Islam to the shores of the Malabar. Following the wishes of the ruler, Cheraman Perumal, who embraced Islam, Dinar and his followers set about constructing mosques in Kerala and preaching their religion. Of the nine mosques built in the Malabar region, only this one in Kasaragod survives.

The original mosque Dinar built was a small structure with a thatched roof, but later, his followers constructed a larger, more elaborate structure to resemble the palace of a local king.

Madhur Sree Madananteshwara Vinayaka Temple (Map pg 111, B2)
Of the four noted temples built by the Mypadi kings of Kumbla around the 10th century, this one at Madhur is the most renowned, both in terms of architecture and importance. Myths and legends tell of the miracles attributed to this Shaivite shrine.

Renovated in the 15th century and built in a distinctive style, this three-storied oval structure has its two highest roofs covered with copper plates.

Note: It is 8 km northeast of Kasargod, on the banks of the River Madhuvahini.

Kappil Beach (Map pg 111, B3)
The secluded Kappil Beach, fringed by palms and occasional casuarina groves, is among the **cleanest and most unpolluted** in all of Kerala. The nearby Kodi cliff offers panoramic views of the sea and the beach, while the Pallikunnam Temple, 2 km away, promises spiritual salvation.

Ananthapura Temple (Map pg 111, B2)
Considered the **only lake temple in Kerala**, this ninth century shrine is unique in other ways as well. Situated in the middle of a picturesque lake, its sanctum sanctorum can be reached only by a bridge. Two other structures stand separately in the lake, housing other deities.

The outer walls of the sanctorum are covered in murals, depicting scenes from

Kasaragod | District Map

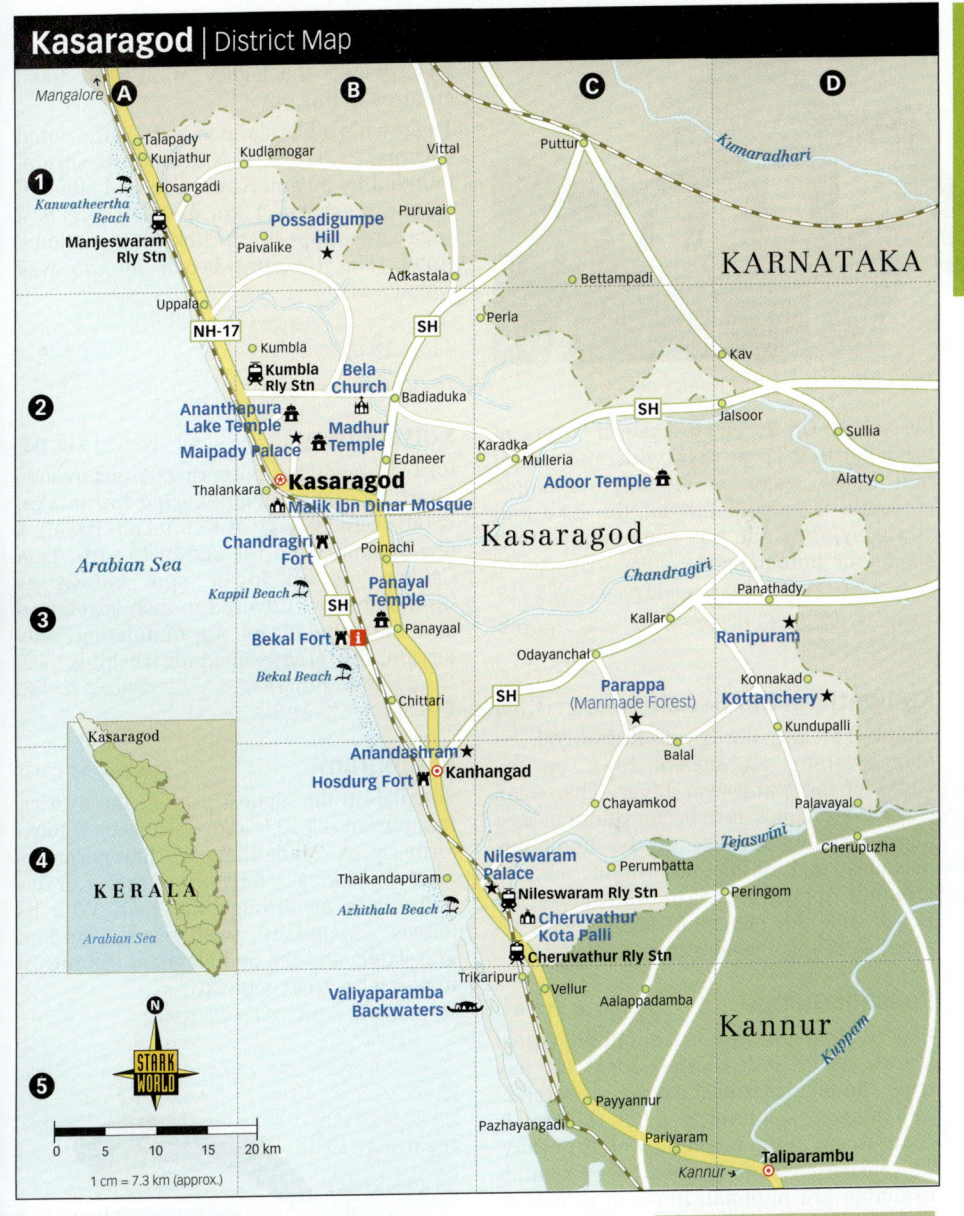

SIGHTS AND ATTRACTIONS	Grid
Adoor Temple	C2
Anandashram (spiritual centre)	B4
Ananthapura Lake Temple	B2
Bekal Fort	B3
Bela Church	B2
Chandragiri Fort	B3
Cheruvathur Kota Palli	C4
Hosdurg Fort	B4
Kottanchery (trekking)	D3
Madhur Temple	B2
Maipady Palace	B2
Malik Ibn Dinar Mosque	B2
Nileswaram Palace	C4
Panayal Mahalingeshwara Temple	B3
Parappa (manmade forest)	C3
Possadigumpe Hill	B1
Ranipuram (trekking)	D3
Valiyaparamba Backwaters	B5

BEACHES

Azhithala Beach	B4
Bekal Beach	B3
Kanwatheertha Beach	A1
Kappil Beach	B3

DON'T MISS

» **Chandragiri Cruises**
Fishermen offer rides in their wooden crafts from near the Chandragiri bridge to small islands scattered on the backwaters of the Chandragiri River
☎ 04994–225 551

MAPS & MORE **KERALA** | 111

The popular Malik Ibn Dinar Mosque

the Vedas. On the north-eastern corner of the lake, is a large cave with a small pit that holds water perennially. A single crocodile is said to inhabit the lake and strangely, only one has been spotted in it since time immemorial.

Note: It is located on the Kumbla-Badiyadka Road, about 14 km north along the national highway from Kasaragod town.

Kanwatheertha Beach (Map pg 111, A1)

About 15 km north of Kasaragod, is Manjeswaram, an ancient town on the banks of the Manjeswar River. This small cashew-growing centre became famous as a pilgrim centre because of the numerous mosques and Jain and Hindu temples around it. Apart from that, the Kanwatheertha Beach and the charming lagoon with its expanse of white sand attract weekenders.

Possadi Gumpe (Map pg 111, B1)

East of Manjeswaram is a small hill resort known as Possadi Gumpe, ideal for day trips and picnics from Kasaragod. Perched 323 m above sea level on a hill, the area is reminiscent of the beautiful woods of Ooty. The nearest village is Paivalike. Facilities available are minimal, hence it is best to carry food and water and go equipped with adequate trekking gear.

Note: Buses ply from Manjeswaram.

Kanhangad/ Hosdurg Fort (Map pg 111, B4)

Following the chain of forts built in this region by the Ikkeri dynasty, the sleepy little town of Kanhangad, 23 km southeast of Kasaragod, was given a new name – Hosdurg. Although only the ruins of the old fort remain, the legacy of the fort town endures to this day.

The town's other claim to fame is the noted spiritual centre, Nithyananthashram, founded by Swami Nithyanda and situated on the outskirts, 4 km away. There is a yoga centre opposite the Bekal International Hotel. The Hosdurg beach too, is well worth a visit.

Note: The Kanhangad/Hosdurg Fort is located 4 km east of Kanhangad town.

TREKKING OPTIONS

Kottanchery (Map pg 111, D3)

East of Kanhangad, bordering the picturesque Coorg district of neighbouring Karnataka, is the scenic village of Konnakad. Barely a few kilometres to the south, close to Tala Cauvery, is an idyllic spot known as 'Kottancherry'. Covered in lush vegetation and surrounded by an undulating hilly terrain, this area is ideal for trekking.

Note: It is 30 km northeast of Kanhangad, and 40 km east of Nileswaram.

Ranipuram (Map pg 111, D3)

Situated on the highest peak in the district, Ranipuram is 750 ft above sea level. Known formerly as 'Madathumala', Ranipuram is ideal trekking territory, and draws enthusiasts all through the year. With its forests, abundant wildflowers, verdant grasslands and the odd elephant sighting, it makes for a great getaway.

Note: It is 46 km from Kanhangad.

The Madhur Temple, famous for its copper-plate-covered roofs

The best travel images. Now just a click away.

STARK WORLD IMAGES
www.starkworld.net

Wildlife
Abundant and thriving

The forests of Kerala, where the wild and the untamed roam freely

1. Neyyar Wildlife Sanctuary
2. Peppara Wildlife Sanctuary
3. Shenduruney Wildlife Sanctuary
4. Periyar Tiger Reserve
5. Idukki Wildlife Sanctuary
6. Eravikulam National Park
7. Chinnar Wildlife Sanctuary
8. Thattekkad Bird Sacnctuary
9. Chimmini Wildlife Sanctuary
10. Peechi-Vazhani Wildlife Sanctuary
11. Parambikulam Wildlife Sanctuary
12. Silent Valley National Park
13. Wayanad Wildlife Sanctuary
14. Aralam Wildlife Sanctuary

Neyyar Wildlife Sanctuary

(Map pg **15**, **D3**)

Getting There

By Air
The nearest airport is Thiruvananthapuram International Airport, 38 km.

By Rail
The nearest railway station is at Thiruvananthapuram, 30 km. Neyyattinkara is 21 km.

By Road
Located 30 km east of Thiruvananthapuram, this sanctuary is well connected by a network of roads to different parts of the district.

For information contact
Chief Conservator of Forests (Wildlife): Thiruvananthapuram
☎ 0471–232 2217

Assistant Wildlife Warden: Neyyar Wildlife Sanctuary, Neyyar Dam, Thiruvananthapuram
☎ 0471–227 2182

Declared a sanctuary as early as in 1958, the lack of sustained conservation efforts hampered Neyyar's growth until 1985, when renewed efforts under a wildlife wing transformed it into a haven for exotic flora and fauna.

With 12,000 hectares of natural vegetation spread across an undulating terrain and the 1,868-m Agasthyamala Peak as its highest point, the sanctuary is interspersed with rushing brooks, flat meadows and gentle slopes, making it an ideal trekking destination. The Neyyar River, which originates from the Agasthya Peak, has an irrigation dam built across it here.

Bonnet macaque

The **Agasthyamala region** supports a wide variety of plant species, and the variety of its flora and forest types make it an ideal gene pool reserve. Elephants, gaur, sambar, barking deer and the endangered Nilgiri tahr are found here, apart from reptiles such as the cobra, python, viper, rat snake and flying snake. The sanctuary is also a popular spot for watching birds.

Peppara Wildlife Sanctuary

(Map pg **15**, **D2**)

The Peppara Wildlife Sanctuary was set up primarily to augment the water supply of Thiruvananthapuram. When a dam was built across the Karamana River in 1983 to meet the increased water supply needs of the city, the Paruthipally range became the catchment area for the dam reservoir. The entire area making up the sanctuary drains into the Peppara Dam reservoir that spreads across nearly 5.82 sq km.

Nestled in the Western Ghats, about 50 km from the city, it lies on the way to Ponmudi. The sanctuary actually consists of part of the **Palode reserve** and part of the **Kottoor reserve**. Apart from the dam and reservoir, forests, eucalyptus plantations and streams spread across 53 sq km.

Tigers, panthers, elephants, sambar and gaur can be seen here. The barking deer, mouse deer and the wild boar are also found. The lion-tailed macaque and the Nilgiri langur represent the simian species, whereas the king cobra and python represent the reptiles.

Getting There

By Air
The nearest airport is Thiruvananthapuram International Airport, 55 km.

By Rail
The nearest railway station is Thiruvananthapuram Central, 50 km.

By Road
It is 50 km from the Thampanoor bus stand. Only a few direct buses operate from Thiruvananthapuram. Board a bus for Vithura (14 km from the sanctuary) or Nedumangad (30 km).

For information contact
Chief Conservator of Forests (Wildlife): Thiruvananthapuram
☎ 0471–232 2217

Assistant Wildlife Warden: Peppara Wildlife Sanctuary
☎ 0472–289 2344

Shenduruney Wildlife Sanctuary

(Map pg **46**, **E2**)

A Peacock Pansy

Part of the **Agasthyamala biosphere reserve**, this sanctuary, located in the southern Western Ghats, derives its name from an endemic tree species, locally known as *chenkurinji*. Declared a wildlife sanctuary in 1984, the region is unique for its bio-diversity, remains of a Stone Age culture, and an important ecotourism resource, Thenmala.

Located on the north of Kulathupuzha valley, and bounded by the Western Ghats on the east, the sanctuary, spread over **100 sq km**, encompasses large tracts of tropical evergreen forests. The area is generally hilly, and at 1,550 m, Alvarkurichi is the highest peak. The long list of species found here includes the lion-tailed macaque, bonnet macaque, mouse deer, elephant, wild boar, sambar, gaur, Nilgiri langur, sloth bear, barking deer, black-naped hare, Malabar giant squirrel, slender loris, brown palm civet and the pangolin. Big cats are comparatively rare. Trekking and boating are allowed within the tourist zone of the sanctuary.

Getting There

By Air
The nearest airport is Thiruvananthapuram International Airport, 85 km.

By Rail
The nearest railheads are Thenmala, and Chenkotta, both 30 km.

By Road
It is 70 km from Kollam on the Kollam-Chenkotta road.

For information contact
Wildlife Warden: Shenduruney Wildlife Sanctuary, Thenmala Dam
☎ 0475–234 4600

Tourist Information Desk Thenmala
☎ 0475–234 4800

Getting There

By Air
The nearest airport is at Madurai, 140 km. Kochi is 190 km.

By Rail
The nearest stations are Theni – 60 km, Kottayam –114 km, and Madurai – 140 km.

By Road
Kottayam – 114 km, Munnar – 110 km, and Madurai – 140 km. Thekkady is on SH 19, which connects Munnar to the Periyar Tiger Reserve. A good road network connects to different tourist centres and major towns in Tamil Nadu and Kerala.

For information contact
District Tourist Information Office: Thekkady
📞 04869–222 620

Eco Tourism Centre of Periyar Tiger Reserve: Ambady Junction, Kumily
📞 04869–224 571

Forest Information Centre: Boat Landing, Periyar Tiger Reserve
📞 04869–222 028

Visiting Hours
6 am to 6 pm.

Getting There

By Air
The nearest airport is Cochin International Airport, 120 km.

By Rail
The nearest railhead is at Kottayam, 113 km.

By Road
It is 115 km from Ernakulam and 55 km from Thodupuzha.

For information contact
Chief Conservator of Forests: Thiruvananthapuram
📞 0471–232 2217

Wildlife Warden:
Idukki Wildlife Division, Vellapara
📞 04862–232 271

Periyar Tiger Reserve

(Map pg **71**, **C5**)

The matriarch leading the herd

Located in the Periyar Valley at Thekkady, this is the oldest and largest tiger reserve in Kerala. Spread across the foothills of the southern Western Ghats, this 777-sq-km forestland is also home to the Asiatic elephant. A repository of rare and endangered flora and fauna, the valley is a major watershed for two important rivers – the Periyar and the Pamba. The famous Sabarimala shrine and the Mangala Devi Temple are also situated in the region.

At the centre of the reserve is the vast artificial lake created by a dam built by the British in 1895. Declared a sanctuary in 1950, the Periyar Reserve became part of **Project Tiger**, a Central Government initiative to protect the animal.

A combination of tropical, deciduous and evergreen forests and grasslands make this an ideal home for 62 species of mammals, 320 species of birds, and 45 species of reptiles. There are numerous varieties of flowers and butterflies as well. A boat ride on the lake is a delightful way of spotting elephants and avifauna, for which the park is well known. If you are fortunate, you might even spot the pride of the sanctuary, the **tiger**. Although tiger sightings are not very common, there are enough of these magnificent felines around. Trackers routinely spot pugmarks.

Idukki Wildlife Sanctuary

(Map pg **71**, **B4**)

A Malabar grey hornbill

Located at an altitude between 450 and 748 m above sea level, this sanctuary covers a total area of 105 sq km. Spread over the Thodupuzha and Udumbanchola taluks, it includes a 33-sq-km scenic lake formed by the three dams – Cheruthoni, Idukki and Kulamavu. A charming canopy of dense tropical evergreen forests, tropical semi-evergreen forests and moist deciduous forests fringe the lake that surrounds this protected area on three sides.

Wildlife found here include herds of elephants, tiger, barking deer, bear, wild boar, sambar, wild dogs, jungle cats, and a large concentration of various species of snakes, including cobra, viper, python, krait, and numerous non-poisonous ones. The sanctuary is home to a variety of bird species and the **extensive reservoir** here attracts a lot of aquatic birds, such as ducks and cormorants. Small groups of tribals, the Adivasis, dwell in the higher areas of the sanctuary. Visitors are taken around in boats. The best time to visit is from November to March.

Eravikulam National Park

(Map pg **71**, **B2**)

This 97-sq-km park of verdant grasslands and wooded valleys is wedged between the picturesque Kannan Devan Hills and Anamudi, South India's highest peak. It is also home to nearly a third of the world's population of the endangered Nilgiri tahr, and the spectacular *neelakurinji* flower that blooms once every 12 years.

Located 13 km from Munnar, the park effectively protects local biodiversity. Stretching over 97 sq km in the tea-growing region of the Western Ghats, it is located on a high rolling plateau next to the Anamudi Peak that soars up to a height of 2,695 m.

Eravikulam's treasure is undoubtedly the endangered Nilgiri tahr that thrives here. The small-clawed otter, ruddy mongoose, the dusky striped squirrel, and the small Indian civet are the other animals found. There are also elephants, sambar, gaur, macaque and the occasional tiger or leopard. The sanctuary is home to about 120 species of birds, including species such as the black and orange flycatcher, Nilgiri pipit, Nilgiri wood pigeon, Nilgiri Verditer flycatcher and the Kerala laughing thrush.

Chinnar Wildlife Sanctuary

(Map pg **71**, **C1**)

The Chinnar Wildlife Sanctuary is considered unique in the whole of the Western Ghats due to its ecological, geological and cultural importance. The grizzly giant squirrel is the star attraction here, as is the white bison, although to a lesser extent. Chinnar also has the richest reptilian fauna, in addition to a treasure trove of medicinal plants and an entire forest of sandalwood.

Contiguous to the Eravikulam National Park and the Indira Gandhi Wildlife Sanctuary, the terrain of this park is highly

Getting There

By Air
The nearest airport is Cochin International Airport, 145 km.

By Rail
The nearest railhead is Pollachi, 72 km.
Aluva is 120 km.

By Road
It is 13 km from Munnar.

For information contact
Wildlife Warden: Forest Information Centre, Munnar
04865–231 587

Visiting Hours
7 am to 5 pm.

A Nilgiri tahr

Getting There

By Air
The nearest airport is at Coimbatore, 115 km. Cochin International Airport is 145 km.

By Rail
The nearest railhead is Pollachi, 72 km.

By Road
It is 60 km from Munnar.

For information contact
Wildlife Warden: Eravikulam National Park, Munnar
04865–231 587

undulating, with varying altitudes. Although it is located in the rain shadow area, nearly **1,000 species of flowering plants** are found here.

Chinnar is also rich in avian diversity and the calls of 225 species of birds have been recorded in the sanctuary. Other animals found here include the spotted deer, rusty spotted cat, wild dog, barking deer, bonnet macaque, porcupine and the wild boar. Larger mammals include the sambar, gaur and the elephant. Trekking options abound.

A bee eater

Getting There

By Air
The nearest airport is Cochin International Airport, 42 km.

By Rail
The nearest railhead is Aluva, 48 km.

By Road
The sanctuary is 13 km northeast of Kothamangalam along the Pooyamkutty Rd.

For information contact
Wildlife Warden: Idukki Wildlife Division, Vellappara, Painavu
☎ 04862–232 271

Assistant Wildlife Warden:
Dr Salim Ali Bird Sanctuary, Nyayappily, Kothamangalam
☎ 0485–258 8302

Thattekkad Bird Sanctuary

(Map pg **27**, **D3**)

Sandwiched between the two branches of the Periyar River and surrounded by the serenity of the Anamalai hills, this pristine 25-sq-km region is a heaven for avid birdwatchers. Also known as Dr Salim Ali Bird Sanctuary, it was the first to be officially recognised as a bird sanctuary in Kerala.

This one-time rubber plantation was declared a sanctuary in 1984, with the help of the late Dr Salim Ali, renowned ornithologist. Nearly 320 species of birds thrive here. Scores of crow pheasants, nightjars, drongos, woodpeckers, robins, babblers and darters colonise the towering trees. Rare birds such as the crimson-throated barbet, bee-eater, fairy blue bird, grey-headed fishing eagle, peninsular bay owl, night heron and the Malabar grey hornbill are also found.

A hoopoe

Sprawled over an undulating area, this sanctuary has tropical evergreen, semi-evergreen and moist deciduous forests, interspersed with plantations of teak and mahogany. The wildlife found here includes elephants, leopards, sloth bears, mongoose, slender loris, porcupines, pythons and king cobras.

Chimmini Wildlife Sanctuary

(Map pg **28**, **D3**)

Established in 1984, this sanctuary covers an area of 85 sq km on the western slopes of Nelliyampathy. With its dense forests, varieties of birds and butterflies, innumerable trekking trails and extensive lake, it is a nature lover's delight.

The park shares a border with the Peechi-Vazhani and Parambikulam wildlife sanctuaries. The dense foliage and rivers provide an ideal habitat for a vast variety of epiphytes and flowering plants.

Indian wild dog (dhole) family

Wildlife here includes the endangered lion-tailed macaque, tiger, and leopard, besides other species such as the mongoose, wild dog, jackal, sloth bear, gaur, sambar, barking deer, wild boar, porcupine, bonnet macaque, Nilgiri langur, slender loris and elephant.

Altitudes range from 40 m at the dam site to 1,116 m atop the highest peak, Pundimudi. With more than 160 species, it is a haven for bird and butterfly watchers. The Forest Department organises trekking and bamboo rafting trips, the highlight being the Moonlight Sonata – rafting on full moon nights.

Getting There

By Air
The nearest airport is Cochin International Airport, 65 km.

By Rail
The nearest railhead is Thrissur, 37 km.

By Road
It is 25 km from Amballur Junction on NH 47 on the way to Thrissur from Kochi.

For information contact
Wildlife Warden: Chimmini Wildlife Sanctuary,
Chimmini Dam
☎ 0487–269 9017

Peechi-Vazhani Wildlife Sanctuary

(Map pg **28**, **D2**)

Spotted deer

Known to be one of the oldest wildlife reserves in Kerala, this 125-sq-km sanctuary was established in 1958. Located 20 km east of Thrissur, it is contiguous with the forest areas of Nelliyampathy and Palappilly reserves, and shares a common boundary with the Chimmini Sanctuary. The undulating terrain varies from 45 to 900 m.

Most of the sanctuary is covered by deciduous forests, but it also has some evergreen and semi-evergreen trees. There are endangered herbs and shrubs, rare medicinal plants, and **innumerable varieties of orchids**. Bird colonies too, are many.

Here, you can expect to spot the bonnet macaque, Nilgiri langur, tiger, leopard, sambar, spotted deer, barking deer, mouse deer, Malabar giant squirrel, porcupine, small Indian civet, common palm civet, elephant, gaur, wild boar, sloth bear, and the wild dog.

The Forest Department organises outdoor activities that include overnight stays in tents, bamboo rafting, bird watching, butterfly safaris and trekking.

Getting There

By Air
The nearest airport is Cochin International Airport, 65 km.

By Rail
The nearest railhead is Thrissur, 20 km.

By Road
It is 5 km from Pattikkad Junction on NH 47, on the way to Palakkad from Thrissur.

For information contact
Wildlife Warden: Peechi Wildlife Division, Peechi, Thrissur
☎ 0487–269 9017, 94479 79103

Getting There

By Air
The nearest airport is at Coimbatore, 120 km.

By Rail
The nearest railhead is Pollachi, 39 km. Coimbatore is 120 km, and Palakkad is 100 km (5 km from Palakkad town).

By Road
Pollachi – 39 km,
Coimbatore – 120 km
and Palakkad – 100 km.

For information contact
Wildlife Warden: Parambikulam Wildlife Sanctuary, Anappady, Thunacadavu
☎ 04253–244 500

A wild boar

Parambikulam Wildlife Sanctuary

(Map pg **88**, **E6**)

This sanctuary, deep in the valley and stretching over 258 sq km, boasts of the first ever scientifically managed teak plantation in the world as well as the world's tallest and oldest teak tree. Besides the astounding array of flora and fauna, it offers challenging treks in the hills and vast lakes for boating. Parambikulam is also a haven for bird watching, and was once the favourite haunt of the legendary ornithologist, Dr Salim Ali.

The Chalakudy River, coursing through the sanctuary, has been dammed at three places, creating vast reservoirs ideal for viewing wildlife and birds.

Habitat types are very diverse and support a variety of wildlife. While deer, sambar and gaur largely inhabit the forest fringes, the lion-tailed macaque, king cobra, tiger, leopard, civet cat, pangolin, porcupine, jungle cat, cane turtle, and the Ceylon frogmouth roam freely in the interiors. The **Parambikulam frog** (*Rana parambikulamana*) is exclusive to the sanctuary. There are plenty of trekking options here. The tribals from the area are usually well-informed guides.

Getting There

By Air
The nearest airport is at Coimbatore, 90 km. Kozhikode is 100 km.

By Rail
The nearest railhead is Palakkad, 58 km. Coimbatore is 90 km.

By Road
Mannarkkad – 40 km, Palakkad – 58 km, and Coimbatore – 90 km through Anakatty and Mukkali. KSRTC and private buses ply between Mannarkkad and Palakkad. Buses leave from Mannarkkad to Mukkali at one-hour intervals.

For information contact
Wildlife Warden: Silent Valley Division, Mannarkkad, Palakkad
☎ 04924–222 056

Silent Valley National Park

(Map pg **88**, **C2**)

Environmentalists call this sanctuary an ecological island, one that contains immense biological and genetic wealth. Today, Silent Valley National Park, located on the western corner of the Nilgiris, is one of the last remnants of an undisturbed tropical evergreen rainforest. With an unbroken ecological history, which has been continuously evolving for millions of years, it is truly a unique region.

The park owes its name to the relative absence of the noisy cicada insects. Covering an area of over 90 sq km, the evergreen forests consist of different kinds of vegetation. The Kuntipuzha River traverses the entire length of the national park's valley.

Orchids and 960 species of other flowers bloom here. Apart from this, there are 25 species of mammals, 35 species of reptiles, 95 species of butterflies, and a number of rare birds. The valley's most famous inhabitant however, is the elusive **lion-tailed macaque**.

Wayanad Wildlife Sanctuary

(Map pg **80**, **E3**)

The Wayanad Wildlife Sanctuary encompasses an area of 344.44 sq km and is made up of two discontinuous pockets – Muthanga in the south and Tholpetty in the north. Located 18 km west of Sulthan Bathery, Muthanga is part of the Nilgiri biosphere region, made up of the Bandipur Tiger Reserve in Karnataka and the Mudumalai Sanctuary in Tamil Nadu.

The terrain of this sanctuary is undulating and dotted with scattered hillocks. At 1,158 m above mean sea level, Karottimala is the highest peak. One-third of the total area, nearly 110 sq km, is covered in teak, sliver oak, rosewood and eucalyptus plantations. The rest consists of deciduous forests, with a few patches of semi-evergreen trees. Bamboo groves are also abundant. There are different varieties of flora, shrubs and creepers in the forest. According to the 2004 census, elephants number a total of 216 in the Muthanga sanctuary alone, there are also four tigers and six leopards. The spotted deer, sambar and bison are the herbivores found here.

Getting There

By Air
The nearest airport is Calicut International Airport, 106 km.

By Rail
The nearest railhead is Thalassery, 80 km. Kozhikode is 100 km.

By Road
It is 100 km from Kozhikode on NH 212.

For information contact
Wildlife Warden: Wayanad Wildlife Sanctuary,
Sulthan Bathery
☎ 04936–220 454

A sambar

Aralam Wildlife Sanctuary

(Map pg **104**, **E3**)

This is the northernmost sanctuary in Kerala, and at 55 sq km, is also one of its smallest. Located on the western slopes of the Western Ghats, it is next to the State farm at Aralam.

Established in 1984, the sanctuary is administered by the Wayanad division and headquartered at Iritty, a small town that lies 10 km to the east. The topography varies from 50 m at the foothills to the highest peak, Katti Betta, at 1,145 m. Copious rainfall, about 3,000 mm annually, keeps the forested areas predominantly evergreen. There are vast tracts of teak and eucalyptus plantations as well. Not far from the sanctuary, flows the Aralam River.

A wide variety of flora can be found here. The fauna includes birds and animals endemic to the Western Ghats, such as deer, boar, bison and elephant. Jungle cats and leopards are found in smaller numbers.

Getting There

By Air
The nearest airport is Calicut International Airport, 115 km.

By Rail
The nearest railhead is Thalassery, 35 km. Kannur is 45 km.

By Road
Accessible by road from Thalassery (35 km), and Kannur (45 km). Buses and taxis ply regularly.

For information contact
Wildlife Warden: Iritty
☎ 0490–249 3160

A gaur

The Good Earth

With resorts that pay respect to nature, the environment and the community, cgh earth helps solve the Zen-like riddle every conscientious traveller likes to unravel - how to indulge without being self-indulgent.

cgh earth comes as a pleasant surprise to travellers accustomed to the high rises of luxury. All cgh earth properties are simple and unassuming, with a raw earthiness to them. You'll find no packaged hospitality here. Which is perhaps why cgh earth prefers to refer to its properties as "experience environments" that offer not just holidays, but "experience holidays" centred on strong core values of respect for the nature, the environment and the community – all for the world to discover itself anew.

Founded by Dominic Joseph Kuruvinakunnel, cgh earth started its journey as the Casino restaurant (later Casino hotel and eventually the Casino Group of Hotels) catering to dock workers and commuters. The Group's commitment to nature can be traced back to its family plantations and today it has a missionary zeal to protect the earth and the environment – which was also what led to its renaming as cgh earth.

All cgh earth properties are today manifestations of this deep respect for nature, of a remarkable understanding of her myriad ways. In fact, the Group is probably the first to have a full-time director for the cause of the environment.

cgh earth
experience hotels
www.cghearth.com

Coconut Lagoon
Kumarakom

Spice Village
Thekkady

Brunton Boatyard
Fort Kochi

Bangaram Island
Lakshadweep

Marari Beach
Alappuzha

Kalari Kovilakom
Palakkad

SwaSwara
Gokarna

Spice Coast Cruises
Houseboats

The journey is the destination

An understanding of cgh earth would be incomplete without a trip across its properties. And the ideal starting point would be Coconut Lagoon, located beside the beautiful backwaters of Kumarakom. Here, you'll have your first glimpse of one of the distinct characters of cgh earth — namely, the seamless blending of the place and the property (this is perhaps why most cgh earth properties have been named after the destinations) as well as its deep concern for the environment, its respect for the earth's fast diminishing resources.

Coconut Lagoon

Enriching the environment

A typical Kerala homestead (tharavadu) painstakingly transplanted and restored, Coconut Lagoon, like all cgh earth properties celebrates Kerala - not just its beauty and charm, but also finer aspects like its architecture, its culture, its cuisine, its rich tradition of Ayurveda. But what adds more value to this resort are the endangered Vechoor cows (the world's smallest cattle of Kerala origin) grazing its lawns, the butterfly park ("The butterflies were there. All we did was to give them an ideal environment to thrive.") and other initiatives at preserving earth's precious resources. It all seems quite natural and that's exactly what makes cgh earth special. For here, cultural and ecological sensitivity is not about keeping a constant watch on what you do, but an integral part of the whole experience itself.

Minimalistic grace

This simple adherence to nature and all her natural designs is what makes an experience at Bangaram Island of Lakshadweep, about 200 miles off the Kerala coast, enriching. When the Group set out to build a resort in Bangaram, the island's fragile ecology - the coral reefs, the turquoise blue lagoons and the lush coconut palms - inspired them to opt for minimalism. So instead of building something new, they worked with the thatched huts that already existed on the island. Nothing was added, nothing taken away. Today the hotel and every little thing about it blend quietly and unobtrusively with the landscape of the island. There is nothing here that does not belong and the island remains what it once was – pristine and untouched.

Bangaram Island

Marari Beach

Celebrating the community

In the district of Alappuzha is Marari, a typical Keralan fishing village. Located here is another of cgh earth's experience hotel, the Marari Beach. There is nothing that tells you that this is a resort, for Marari so well blends in with the village

A rich taste of tradition

cgh earth experiences are also exclusive culinary experiences and Casino Hotel, with its Tharavadu and Fort Cochin restaurants (the latter was acclaimed by 'Good Housekeeping' as one of the best seafood restaurants in India) figures high on the list. Freshness is the first rule when it comes to food at cgh earth. This is well taken care of by the fresh fruits and vegetables grown in cgh earth's own organic farms and fresh spices sourced from the local farmers (cgh earth engages in organic farming with the farmers around its properties and in partnership seeks global markets for their spices).

Every cgh earth property lays special emphasis on local cuisine. At Brunton Boatyard, for instance, surrounded as it is by several communities, a mélange of Portuguese, Dutch, English, Arab and Jewish cuisines - some of the recipes sourced from traditional homes - is offered. Similarly, Coconut Lagoon offers Kerala cuisine in its most authentic form. And those who want to take home an enriching taste of the land can take a lesson or two from the ever-obliging chefs.

Spice Village

ambience, with cottages designed after the fishermen's huts. All that separates the resort from the sea are rows of coconut trees - which lets you take in the splendours of the beach like never before and touch its living heart. The simplicity and charm of village life that pervades the resort, both in form and spirit, make you feel one with nature and the environs. Marari is a beautiful manifestation of cgh earth's belief that a holiday comes alive only when it breathes the life of the community around.

In the nature of things

cgh earth's concern for nature and the environment reaches new heights at the Spice Village, located in the forests of the Periyar on the lofty Western Ghats. Here, there is no air-conditioning, no TV – all to renew our connection with nature. Spice Village has cottages built with brick, split bamboo and elephant-grass, and simple pine furniture and plain terracotta floors to adorn them. The resort itself is like an integral part of nature's design, blending with the lush greenery around – all of which makes way for an unhindered journey back to nature. Like most cgh earth properties, Spice Village too has been modelled after the dwellings of the area – that of the local tribal inhabitants – and has been built by the tribals themselves. For cgh earth, this is a way of paying tribute to the community which has been a source of inspiration.

Brunton Boatyard

Past perfected

cgh earth has a fine sense of perfection, an obsession for detail. This is most evident in Brunton Boatyard, built on the site of the century-old private boatyard of Geo Brunton and Sons. The hotel has been built with the same materials used to build the boatyard. And from the enormous Indo-Portuguese punkahs in the lobby, to the ancient anchor in the green courtyard and the food served in the restaurant, every detail keeps alive the spice-scented history of the land. This re-creation of history becomes total with the vast expanse of the Arabian Sea in the foreground through which sailed many a trading vessel of yore and the priceless monuments of Fort Kochi in the background. All of which will transport you to another world, where you will relive grandma's old tales.

Balancing acts

Conservation efforts are a critical part of cgh earth's operations. And apart from the Vechoor cows and the butterfly park, there are other initiatives that often miss the eye of the visitor. This includes biodigesters and waste treatment plants that convert effluents into clean fuel, vermiculture pits that process garbage into manure which goes into cgh earth's organic farms and rain harvesters dug in discreet corners to take advantage of Kerala's abundant rainfall. Small steps which ensure that the natural balance remains intact.

Rejuvenating tradition

History comes alive once again at Kalari Kovilakom – this time to give life to the 5000 year-old system of Ayurveda. This centuries-old palace belonging to the Kollengode royal family echoes the group's sensitiveness to the royal legacy and the age-old tradition of Ayurveda - well evident in the unique lifestyle at the Kovilakom today. Here, you will be required to take off your shoes when you check in and non-vegetarian fare or liquor will not be served. You will wake up at dawn, drink warm water, meditate, do Yoga. And there is nothing here to hinder this healing experience - not even telephone or the television.

Kalari Kovilakom is restricted only to those guests wanting Ayurvedic treatment and the minimum stay will be for fourteen days as required by this ancient therapeutic system.

KALARI KOVILAKOM
VENGUNAD

The Palace For Ayurveda
| a cgh earth experience |

A touch of green

Ayurveda is part of every cgh earth experience and almost all properties have Ayurveda centres - fully equipped and run by resident physicians who are experts in the field. The restaurants too offer Ayurvedic food and drinks that have special restorative powers. Also offered are special wellness holiday packages.

Kalari Kovilakom

SwaSwara

Inspiring the journey within

If Kalari Kovilakom welcomes you to a healing experience based on Ayurveda, SwaSwara, the latest cgh earth initiative offers Yoga by the beach. Spread across 30 acres of land on the cove of one of the finest beaches in India – the serene and secluded Om Beach in Gokarna – is this resort. Designed and built like a typical Konkan Village, SwaSwara, like all other cgh earth properties, echoes the ethos of the land. As in Marari, the sea is a living part of the holiday experience that is centred on Yoga offered by experts. The centrepiece of SwaSwara is a special dome for meditation named the 'Blue Dome' and which represents the cosmic sphere of harmony. In fact, SwaSwara which in Sanskrit means "inner vibration" is all about harmony - of the body with the elements, of life with nature, of the self with the music of the soul.

Simple abundance

cgh earth's philosophy of life reflects once again in Spice Coast Cruises, that take you on a journey through the heartland of Kerala in Kerala's own traditional houseboat. Like all the cgh earth's properties, these cruises also capture the Group's trademark simplicity and lack of

Art of the matter

cgh earth for whom the community is part of every experience celebrates its commitment to traditional art and culture by conducting art camps at its properties. Artists from India and abroad participate in these camps, one of which focused on the mural tradition of Kerala, once confined to the walls of the temples.

The paintings created in these camps are showcased to the world through exhibitions conducted worldwide. A website www.cghearthgallery.com enables people to view and buy these paintings online. Several of these works today adorn the walls of cgh earth International's headquarters at Swabish Hall, Germany.

pretense. The crew comprises people from the local community (most of cgh earth's staff are in fact members of the local community). Only natural and local materials are used for the interiors - coir matted decks and canopies made of split bamboo and palm fronds. Even the meals that the cook serves on board are simple, which on a typical day would include among other divine dishes, the famed Karimeen (pearlspot) of the backwaters and enormous freshwater prawns.

Future perfect

Today cgh earth is a byword for sustainable, sensitive tourism. The Group strongly believes that the way ahead for the tourism industry is on the path of responsible tourism – which seems to be well-founded with the emergence of the new alert, independent traveller. cgh earth's efforts have been well received worldwide and it has played host to some of the world's famous personalities including Sir Paul McCartney. Like Anthony Weller of the 'National Geographic Traveler' noted in a travelogue, "cgh earth's properties represent the kind of architecturally and aesthetically sound tourism now rare elsewhere in India." In today's fast-paced world, cgh earth is a reminder that God is in the details.

To discover more about cgh earth experiences, call +91-484-3011711; email contact@cghearth.com or log on to www.cghearth.com

Accommodation

Thiruvananthapuram

Muthoot Plaza (L)
☎ 0471–233 7733
🌐 www.muthoot.com/plaza

Hotel Saj Lucia (T)
☎ 0471–246 3443
🌐 www.sajlucia.com

Duke's Forest Lodge (T)
☎ 0472–285 9273
🌐 www.dukesforest.com

Mascot Hotel (T)
☎ 0471–231 8990
🌐 www.ktdc.com

The South Park (T)
☎ 0471–233 3333
🌐 www.thesouthpark.com

The Residency Tower (T)
☎ 0471–233 1661
🌐 www.residencytower.com

Jas Hotel (T)
☎ 0471–232 4881

Hotel Horizon (T)
☎ 0471–232 6888
🌐 www.thehotelhorizon.com

Hotel Pankaj (T)
☎ 0471–246 4645
🌐 www.pankajhotel.com

Surya Hotel (M)
☎ 0472–281 2088
🌐 www.thehotelsurya.com

Hotel Kyvalya (M)
☎ 0471–233 0724

Comfort Inn Grand (M)
☎ 0471–247 1286

Hotel Geeth (M)
☎ 0471–247 1987

Wild Palms Guesthouse (M)
☎ 0471–247 1175
🌐 www.wildpalmshomestay.org

Hotel Thara International (M)
☎ 0471–249 4888

Chaitram (M)
☎ 0471–233 0977

Hotel Arya Nivas (B)
☎ 0471–233 0789

Hotel Thampuri International (B)
☎ 0471–232 1687

Venus International (B)
☎ 0471–233 1963

Kochi

Ernakulam

Le Meridian (S)
☎ 0484–270 5777
🌐 www.lemeridien-cochin.com

Riviera Suites (L)
☎ 0484–266 5533
🌐 www.rivierasuites.org

Taj Residency (L)
☎ 0484–237 1471
🌐 www.tajhotels.com

The Avenue Regent (T)
☎ 0484–237 7977
🌐 www.avenueregent.com

Bolgatty Palace (T)
☎ 0484–275 0500
🌐 www.ktdc.com

Abad Plaza (T)
☎ 0484–238 1122
🌐 www.abadhotels.com

Harbour View Residency (T)
☎ 0484–235 8444
🌐 www.harbourviewresidency.com

Gokulam Park Inn (T)
☎ 0484–240 0707
🌐 www.sarovarhotels.com

Mermaid Days Inn (T)
☎ 0484–230 7999
🌐 www.milmermaid.com

The Avenue Center (T)
☎ 0484–231 5301
🌐 www.avenuehotels.com

The International Hotel (T)
☎ 0484–238 2091
🌐 www.theinternationalhotel.com

Hotel Highland (B)
☎ 0471–233 3200
🌐 www.highland-hotels.com

Oasis International (B)
☎ 0471–233 3223

Hotel Fort View (B)
☎ 0471–245 2194

Hotel Silver Sand (B)
☎ 0471–246 0318

Agasthya House (B)
☎ 0471–227 t2160

Neyyar House (B)
☎ 0471–230 3189

Government Guest House (B)
☎ 0472–289 0320

The Renaissance Cochin (T)
☎ 0484–234 4463
🌐 www.renaissancecochin.com

Hotel Wyte Fort (T)
☎ 0484–270 6952
🌐 www.thewhitefort.com

Yuvarani Residency (T)
☎ 0484–237 7040
🌐 www.yuvaraniresidency.com

Woods Manor (T)
☎ 0484–238 2059
🌐 www.thewoodsmanor.com

Woodlands (T)
☎ 0484–236 8900
🌐 www.woodlandscochin.com

Abad Atrium Hotel (T)
☎ 0484–238 1122
🌐 www.abadhotels.com

Quality Inn Presidency (T)
☎ 0484–239 4040
🌐 www.presidencyhotel.com

Grand Hotel (T)
☎ 0484–238 2061

Cochin Tower (M)
☎ 0484–240 1910
🌐 www.hotelcochintower.com

Hotel Mercy Estate (M)
☎ 0484–236 7372
🌐 www.themercy.in

Dwaraka Hotel (M)
☎ 0484–238 3236

Hotel Alapatt Regency (M)
☎ 0484–234 4413

The Metropolitan (M)
☎ 0484–237 6931
🌐 www.metropolitancochin.com

BTH Sarovaram (M)
☎ 0484–230 5591
🌐 www.sarovaram.com

Bharat Tourist Home (BTH) (M)
☎ 0484–235 3501
🌐 www.bharathotel.com

Hotel Sealord (M)
☎ 0484–238 2472

Abad Metro (M)
☎ 0484–236 4102
🌐 www.abadhotels.com

Hotel Mareena Regency (B)
☎ 0484–236 6618

Hotel Excellency (B)
☎ 0484–237 8251
🌐 www.hotelexcellency.com

Star Homes Hotel (B)
☎ 0484–232 3051/0192
🌐 www.starhomes.co.in

Fort Kochi and Mattancherry

Brunton Boatyard (S)
☎ 0484–221 5461
🌐 www.cghearth.com

Koder House (S)
☎ 0484–221 8485
🌐 www.koderhouse.com

Malabar House (L)
☎ 0484–221 6666
🌐 www.malabarhouse.com

PRICE CATEGORIES

Accommodation listing is arranged on the basis of average room tariff per room on twin sharing basis.

- (S) **Super Luxury** – Rs 10,000 upwards
- (L) **Luxury** – Rs 5,000 to Rs 10,000
- (T) **Top-End** – Rs 2,000 to Rs 5,000
- (M) **Mid Range** – Rs 1,000 to Rs 2,000
- (B) **Budget** – Less than Rs 1,000

Trinity Malabar Escapes (L)
☎ 0484–221 6669
🌐 www.malabarhouse.com

Old Courtyard (T)
☎ 0484–221 6302
🌐 www.oldcourtyard.com

Fort Heritage (T)
☎ 0484–221 5333
🌐 www.fortheritage.com

Hotel Arches (T)
☎ 0484–221 5050
🌐 www.hotelarches.com

Rossitta Wood Castle (T)
☎ 0484–221 8590
🌐 www.rossittawoodcastle.com

Kimansion (T)
☎ 0484–221 6730
🌐 www.kimansion.com

Ballard Bungalow (T)
☎ 0484–221 5854
🌐 www.cochinballard.com

Ann's Residency (T)
☎ 0484–221 8024
🌐 www.annsresidency.com

Sonnetta Residency (T)
☎ 0484–221 5744

Casa Linda (M)
☎ 0484–221 6888
🌐 www.casalindahotel.com

Hotel Abad (M)
☎ 0484–222 8211
🌐 www.abadhotels.com

The Fort House (M)
☎ 0484–221 7103
🌐 www.forthousecochin.com

Jewel Cottage (M)
☎ 0484–221 5330

Vintage Inn (B)
☎ 0484–221 5064
🌐 www.vintageresorts.in

Fort Avenue (B)
☎ 0484–221 5219

Santa Cruz Tourist Home (B)
☎ 0484–221 6250

Hotel Mareena Regency (B)
☎ 0484–236 6618

Hotel Park Avenue (B)
☎ 0484–221 6671/5676

Brunton Boatyard, Fort Kochi

Birds Lagoon Village, Thattekkad

HOMESTAYS

Chiramel Residency (M)
☎ 0484–221 7310
🖥 www.chiramelhomestay.com

Napier House Homestay (M)
☎ 0484–221 6296
🖥 www.napierhouse.com

Geo Maria Homestay (M)
☎ 0484–221 8061

Tom Heritage Villa Homestay (B)
☎ 0484–221 8409
🖥 www.fortcochinhomestay.com

Delight Homestay (B)
☎ 0484–221 7658
🖥 www.delightfulhomestay.com

Rosa-Rio Homestay (B)
☎ 0484–221 5495

Vasco Homestay (B)
☎ 0484–221 6267

Spice Holidays Homestay (B)
☎ 0484–221 6650

Sea View Homestay (B)
☎ 0484–221 5287/0208

Willingdon Island

Taj Malabar (S)
☎ 0484–266 6811
🖥 www.tajhotels.com

Casino Hotel (L)
☎ 0484–266 8221
🖥 www.cghearth.com.

Trident Hilton Cochin (L)
☎ 0484–266 9595
🖥 www.trident-hilton.com

Around Kochi

Riverdale Holiday Homes (L)
☎ 0484–278 4282
🖥 www.riverdale.in

Kamyakam Haven (T)
☎ 0484–243 2701
🖥 www.kamyakamhaven.com

Royal Village (T)
☎ 0484–254 6042
🖥 www.royalindian.com

Punarnava Ayurveda Hospital (B)
☎ 0484–280 1415
🖥 www.punarnava.net

HOMESTAYS

Gramam Backwater Homestay (T)
☎ 0484–224 0278
🖥 www.keralagramam.com

Thani Illam (B)
☎ 0484–264 9679
🖥 www.thaniillam.org

Nedumbassery

Saj Earth Resort (L)
☎ 0484–261 0356
🖥 www.sajhotels.com

The Surya (T)
☎ 0484–245 5570
🖥 www.suryahotels.com

Abad Airport Hotel (T)
☎ 0484–261 0411
🖥 www.abadhotels.com

Cochin Durbar (T)
☎ 0484–261 1520
🖥 www.cochindurbar.com

Quality Airport Hotel (T)
☎ 0484–261 0366
🖥 www.qualityairporthotel.com

NedStar Airport Hotel (T)
☎ 0484–247 7411
🖥 www.nedstarhotels.com

Lotus 8 (M)
☎ 0484–261 0640
🖥 www.lotus8hotels.com

Athirappally

Rainforest (S)
☎ 0480–276 9062
🖥 www.avenuehotels.in

Riverok Villas (M)
☎ 0480–276 9140
🖥 www.riverokvillas.com

Richmond Cascade (M)
☎ 0480–276 9024

Thattekkad Bird Sanctuary

Kothamangalam Plantation Bungalow (L)
☎ 93886 20399
🖥 www.mundackalhomestay.com

Birds Lagoon Village (T)
☎ 0485–257 2444

Periyar River Lodge (T)
☎ 0484–220 7173
🖥 www.periyarriverlodge.com

Hornbill Camp (M)
☎ 0484–209 2280
🖥 www.thehornbillcamp.com

Hornbill Inspection Bungalow (B)
☎ 0485–258 8302

Thrissur

Kadappuram Beach Resort (L)
☎ 0487–239 4988
🖥 www.kadappurambeachresorts.com

Trichur Towers Hotel (T)
☎ 0487–242 5290
🖥 www.hoteltrichurtowers.com

Majlis Health Park (M)
☎ 0487–221 2845

Hotel Elite International (M)
☎ 0487–242 1033
🖥 www.hoteleliteinternational.com

Casino Hotels (M)
☎ 0487–242 4699
🖥 www.casinohotels.com

Hotel Sidhartha Regency (M)
☎ 0487–242 4773
🖥 www.hotelsidharegency.com

Sreedhari Ayurvedic Resorts (M)
☎ 0487–228 2441
🖥 www.sreedhariresorts.com

Hotel Luciya Palace (B)
☎ 0487–242 4731

Green Hattu Resorts (B)
☎ 04885–240 736
🖥 www.greenhatturesorts.com

Ayuryogashram (B)
☎ 04884–237 976
🖥 www.ayuryogashram.com

The Highway Castle (B)
☎ 0480–275 2606
🖥 www.thehighwaycastle.com

Hotel Sea Fort (B)
☎ 0487–242 4067

Hotel Merlin International (B)
☎ 0487–238 5520/5619

Hotel Pearl Regency (B)
☎ 0487–244 6661/65

HOMESTAYS

Coconut Island (L)
☎ 0487–242 0556
🖥 www.keralaislandresort.com

Nakshathra Inn (L)
☎ 0487–255 0500

Guruvayur

Rajah Island Ayurvedic Hospital (T)
☎ 0487–253 2352
🖥 www.island.ayurveda-in.com

Mayura Residency (T)
☎ 0487–255 7174
🖥 www.mayuraresidency.com

Thalikulam Beach Resorts (T)
☎ 0487–239 9843
🖥 www.thalikkulambeachresorts.com

Hotel Vysakh International (M)
☎ 0487–255 6188

Hotel Sopanam Heritage (M)
☎ 0487–255 5442
🖥 www.sopanamguruvayoor.com

Krishna Inn (M)
☎ 0487–255 0777
🖥 www.krishnainn.com

Hotel Elite (M)
☎ 0487–255 6215
🖥 www.eliteguruvayur.in

Gokulam Vanamala Kusumam (M)
☎ 0487–255 6702

Hotel RVEE's Regency (M)
☎ 0487–255 4444
🖥 www.hotelrveesregency.com

Surya Ayurvedics (M)
☎ 0487–231 2366
🖥 www.ayurvedaresorts.com

Zamorin's Health Retreat (M)
☎ 04885–222 349
🖥 www.zamorins.com

Hotel Bhasuri Inn (B)
☎ 0487–255 8888
🖥 www.bhasuriinn.com

Kozhikode

Kadavu (L)
☎ 0483–283 0570
🖥 www.kadavuresorts.com

Taj Residency (L)
☎ 0495–276 5354
🖥 www.tajhotels.com

Harivihar (Homestay) (T)
☎ 0495–276 5865
🖥 www.harivihar.com

Malabar Palace (T)
☎ 0495–272 1511
🖥 www.malabarpalacecalicut.com

Harivihar, Kozhikode

RESOURCES — **Accommodation**

MAPS & MORE **KERALA** | 133

Punnamada Backwater Resort, Alappuzha

PRICE CATEGORIES

Accommodation listing is arranged on the basis of average room tariff per room on twin sharing basis.

- **S** Super Luxury – Rs 10,000 upwards
- **L** Luxury – Rs 5,000 to Rs 10,000
- **T** Top-End – Rs 2,000 to Rs 5,000
- **M** Mid Range – Rs 1,000 to Rs 2,000
- **B** Budget – Less than Rs 1,000

Fortune Hotel (T)
0495–276 8888
www.fortuneparkhotels.com

Hotel Malabar Gate (T)
0495–272 4534

Beach Hotel (M)
0495–276 2055
www.beachheritage.com

Hotel Hyson Heritage (M)
0495–276 6726
www.hysonheritage.com

Hotel Span (M)
0495–270 0037
www.spanhotel.com

Calicut Towers (M)
0495–272 3202

Kovilakom Residency (M)
0495–274 3500

Hotel Maharani (B)
0495–272 3101
www.hotelmaharani.com

East Avenue Suites (B)
0495–236 7175
www.eastavenuesuites.com

Alakapuri Hotels (B)
0495–272 3451
www.alakapurihotels.com

Hotel Asma Tower (B)
0495–272 3560
www.asmatower.com

The Renaissance Classic (B)
0495–272 2339
www.therenaissanceclassic.com

Around Kozhikode

Musselbay (T)
98471 00528
www.musselbay.com

The Renaissance Cochin Kappad Beach Resort (T)
0496–268 8777
www.renaissancekappadbeach.com

Waterfront (M)
0495–276 8996

HOMESTAYS

Tasara Centre for Creative Weaving (M)
0495–241 4832
www.tasaraindia.com

Kasa Marina (M)
0495–246 2162

Misty Grove (M)
0495–276 2020, 944727 6352

Thalassery

Ayisha Manzil (L)
0490–234 1590

Pearl View Regency (M)
0490–232 6702
www.pearlviewregency.com

Beach Pavilion Resort (B)
0497–283 3471

Hotel Paris Presidency (B)
0490–234 2666
www.parispresidency.com

Mahe

Zara Resorts (B)
0490–233 2503

Tourist Home (B)
0490–233 2560

Backwaters

Kollam

Ashtamudi (L)
0476–288 2470
www.ashtamudiresort.com

Aquaserene (T)
0474–251 2410
www.aquasereneindia.com

Vijaya Palace (T)
0476–268 2910
www.vijayapalace.com

Fragrant Nature Resort (T)
0474–251 8020
www.fragrantnature.com

Sarovaram Ayurvedic Backwater Resort & Spa
0474–270 4686
www.sarovaramkollam.com

Nila Palace (T)
0474–252 9301
www.nilapalace.com

Vijaya Castle (T)
0476–283 1348
www.vijayacastle.com

Hotel Sea Bee (M)
0474–274 4696
www.hotelseabee.com

Valiyavila Family Estate (M)
0474–270 1546
www.kollamlakeviewresort.com

Palm Lagoon Resorts (M)
0474–254 8974
www.palmlagoon.com

Lake Sagar Resort (B)
0474–251 4300
www.puthooram.com

Hotel Ramkamal Residency (B)
0474–276 8101
www.ramkamalresidency.com

Karunagapally

Hotel Comfort Regency (M)
0476–262 3888

Hotel New Excellency (M)
0476–262 0749

Green Channel (B)
0476–262 8134

Alappuzha

Lake Palace (S)
0477–223 9701
www.lakepalaceresort.com

Punnamada Backwater Resort (L)
0477–223 3690
www.punnamada.com

Kayaloram Lake Resort (L)
0477–223 2040
www.kayaloram.com

Pristine Isle Resorts (T)
0478–256 1900
www.pristineisle.in

Kovilakam Lakeside Villa (T)
0478–286 1275
www.ananyahillresorts.com

Coir Village Lake Resort (T)
0477–224 3462
www.coirvillage.com

Sea Lamp Shimmer (T)
0477–225 1070/1432
www.shyamavarna.com

Arcadia Regency (T)
0477–223 0414
www.arcadiaregency.com

Pagoda Resorts (T)
0477–225 1697
www.pagodaresorts.com

Green Palace Health Resort (T)
0477–273 6262
www.greenpalacekerala.com

Alleppey Prince Hotel (T)
0477–224 3752
www.alleppeyprincehotel.com

Shanthitheeram (T)
0478–258 2333
www.shanthitheeram.com

Kuttanadu River Resort (M)
0477–273 6248
www.kuttanaduresorts.com

Hotel Royal Park (M)
0477–223 7828
www.hotelroyalepark.com

Keraleeyam Ayurvedic Resort (M)
0477–225 4501
www.keraleeyam.com

Palm Grove Lake Resort (M)
0477–223 5004
www.palmgrovelakeresort.com

ATDC Residency (M)
0477–224 3462
www.atdcalleppey.com

Tharayil Tourist Home (B)
0477–223 6475
www.tharayiltouristhome.com

KTC Guest House (B)
0477–225 4275
www.ktchouseboat.com

Palmy Lake Resorts (B)
0477–223 5938
www.palmyresorts.com

HOMESTAYS

Mankotta (L)
0477–221 2245

Olavipe (L)
9447 142410
www.olavipe.com

Raheem Residency (L)
0477–223 0767
www.raheemresidency.com

Motty's Homestay (L)
0477–224 3535

Emerald Isle (T)
0477–270 3899
www.emeraldislekerala.com

Philipkutty's Farm, Kumarakom

134 | KERALA MAPS & MORE

Privacy at Sanctuary Bay (T)
☎ 0484–221 6666
🌐 www.malabarescapes.com

Ayanat House (T)
☎ 0478–253 2233
🌐 www.ayanathouse.com

La Casa del Fauno Homestay (T)
☎ 0478–286 0862
🌐 www.casadelfauno.com

Granary Riverside Inn (T)
☎ 0477–270 3466
🌐 www.granaryinn.com

Alleppey Beach Resorts (T)
☎ 0477–226 3408
🌐 www.thealleppeybeachresorts.com

Pamba Heritage Villa (T)
☎ 0477–276 2806
🌐 www.pambaheritage.com

Arakkal Heritage (T)
☎ 0478–286 5545

Pooppally's Homestay (T)
☎ 0477–276 2034
🌐 www.pooppallys.com

Backwater Bliss (T)
☎ 0477–224 3535, 98470 32836

Tharavad Heritage Home (M)
☎ 0477–224 4599
🌐 www.tharavadheritageresort.com

Navalli (Community) Green Palm Homes (M)
☎ 0477–276 2034, 3090800

Anamika the villa (M)
☎ 0477–224 2044
🌐 www.anamikahome.com

Penguin Lake Resort (M)
☎ 0477–226 1522
🌐 www.penguinlakeresort.com

Neelambari Heritage Villa (B)
☎ 0477–272 4599

Gowri Heritage Residence (B)
☎ 0477–223 6371
🌐 www.gowriresidence.com

Kooplikaat Homestay (B)
☎ 0478–258 2194

Kunnekkattu Homestay (B)
☎ 0477–2710076, 98460 43217
🌐 www.kunnekkattuhomestay.in

Sona (B)
☎ 0477–223 5211
🌐 www.sonahome.com

Johnson's – The Nest (B)
☎ 0477–224 5825

Xoticaa Heritage Home (B)
☎ 0932318 2576
🌐 www.xoticaa.in

Kainady Heritage (B)
☎ 0477–271 0293, 94471 17845

Kumarakom

Kumarakom Lake Resort (S)
☎ 0481–252 4900
🌐 www.klresort.com

Coconut Lagoon (S)
☎ 0481–252 4491
🌐 www.cghearth.com

Taj Garden Retreat (S)
☎ 0481–252 5711
🌐 www.tajhotels.com

Golden Waters (L)
☎ 0481–2525 826
🌐 www.goldenwaters.com

Whispering Palms (L)
☎ 0481–252 3820
🌐 www.abadhotels.com

Backwater Ripples (L)
☎ 0481–252 3600
🌐 www.backwaterripples.com

Kalathil Health Resorts (L)
☎ 04829–271 034
🌐 www.kalathilresorts.com

Thanneermukkom Lake Resort (T)
☎ 0478-258 3218
🌐 www.ktdc.com

Water Scapes (T)
☎ 0481–252 5861
🌐 www.ktdc.com

Cocobay Resort (T)
☎ 0481–252 3200
🌐 www.cocobayresort.net

The Backwater Resort (T)
☎ 0481–252 5388
🌐 www.thebackwater.co.in

Lakshmi Hotel & Resorts (T)
☎ 0481–252 3313
🌐 www.lakshmiresorts.com

Paradise Resorts (T)
☎ 0481–252 4983
🌐 www.paradisein.com

Illikkalam Lake Resort (M)
☎ 0481–252 3282/4234, 94470 24234
🌐 www.illikkalamlakeresort.com

HOMESTAYS

Philipkutty's Farm (L)
☎ 04829–276 529
www.philipkuttysfarm.com

Cruise N Lake (M)
☎ 0481–252 5804
🌐 www.homestaykumarakom.com

Tharavadu Heritage Home (T)
☎ 0481–252 5230
🌐 www.tharavaduheritage.com

GK'S Riverview (M)
☎ 0481 259 7527
🌐 www.gkhomestay-kumarakom.com

Midlands

Kottayam

Lake Village Heritage Resort (T)
☎ 0481–236 3637
🌐 www.thewindsorcastle.net

Puzhayoram Heritage Resorts (L)
☎ 0481–239 2612
🌐 www.sangamamresorts.in

Serenity at Kanam Estate (T)
☎ 0481–245 6353
🌐 www.malabarescapes.com

The Windsor Castle (T)
☎ 0481–236 3637
🌐 www.thewindsorcastle.net

Aymanam Village Backwater Resort (T)
☎ 0481–251 8478
🌐 www.sangamamresorts.in

Sangamam Health Resort (T)
☎ 0481–258 1044
🌐 www.sangamamresorts.in

Pearl Regency (M)
☎ 0481–256 1123/25

Hotel Aida (B)
☎ 0481–256 8391
🌐 www.hotelaidakerala.com

Spice Village, Thekkady

Vembanad Lake Resort (B)
☎ 0481–236 0866
🌐 www.vembanadlakeresort.com

HOMESTAYS

Kaithayil Paddy Side Nest (M)
☎ 0481–246 2295

Pathanamthitta

Contour Hill Resorts (T)
☎ 0475–237 9900
🌐 www.contourresorts.com

Mannil Regency (B)
☎ 0468–232 0364

HOMESTAYS

Viswadarsanam (B)
☎ 0468–235 0543
🌐 www.viswadarsanam.8m.com

Mampra House (B)
☎ 0468–222 2645

Tulasidalam (B)
☎ 0469–266 2190
🌐 www.tulasidalam.com

Lal Residency (B)
☎ 04734–226 008
🌐 www.lalsresidency.com

Thiruvalla

Hotel Elite Continental (M)
☎ 0469–260 2302

Vanjipuzha Palace (B)
☎ 0479–245 2004
🌐 www.vanjipuzhapalace.com

Hotel Panchami (B)
☎ 0469–263 0539

HOMESTAYS

Tharayil House (B)
☎ 93802 85626
🌐 www.illamtraveler.com

Pala

Nazarani Tharavad (T)
☎ 04822–212 438
🌐 www.nazaranitharavad.com

Ann's Homestay (T)
☎ 04822–221 287
🌐 www.annshomestay.org

Hotel Maharani (B)
☎ 04822–212 520

Hotel Rose Meriya (B)
☎ 04822–211 117

Hotel Meriya (B)
☎ 04822–212 476

Vazhayil Residency (B)
☎ 04822–212 893

HOMESTAYS

Planters Homestay (M)
☎ 04822–236 250, 237 850
🌐 www.plantershomestay.com

Kanjirapally

Chamundi Hill Palace (T)
☎ 04828–251 246
🌐 www.chamundihillpalace.org

Hotel Hilltop (B)
☎ 04828–202 273

HOMESTAYS

Kalaketty Estate Bungalow (L)
☎ 04828–235 223
🌐 www.kalakettyestate.com

Manjappally Plantation Bungalow (T)
☎ 98470 39874
🌐 www.plantationbungalow.com

Thekkady

Shalimar Spice Garden (S)
☎ 04869–222 132
🌐 www.shalimarkerala.com

The Elephant Court (S)
☎ 98951 67199
🌐 www.theelephantcourt.com

Spice Village (L)
☎ 04869–222 314
🌐 www.cghearth.com

Jungle Village (L)
☎ 04869–223 363
🌐 www.sajhotels.com

Cardamom County (L)
☎ 04869–224 501
🌐 www.cardamomcounty.com

Taj Garden Retreat (L)
04869–222 273
🌐 www.tajhotels.com

Hotel Treetop (L)
☎ 04869–223 287
🌐 www.hoteltreetop.com

The Wildernest (T)
☎ 04869–224 030
🌐 www.wildernest-kerala.com

Carmelia Haven (T)
☎ 04868–270 252
🌐 www.carmeliahaven.com

Silver Crest Resort (T)
☎ 04869–222 481
🌐 www.sealordhotels.com

Tall Trees, Munnar

T&U Leisure Hotel (T)
☎ 04865–233 081
🌐 www.tanduleisurehotel.com

Black Berry Hills (T)
☎ 04865–232 978
🌐 www.blackberryhillsindia.com

Oak Fields Resorts (T)
☎ 04865–231 016
🌐 www.oakfieldsmunnar.com

Olive Brook (T)
☎ 04865–230 588
🌐 www.olivebrookmunnar.com

Westwood Riverside Garden Resort (T)
☎ 04865–230 884
🌐 www.westwoodmunnar.com

Isaacs Residency (T)
☎ 04865–230 501
🌐 www.issacsresidency.com

Edassery East End (T)
☎ 04865–230 451
🌐 www.edasserygroup.com

Tallayar Valley Bungalow (T)
☎ 04865–257 314
🌐 www.unusualplaces.info

Ela Eco Land (T)
☎ 04864–278 322, 98410 30553
🌐 www.elaecoland.com

Forest Haven Resort (M)
☎ 04864–278 401
🌐 www.foresthavenresort.com

High Range Club (M)
☎ 04865–230 724
🌐 www.highrangeclubmunnar.com

B Six Holiday Resorts (T)
☎ 04865–230 527
🌐 www.bsixtoursandtravels.com

SN Annexe (M)
☎ 04865–232 022
🌐 www.snmunnar.com

Elysium Garden (M)
☎ 04865–230 510
🌐 www.elysiumgarden.com

Poopada Tourist Home (M)
☎ 04865–230 223
🌐 www.poopada.com

Springdale Resort (M)
☎ 04865–264 268
🌐 www.springdaleresort.com

SN Tourist Home (B)
☎ 04865–230 212
🌐 www. snmunnar. com

Chinnakanal

Club Mahindra Lake View (L)
☎ 04868–249 226
🌐 www.clubmahindra.com

Hotel Fort Munnar (L)
☎ 04868–249 312
🌐 www.royalindian.com

The Siena Village (T)
☎ 04868–249 261
🌐 www.thesienavillage.com

Sterling Days Inn Resorts (B)
☎ 04868–249 206
www.sterlingresorts.org

Peermede

Hotel Himarani International (M)
☎ 04869–232 211
🌐 www.eastwesthospitalities.com

PRICE CATEGORIES

Accommodation listing is arranged on the basis of average room tariff per room on twin sharing basis.

- **S** Super Luxury – Rs 10,000 upwards
- **L** Luxury – Rs 5,000 to Rs 10,000
- **T** Top-End – Rs 2,000 to Rs 5,000
- **M** Mid Range – Rs 1,000 to Rs 2,000
- **B** Budget – Less than Rs 1,000

Sahyadri (B)
☎ 04869–232 496
🌐 www.ayurvedaexcellence.com

Kuttikkanam

Paradisa Plantation Retreat (L)
☎ 0469–270 1311
🌐 www.paradisaretreat.com

Rock Palace Resorts (L)
☎ 04869–233 778
🌐 www.eastwestgroup.co.in

Misty Mountain (T)
☎ 04869–233 265
🌐 www.glenrock-group.com

Wood Palace Resort (T)
☎ 04869–232 266
🌐 www.eastwesthospitalities.com

Thrisangu Haven (T)
☎ 04869–232 633
🌐 www.thrisanguhaven.com.

Orma House (T)
☎ 04869–233 543

Dreamland Hill Resort (T)
☎ 04869–233 220
🌐 www.dreamlandhillresort.com

HOMESTAYS

Ashley Bunglow (T)
☎ 04869–232 282, 989584 30300
🌐 www.stayhomz.in

Kurisumala Ashram Guest House (B)
☎ 04822–289 277/477

Elappara

Chinnar Heritage Plantation Resort (L)
☎ 04869–242 224
🌐 www.stayhomz.in

Henwoods Bungalow (T)
☎ 04828–284 310
🌐 www.stayhomz.in

Green Acre Backpackers Inn (T)
☎ 04828–284 310
🌐 www.stayhomz.in

Koottikkal

Evergreen Estate (T)
☎ 04828–284 310
🌐 www.stayhomz.in

Erunnakutty Estate Bungalow (T)
☎ 094971 18494
🌐 www.stayhomz.in

Little Bungalow (M)
☎ 04828–284 310
🌐 www.stayhomz.in

Mayapott Plantations (T)
☎ 04828 284144, 224271
🌐 www.mayapott.com, www.marveltours.in

Hotel Ambadi (M)
☎ 04869–222 193
🌐 www.hotelambadi.com

Michaels Inn (M)
☎ 04869–222 355
🌐 www.michaelsinnthekkady.com

Hotel SN International (M)
☎ 0989569 9550
🌐 www.snthekkady.com

Hotel Lake Queen (M)
☎ 04869–222 084

Periyar

Periyar reserve Bungalow (S)
☎ 04869–284 310
🌐 www.stayhomz.com

Lake Palace (L)
☎ 04869–222 023
🌐 www.ktdc.com

Aranya Nivas (L)
☎ 04869–222 023
🌐 www.ktdc.com

Periyar House- KTDC (M)
☎ 04869–222 026
🌐 www.ktdc.com

The Bamboo Grove (M)
☎ 04869–224 571
🌐 www.periyartigerreserve.org

Jungle Inn (M)
☎ 04869–224 571
🌐 www.periyartigerreserve.org

Green Mansion (M)
☎ 0481–258 1204/1236
🌐 www.kfdcgavi.com

The Hills

Thenmala

Evergreen Estate Bungalow (L)
☎ 0475–235 2610
🌐 www.stayhomz.com

Ambanaad Estate Bungalow (L)
☎ 0475–234 4536

The Larc Resorts (M)
☎ 0475–234 4270

Highland Hotel and Resort (T)
☎ 0474–245 1442
🌐 www.highlandindia.com

Lake View Ayurvedic Resort & Research Centre (T)
☎ 0475–234 4270/4899, 278 3222

Thenmala Tourism Development Cooperative Society (B)
☎ 0475–234 4800

Tented Accommodation (B)
☎ 0475–234 4800
🌐 www.naftvm.org

Idukki

Greenberg Resorts (T)
☎ 04862–259 954
🌐 www.greenbergresorts.com

Ranger Woods Hill Resort (T)
☎ 04865–230 408/183
🌐 www.rangerwoodsmunnar.com

Hotel Stone Age (B)
☎ 04862–235 477

Thodupuzha

River Banks (M)
☎ 04862–224 942
🌐 www.theriverbanks.com

Maurya Monarch (B)
☎ 04862–222 697
🌐 www.mauryamonarch.com

Sicilia Hotels (T)
☎ 04862–22 2117

Geminy Tourist Home (B)
☎ 04862–224 364

Charakas (B)
☎ 04862–200 756
🌐 www.charakas.org

HOMESTAYS

The Pimenta Farmstay (T)
☎ 0485–226 0216
🌐 www.harithafarms.com

Munnar

Tall Trees (L)
☎ 04865–230 641
🌐 www.ttr.in

Windermere Estate (L)
☎ 04865–230 512
🌐 www.windermeremunnar.com

Tea County (L)
☎ 04865–230 968
🌐 www.ktdc.com

Deshadan Mountain Resort (T)
☎ 0486–523 2910
🌐 www.deshadan.com

Abad Copper Castle (T)
☎ 04865–231 201
🌐 www.abadhotels.com

---

136 | KERALA MAPS & MORE

Vagamon

Vagamon Hideout (L)
04869–248 540
www.sajvagamon.com

The Retreat (L)
94470 84310
www.stayhomz.com/in

Ananya Hill Resorts (T)
04869–248 444
www.ananyahillresorts.com

Vagamon Heights (T)
04869–248 206
www.vagamonheights.com

Indo-American International Gurukulam (B)
04822–289 255
www.gurukulam.com

HOMESTAYS

Vanilla County (T)
0482–228 1225
www.vanillacounty.in

Nelliyampathy

Tropical Hill (T)
04923–246 328
www.tropicalhillresorts.com

ITL Holidays and Resorts (M)
04923–246 357

Greenland Farmhouse (M)
04923–246 246

HOMESTAYS

Whistling Thrush Bungalow (T)
93494 00061
www.nelliampathy.com

Kakkanat Homestay (B)
04923–242 087
www.kakkanat-tourism.com

Ciscilia Heritage (B)
094470 33560
www.cisciliaheritage.com

Vythiri

Green Magic Nature Resort (L)
98474 12266
www.jungleparkresorts.com

Jungle Park Resort (L)
04936–326 868
www.jungleparkresorts.com

Wayanad Resorts (L)
04936–329 302
www.bluegingerresorts.com

Vythiri Resort (T)
04936–255 366
www.vythiriresort.com

Rain Country (T)
04936–205 306
www.raincountryresort.com

Greeshmam Resorts (M)
04936–255 716
www.greeshmamresorts.com

HOMESTAYS

Pranavam Holidays (M)
04936–255 308

Stream Valley Cottages (M)
04936–255 860
www.streamvalleycottages.com

Kalpetta

Wynberg Resorts (T)
04936–247 823
www.wynbergresorts.com

Green Gates Hotel (T)
04936–202 010
www.greengateshotel.com

Haritagiri Ecotel (M)
04936–203 145
www.hotelharitagiri.com

The Woodlands Hotel (M)
04936–202 547
www.thewoodlandshotel.com

Royal Palm Holiday Home (M)
04936–206 096
www.royalpalmwayanad.com

HOMESTAYS

Ayurkendra (B)
04936–203 953
www.ayurkendra.com

Sulthan Bathery

Edakkal Hermitage (T)
04936–221 860
www.edakkal.com

Orchid Resort (T)
04936–262 844
www.orchidresorts.com

HOMESTAYS

Tranquil (L)
04936–220 244
www.tranquilresort.com

Hill View Resorts (T)
04936–217 404
www.hillviewhomestay.com

Mountain View (M)
04936–260 312
www.mountainviewayurvedaretreat.com

Vythiri Resort, Vythiri

Mananthavady

Pachyderm Palace (T)
0484 237 1761
www.costamalabari.com

Fringe Ford (T)
080–2672 2750
www.fringeford.com

Pancha Theertha Rest House (T)
04935–210 055

River Nila

Palakkad

Kairali Ayurvedic Health Resort (S)
04923–222 623
www.kairali.com

Kandath Tharavad (L)
04922–284 124
www.tharavad.com

Poomully Aramthampuran's Ayurveda Mana (M)
0466–237 0660
www.ayurvedamana.com

Rajah Healthy Acres (M)
0466–237 1741
www.ayurveda-in.com

Sri Chakra International (M)
0491–257 0901
www.hotelsrichakra.com

Hotel Indraprastha (M)
0491–253 4641
www.hotelindraprastha.com

Marhaba Residency (M)
0491–252 5262

The Fort Palace Hotel (M)
0491–253 4621\4625

Hotel Kapilavasthu (M)
0491–254 0029

Kalari Kovilakom (B)
04923–263 155
www.cghearth.com

HOMESTAY

Olappamanna Mana (M)
0466–228 5383

Kuttippuram

NC Gardens and Beach Resort (T)
0494–247 1480
www.ncbeachresort.com

The Riverside Retreat (M)
0494–269 8825
www.theblueyonder.com/rr.htm

Tirur

Hotel Navaratna (B)
0494–242 1379

Tranquil Homestay, Sulthan Bathery

Hotel Zodiac International (B)
0494–242 2728

Gulf Tourist Home (B)
0494–242 2747

Kohinoor Tourist Home (B)
0494–242 2411

Ponnani

Safa Lodge (B)
0494–266 6060

Ponnani Tourist Bungalow (B)
0494–266 6082

Manjeri

Hotel Woodbyne (B)
0483–276 2035

Malabar Tower (B)
0483–276 6449

Perinthalmanna

KPM Residency (B)
04933–227 590

Hotel Sabrina (B)
04933–227 196

Kottakkal

KKM Tourist Home (B)
0483–274 4801

Reem International (B)
0483–274 2302

Hotel Vijraj (B)
0483–274 3269

Thrayambaka Tourist Home (B)
0483–274 3078

Nilambur

Hotel Nilambur Manor (B)
04931–221 982

Nilambur Tourist Home (B)
04931–220 373

Sinai Tourist Home (B)
04931–220 785

Chaliyar View(Forest IB) (B)
04931–220 307

HOMESTAY

Thayyil Farm (T)
09380–94471 85668

Cheruthuruthy

The River Retreat (T)
04884–262 244
www.riverretreat.in

Nilayoram Resorts (M)
04884–262 788
www.nilayoram.com

RESOURCES | Accommodation

MAPS & MORE **KERALA** | 137

Al Sulaithy Resorts (M)
04884–262 964

Shoranur

Hotel Apsara (B)
0466–222 2458

Welcome Tourist Home (B)
0466–222 2087

Nakshatra Tourist Home (B)
0466– 320 2454

Coastal Circuit

Kovalam

The Leela Kovalam (S)
0471–248 0101
www.theleela.com

Taj Green Cove (S)
0471–248 7733
www.tajhotels.com

Surya Samudra (S)
0471–226 7333
www.suryasamudra.com

Somatheeram (S)
0471–226 8101
www.somatheeram.in

Travancore Heritage (L)
0471–226 7828
www.thetravancoreheritage.com

Manaltheeram (L)
0471–226 8610
www.manaltheeram.com

Uday Samudra (L)
0471–248 1654
www.udaysamudra.com

Hotel Samudra KTDC (L)
0471–248 0089
www.ktdc.com

Coconut Bay (T)
0471–248 0566
www.coconutbay.in

Lagoona Davina (T)
0471–238 0049
www.lagoonadavina.com

Hotel Rockholm (T)
0471–248 0306
www.rockholm.com

Hotel Abad Palm Shore (T)
0471–248 1481
www.abadhotels.com

Swagath Holiday Resorts (T)
0471–248 1148
www.swagathresorts.com

Kadaloram Beach Resort (T)
0471–248 1116
www.kadaloram.com

Hotel Neelakanta (T)
0471–248 0321
www.hotelneelakantakovalam.com

Hotel Seaface (T)
0471–248 1591
www.seaface.com

Jasmine Palace (T)
0471–248 1475
www.jasminepalace.net

Hotel Jeevan Ayurvedic House (T)
0471–248 0662
www.jeevanresorts.com

Beach and Lake Ayurvedic Resort (T)
0471–238 2086
www.beachandlakeresort.com

Hotel Marine Palace (T)
0471–248 1428
www.hotelmarinepalace.com

Hotel Puja Mahal (T)
0471–657 6133
www.hotelpujamahal.com

Hotel Sea Rock (T)
0471–248 0422
www.hotelsearock.com

Hotel Beach Castle (T)
0471–248 0252
www.hotelbeachcastle.com

Sagara Beach Resorts (T)
0471–248 4077
www.sagarabeachresort.com

Varma's Beach Resort (M)
0471– 248 0478

Golden Sands Beach Resort (M)
0471–248 4077
www.goldensands.com

Temple Garden (M)
0471–248 1972
www.templegarden.in

Surya Samudra, Kovalam

Sea Flower Beach Resort (M)
0471–248 0554
www.seaflowerbeachresort.com

Hotel Orion Beach Resort (B)
0471–248 0999
www.orionbeachresort.com

Alitalia Beach House (B)
0471–248 0042

Sandy Beach Resort (B)
0471–248 0012
www.sandykovalam.com

Ashatheeram Beach Resort (B)
0471–226 7566
www.ashatheeram.net

HOMESTAYS

Karikkathi Beach House (L)
0471–240 0956
www.karikkathibeachhouse.com

Poovar and Chowara

Poovar Island Resort (L)
0471–221 2069
www.poovar-island.com

Isola Di Cocco Ayurvedic Beach Resort (L)
0471–2210008
www.isoladicocco.com

Estuary Island (L)
0471–221 4355
www.estuaryisland.com

Thapovan Heritage Home (T)
0471–248 0453
www.thapovan.com

Varkala

Hindustan Beach Retreat (L)
0470–260 4254
www.hindustanbeachretreat.com

Taj Garden Retreat (T)
0470–260 3000
www.tajhotels.com

Krishnatheeram Ayur Holy Beach Resort (T)
0470–2156 444
www.krishnatheeram.com

Raja Park Beach Resort (T)
0470–260 7060
www.rajapark.com

Deshadan Cliff & Beach Resort (T)
9447459912

Le Mangalath (T)
0470–261 1805
www.lemangalath.com

Green Palace Sea Side Hotel (M)
0470–261 0055

Preeth Beach Resort (M)
0470–260 0942
www.preethbeachresort.com

PRICE CATEGORIES

Accommodation listing is arranged on the basis of average room tariff per room on twin sharing basis.

(S) Super Luxury – Rs 10,000 upwards

(L) Luxury – Rs 5,000 to Rs 10,000

(T) Top-End – Rs 2,000 to Rs 5,000

(M) Mid Range – Rs 1,000 to Rs 2,000

(B) Budget – Less than Rs 1,000

Sea Breeze (M)
0470–329 2685
www.seabreezevarkala.com

SB Regency (M)
0470–329 0288
www.sbregency.com

Oceano Cliff (M)
0470–329 4978
www.oceanocliff.com

Ever Green Beach Resort (M)
0470–260 9808
www.evergreenskm.com

Panchavadi Beach Resort (M)
0470–260 0200
www.panchavadi.com

SS Beach Resort (M)
0470–329 1110
www.ssbeachresortvarkala.com

Dreams Beach Resort (M)
0470–214 6308
www.dreamsvarkala.com

Thiruvambadi Beach Retreat (M)
0470–260 1028
www.thiruvambadihotel.com

Golden Beach Resort (M)
0472–260 9555
www.varkalagoldenbeach.com

Samudra Garden Resort (M)
0470–395 7298
www.arunstours.com

Kattil Beach Resort (B)
0470–266 2226

Eden Garden Ayurvedic Health Retreat (B)
0470–263 3910
www.eden-garden.net

Palm Ayurvedic Beach Resort (B)
0470–279 5949
www.palmbeachresort.net

Varkala Marine Palace Beach Resort (B)
0470–260 3204
www.varkalamarinepalace.com

Hill Palace Beach Resort (B)
0470–261 0142
www.hillpalaceresort.com

Clafouti Beach Resort (B)
0470–2601 414
www.clafoutiresort.com

Mararikulam

Marari Beach Resort (S)
0478–286 3801
www.cghearth.com

Poovar Island Resort

138 | KERALA MAPS & MORE

Marari Beach Homes (L)
☎ 0477–224 3535
🌐 www.mararibeachhomes.com

Alleppey Fisherman Village Beach Resort (L)
☎ 0477–224 3462
🌐 www.atdcalleppey.com

Cherai

Rock Springs (T)
☎ 0484–249 2657

Cherai Beach Resorts (T)
☎ 0484–241 6949
🌐 www.cheraibeachresorts.com

Baywatch Beach Homes (T)
☎ 0484–248 0299
🌐 www.baywatchbeachhomes.com

Sea Palace (M)
☎ 98477 88099
🌐 www.seapalaceresorts.com

Kadalkkara Lake Resort (M)
☎ 0484-248 1999
🌐 www.kadalkkaralakeresorts.com

Kannur

Kairali Heritage Riverside Resort (T)
☎ 0460–224 1665
🌐 www.kairaliheritage.com

Costa Malabari (M)
☎ 0484–237 1761
🌐 www.costamalabari.com

Mascot Beach Resort (M)
☎ 0497–270 8445
🌐 www.mascotresort.com

Royal Omar's (M)
☎ 0497–276 9091
🌐 www.royalomars.com

Malabar Residency (M)
☎ 0497–270 1654

Cliff Exotel International Beach Resort (M)
☎ 0497–271 2197
🌐 www.holidayinmalabar.com

Kamala International (M)
☎ 0497–276 6910

Beach House (B)
☎ 98471 84535
🌐 www.kannur.biz

Hotel Meridian Palace (B)
☎ 0497–270 1676
🌐 www.hotelmeridianpalace.com

Sweety International (B)
☎ 0497–270 8283

Kasaragod

Bekal International (B)
☎ 0467–220 4271
🌐 www.hotelbekal.com

Houseboats

Alappuzha

Muthoot River Escapes
☎ 0484–550 3044
🌐 www.muthoothotels.com

Lakes and Lagoons Tour Co
☎ 0477–225 1118, 225 4881
🌐 www.lakeslagoons.com

Rainbow Cruises
☎ 0477–224 1375
🌐 www.backwaterkerala.com

ATDC
☎ 0477–2231 145, 224 3462
🌐 www.atdcalleppey.com

Amritha Houseboats & Resorts
☎ 98478 62771
🌐 www.amrithahouseboats.com

Aria Holidays & Resorts
☎ 0477–329 0403

Bharath Tourist Services Society
☎ 0477–226 2262, 226 4860
🌐 www.btsstourism.com

Evergreen Tours
☎ 0477–2264 654, 223 9387
🌐 www.evergreen-kerala.com

Guardian Tours & Travels
☎ 98474 36662, 0477–224 4741
🌐 www.guardianhouseboat.com

JCT Houseboats
☎ 0477–329 0495

Lake Lands Cruise
☎ 0477–2868985, 2868986
🌐 www.lakelandcruise.com

Hotel City Tower (B)
☎ 04994–230 562

Apsara Regency (B)
☎ 04994–230 124

Government Guesthouse (B)
☎ 0499–423 0666

Victoria Tourist Home (B)
☎ 0499–423 046

Marvel Cruise
☎ 0477–226 4341, 223 7108
🌐 www.marvelcruise.com

Minar De Lake
☎ 94477 46327
🌐 www.minardelake.com

Morning Mist Backwater Cruises
☎ 0477–223 5020
🌐 www.morningmistcruise.com

Pulickattil Houseboats
☎ 0477–226 4558
🌐 www.pulickattilbackwaters.com

Punnamada Houseboat
☎ 0477–223 3690
🌐 www.punnamada.com

River Homes Cruise
☎ 0477–329 0753
🌐 www.houseboattourism.com

River & Country Tours
☎ 0477–224 3581
🌐 www.riverandcountry.com

Indigenous House Boats
☎ 0484–329 7245, 358678
🌐 www.indigenoustour.com

Kumarakom

Kumarakom Lake Resort
☎ 0481–252 4900
🌐 www.klresort.com

Spice Coast Cruises
☎ 0484–266 8221, 266 6821
🌐 www.cghearth.com

Gitanjali Heritage (T)
☎ 0467–223 4159
🌐 www.gitanjaliheritage.com

Nileswaram

Gokulam Nalanda (M)
☎ 0467–228 2662
🌐 www.nalandaresorts.com

Neelambari Resorts and Spa (L)
☎ 0467–222 8957
🌐 www.neelambari.com

Lake View House Boats
☎ 0481–252 3966
🌐 www.lakeviewhouseboat.com

Kollam

Southern Backwaters
☎ 0474–2746037, 94471 46037
🌐 www.southernbackwaters.com

Kochi

Emerald Star Tourism
☎ 0484–266 9553
🌐 www.emeraldkeral.comcom

Golden Gate Tours & Travels
☎ 0484–231 6007
🌐 www.ayurcruise.com

Taj House Boat Cruises
☎ 0484–237 1471
🌐 www.tajhotels.com

The Oberoi MV Vrinda
☎ 0484–266 9595
🌐 www.hilton.com

Thiruvananthapuram

Soma Houseboats
☎ 0471–226 8101, 226 4112
🌐 www.somahouseboats.com

Valiyaparamba

Bekal Boat Stay
☎ 0467–228 2633, 325 3311
🌐 www.bekalboatstay.com

Note: Only a representative list of accommodation and houseboat options has been given. The listing should not be construed as recommendations by the publisher.

Spice Coast Cruises

Useful Information

Airports and Airlines

Thiruvananthapuram International Airport
☎ 0471–250 1424
Location: 6 km south of Thiruvananthapuram.
Air India	☎ 0471–250 1426
Air India Express	☎ 0471–231 9595
Deccan	☎ 0471–250 8988
Emirates	☎ 0471–250 7861,78
Gulf Air	☎ 0471–250 1205, 06
Indian	☎ 0471–250 0419
Jet Airways	☎ 0471–250 0710, 0860
Kuwait Airways	☎ 0471–250 0437
Oman Air	☎ 0471–250 1387
Qatar Airways	☎ 0471–250 2548
Singapore Airlines /SilkAir	☎ 0471–250 4141
SriLankan Airlines	☎ 0471–250 1140

Cochin International Airport, Nedumbassery ☎ 0484–261 0115
Location: 34 km north of Kochi.
Air Arabia	☎ 0484–261 1153, 54
Air India	☎ 0484–261 0040, 70
Air India Express	☎ 0484–261 0040
Deccan	☎ 0484–261 0288
Emirates	☎ 0484–261 1194, 95
Gulf Air	☎ 0484–261 1346-48
Indian	☎ 0484–261 0041
Jet Airways	☎ 0484–261 0037, 65
Jet Lite	☎ 0484–261 1340-42
Kingfisher Airlines	☎ 0484–261 0055
Kuwait Airways	☎ 0484–261 0252
Oman Air	☎ 0484–261 0169, 70
Qatar Airways	☎ 0484–261 1305
Saudi Arabian Airlines	☎ 0484–261 1288
Singapore Airlines/Silk Air	☎ 0484–235 8132
SriLankan Airlines	☎ 0484–261 1313, 14

Calicut International Airport, Karipur
☎ 0483–271 1314
Location: 26 km south of Kozhikode.
Air India	☎ 0483–271 5646
Air India Express	☎ 0483–271 2401
Deccan	☎ 0483–271 5102
Indian	☎ 0483–271 0100
Jet Airways	☎ 0483–271 2375
SriLankan Airlines	☎ 0483–271 7757

The Government

Thiruvananthapuram
Chief Minister's Office
☎ 0471–233 3682
✉ chiefminister@kerala.gov.in
🌐 www.kerala.gov.in
District Collectorate
☎ 0471–246 2471
✉ tvm_collectorate@messaging.kerala.gov.in

Kochi
District Collectorate
☎ 0484–242 3001
✉ ekm_collectorate@messaging.kerala.gov.in

Kozhikode
District Collectorate
☎ 0495–237 1400, 237 0582
✉ kkd_collectorate@messaging.kerala.gov.in

International Organisations

Thiruvananthapuram
Alliance Francaise de Trivandrum
☎ 0471–232 0666
🌐 www.afindia.org

British Council Library
☎ 0471–233 0716
🌐 www.library.britishcouncil.org.in
Indian Red Cross Society
☎ 0471–247 8106
🌐 www.indianredcross.org
Russian Cultural Centre
☎ 0471–233 8399
🌐 www.russianculturalcentre.org

Kochi
Alliance Francaise de Cochin
☎ 0484–237 6220
🌐 www.afindia.org
Indo-American Chamber of Commerce
☎ 0484–237 5434
🌐 www.iaccindia.com

New Names

All cities and towns in Kerala are now referred to by their new names (actually old names before they were anglicised by the British).

Old name	New name
Alleppey	Alappuzha
Badagara	Vatakara
Calicut	Kozhikode
Cannanore	Kannur
Cranganore	Kodungallur
Cochin	Kochi
Palghat	Palakkad
Quilon	Kollam
Sultan's Battery	Sulthan Bathery
Telicherry	Thalassery
Trichur	Thrissur
Trivandrum	Thiruvananthapuram

Police

100 is the emergency code for police assistance. To report crimes, call the Crime Stopper Cell at 1090.
🌐 www.keralapolice.org

Thiruvananthapuram
Commissioner of Police
☎ 0471–232 0579, 232 9092
🌐 www.tvmcitypolice.org

Kochi
Commissioner of Police
☎ 0484–239 4770
🌐 www.kochicitypolice.org

Kozhikode
Commissioner of Police
☎ 0495–272 2911, 272 2116

Public Holidays

Kerala is famous for its *bandhs* and *hartals*, which means a forced holiday whether you like it or not. In addition, there are National and State holidays. Places such as museums, dam sites and palaces, remain closed to the public on these days.

- Id-ul-Azha (Bakrid)
- Muharram
- Maundy Thursday
- Vishu
- Karkkadaka Vavu
- First Onam
- Fourth Onam
- Birthday of Dr BR Ambedkar
- Sree Narayana Guru Jayanthi
- Sree Krishna Jayanthi
- Sree Narayana Guru Samadhi Day
- Gandhi Jayanthi/ Vijayadasami
- Deepavali
- Id-ul-fitr (Ramzan)
- Christmas
- Republic Day
- Milad-i-sherif
- Good Friday
- May Day
- Independence Day
- Thiruonam

Trains

For long journeys, trains are the best for panoramic views and relatively relaxed travel. There are four main classes. Second class unreserved, second class sleeper, first class and air - conditioned travel, which again has AC chair car for day journeys. For overnight journeys, there is AC III sleeper, and AC II sleeper. There are also ladies compartments for women travelling alone.
🌐 www.indianrail.gov.in

Important railway stations
Alappuzha	☎ 0477–225 3865
Ernakulam	☎ 0484–237 5131
Kannur	☎ 0497–270 5555
Kollam	☎ 0474–274 6194
Kottayam	☎ 0481–256 2933
Palakkad	☎ 0491–253 2156
Thiruvananthapuram	☎ 0471–232 1568
Thrissur	☎ 0478–242 3150

Useful Websites

🌐 www.keralatourism.org
🌐 www.starkworld.net
🌐 www.kerala.com
🌐 www.kerala.gov.in
🌐 www.keralaforest.org
🌐 www.keralapolice.org
🌐 www.keralapwd.net
🌐 www.prd.kerala.gov.in

Visas

All foreigners need to possess a valid visa issued by any Indian Embassy or High Commission to enter Kerala. Visas are usually non-extendable but 15-day extensions are issued under special circumstances. Anyone who stays in India for more than four months on a tourist visa needs an Exemption Certificate (from paying tax) on leaving the country.
For visa extension, contact:
Office of the Commissioner of Police, Thiruvananthapuram
☎ 0471–320 555

Making Calls

Calling India from another country
- To a landline – If the number is 240 9430 and the STD code is 0484, you have to dial 0091484–240 9430.
- To a mobile – If the number is 98466 01236, then dial 0091–98466 01236.

Calling from a landline in India
To call a landline number within India but outside the State of residence, prefix the STD code of the particular place. Eg: To call the number 4125 5036 in Bangalore, prefix the STD code of Bangalore (080).
Making a local call
To call a local landline number, dial the number directly without the STD code.
Calling a mobile phone
To call a mobile phone within the State dial the 10-digit number directly. eg: 98466 01236. To call a mobile phone within India, outside the State, prefix '0' to the 10 digit number given.
eg: 098865 04963

From a mobile phone
- Calling a local landline number – prefix the STD code of particular destination and then dial the number, eg: 0484–240 9430.
- To call another mobile number within the State of residence, dial the 10-digit number directly, eg: 98466 01236
- To make a call to a mobile number outside the State of residence, prefix '0' to the 10 - digit number given, eg: 09886 504963.

140 | KERALA MAPS & MORE

Index–Places and Tourist Attractions

A
Aakulam Tourist Complex 14
Adventure Park 47
Agasthyakoodam Mountains 17
Alappuzha 42, 48
Alumkadavu Boat Building Yard 44
Ambalappuzha Sree Krishna Temple 50
Ananthapura Temple 110
Anjengo Fort 102
Antique Shops in Jew Street 25
Aralam Wildlife Sanctuary 121
Aranmula boat race 62
Art Gallery 12
Aruvikkara Dam and Devi Temple 17
Ashtamudi Backwaters 45
Athirappally Waterfalls 26
Ayyampara hills 59

B
Backwaters 7, 40
Backwater Cruise 97
Beach Road 34
Beemapalli 14
Bekal Fort 109
Beypore 35
Bhoothathankettu 26
Bishop's House/Indo-Portuguese Museum 23
Blossom International Park 73
Boating at Kootai 93
Boating in Tirur Puzha 93
Broadway 19

C
Chakkulathukavu Bhagavathi Temple 50
Chandragiri Fort 109
Chavara Bhavan 50
Chellarkovil 67
Chembra Peak 79
Chendamangalam 26
Cherai Beach 26
Cheraman Perumal Juma Masjid 30
Cheriyapalli 55
Cheruthuruthy 94
Cheruvathur Kota Palli 108
Chimmini Wildlife Sanctuary 118
Chinese Fishing Nets 20
Chinnar Wildlife Sanctuary 117
Chottanikkara temple 20
Chowara 99
Clock tower at Mattancherry 25
COMTRUST 33
CSI Church, Kozhikode 34
CSI Church, Munnar 73
CSI Church, Pallikkunnu 76

D
Devikulam Lake 75
Dharmadom Island 38
Driftwood Museum 53
Dutch Cemetery 23

E
Eagle Rock or Parunthumpara 76
Edakkal Caves 82
Eravikulam National Park 117
Ernakulam 19
Erumely 61

F
Fort Kochi 20
Fort Kochi beach 23
Fort St Angelo 105

G
Ganapathiyar Kovil 61
Gavi 67
Good Shepherd Church 57
Guruvayur 31

H
Hill Palace Museum 19

I
Idukki 70
Idukki Arch Dam 70
Idukki Wildlife Sanctuary 116

J
Jain Temple, Sulthan Bathery 82
Jain Temple, Palakkad 90
Janardhana Temple 102

K
Kadalundi 35
Kakki Reservoir 64
Kala Mandapam at Vyloppilly Sanskrithi Bhavan 14
Kallai 35
Kalpetta 82
Kalvary Mount 70
Kanhangad/ Hosdurg Fort 112
Kanhirode Weaving Co-operative 106
Kanjirapally 60
Kannur 103
Kanwatheertha Beach 112
Kappad Beach 35
Kappil Beach 102
Karalad Lake 83
Karumadi Kuttan 51
Kasaragod 109
Kaviyoor 64
Kayyoor Temple 59
KCS Panicker Gallery 13
Kerala Folklore Academy 106
Kerala Lalitha Kala Akademi 20
Kerala State Science and Technology Museum 13
KIRTADS 35
Kochambalam 61
Kochi 18
Kodungallur 30
Kollam 44
Kolukkumalai 75
Konni 62
Koodalmanikyam Temple, Irinjalakuda 30
Kottanchery 112
Kottayam 55
Kottiyoor Shiva Temple 106
Kovalam 97
Koyikkal Palace/ Numismatics Museum 17
Kozhikode 32
Krishnapuram Palace Museum 51
Kumarakom 52
Kumbalangi 26
Kumily and Thekkady 65
Kundala 73
Kurisumala 77
Kurisumala Ashram 77
Kurumba Bhagavathi Temple 30
Kuruva Dweep 83

L
Lakkidi's Chain Tree 79
Lighthouse, Kovalam 97
Lighthouse, Anjengo 102

M
Madhur Sree Madananteshwara Vinayaka Temple 110
Mahalingeshwara Temple 108
Mahe 37
Malanadu Development Society (MDS) 26
Malayala Kalagramam 37
Malik Ibn Dinar Mosque 110
Mampara Grasslands 78
Mananchira Square 36
Mananthavady 83
Mannadi 64
Mannarassala Snake Temple 51
Mar Thoma Pontifical Shrine 30
Maramon 64
Marayoor 75
Marine Drive 19
Maritime Museum 25
Mata Amritanandamayi Ashram 44
Mattancherry 25
Mattupetty 73
Mayiladumpara Sanctuary 90
Meenmutti Waterfalls 17
Meenmutty Falls 81

Methan Mani 15
MG Road 19
Midlands 54
Mishkal Mosque 34
Mother of God Cathedral 34
Mount Carmel Church 73
Muchundipalli 34
Munnar 72
Munroe Island 47
Murugan Para 77
Museum of Kerala History 20
Muzhappilangad Beach 38

N
Napier Museum 12
Natural History Museum 12
Nelliyampathy 78
Neyyar Wildlife Sanctuary 114
Nileswaram 107
Nritha Mandapam 14

O
Ochira Parabrahma Temple 45
Odathil Palli 38
Orange and Vegetable Farm 78

P
Padmanabha Swamy Temple 10
Padmanabhapuram Palace 16
Pakshipatalam 83
Pala 58
Palakkad 89
Palayur Church 31
Panchalimedu 76
Pandikuzhi 65
Panthalayini Kollam 35
Parambikulam Wildlife Sanctuary 120
Parassini Kadavu Temple 105
Pardesi Synagogue 25
Pathanamthitta 62
Pathiramanal Island 51
Payyambalam Beach 105
Payyoli Beach 35
Pazhassi Museum 83
Pazhassiraja Museum and Art Gallery 35
Peechi-Vazhani Wildlife Sanctuary 119
Peermede 76
Peppara Wildlife Sanctuary 115
Periyar Tiger Reserve 116
Perumthenaruvi Falls 62
Pine Forests, Vagamon 77
Planetarium and Science Centre, Kozhikode 35
Ponnani 91
Ponnumthuruthu Island 102
Pookot Lake 81
Poonjar Palace 59
Poovar 99
Possadi Gumpe 112
Pothundy 78
Priyadarshini Planetarium 13
Punnathoor Kotta 31
Puthen Malika 13
Puthenveedu 61

R
R Block 51
Rajarajeshwara Temple 106
Ranga Mandapam at Vyloppilly sanskrithi bhavan 14
Ranipuram 112
River Nila 84
River Rafting at Ponnani 93

S
Sabarimala 64
Santa Cruz Basilica 20
Sasthamkotta Dharmasastha Temple 45
Seetharkundu 78
Shankhumugham Beach 16
Shenduruney Wildlife Sanctuary 115
Shiva Temple, Ernakulam 19
Shiva Temple, Kodungallur 30

Shrine of our Lady of Immaculate Conception 59
Silent Valley National Park 120
Sivagiri Mutt 100
SM Street 33
Snake Boats 42
SNC Maritime Museum 26
Soochipara and Kanthampara Falls 81
Spice Market 25
Sree Chithra Art Gallery 12
Sree Chithra Enclave 12
Sree Krishna Temple 31
Sree Rama Temple, Thriprayar 30
St Dominic's Cathedral 60
St Francis Church 23
St George Church, Aruvithura 59
St George Orthodox Syrian Church 51
St Mary's Church, Bharananganam 59
St Mary's Church, Kanjirapally 60
St Mary's Church, Champakulam 50
St Mary's Forane Church 59
St Teresa's Church 37
St Thomas Benedictine Abbey 61
Subrahmanya Temple 51
Sulthan Bathery 82
Summer Palace 76

T
Tali Temple 34
Tasara Creative Weaving Centre 35
Tea Museum 72
Thalassery 38
Thalassery Fort 38
Thangasseri 45
Thattekkad Bird Sanctuary 118
The Cave temple 99
The Hills 68
The Zoo, Thiruvananthapuram 12
The Zoo and Museum Complex, Thiruvananthapuram 12
Thenmala 69
Thevally Palace 45
Thirumala Devaswom Temple 25
Thirunakkara Temple 57
Thirunelly Temple 83
Thiruvananthapuram 10
Thommankuthu 70
Thrisangu Hills 76
Thrissileri Temple 83
Thrissur 29
Tipu's Fort 89
Top Station 75
Tribal Heritage Museum 66
Trithala 90

U
Ummichipoyil and Varikulam 108

V
Vagamon 77
Valayanadu Devi Kshetram 35
Valiyambalam 61
Valiyapalli, Pala 59
Valiyapalli, Kottayam 55
Valiyaparamba Backwaters 108
Valiyathura Pier 97
Varahamoorthi Kshetram 90
Varkala 100
Vastu Vidya Gurukulam 64
Vavar Mosque 61
Veli Tourist Village 14
Vellayani Lake 97
Velliamkallu 35
Viewpoints, Munnar 75
Vijnana Kala Vedi Cultural Centre 64
Vizhinjam 99
Vyloppilly Sanskrithi Bhavan 14
Vythiri 79

W
Waterfalls of Munnar 75
Wayanad 79
Wayanad Heritage Museum 82
Wayanad Wildlife Sanctuary 121
Willingdon Island 26

MAPS & MORE KERALA | 141

Index–Places-Location on the Map (Place, Page number, Grid number)

A
Achankovil 46, E2
Adimali 71, C2
Adkastala 111, B1
Adoor 63, B4
Alakode 104, C2
Alamkodu 15, B2
Alangad 27, A3
Alangad 88, C3
Alappadamba 104, B1
Alappuzha (Alleppey) 49 -B4, 42- C5
Alathur 88, D4
Alumkadavu 42, C7
Aluva 27, B3
Amarambalam 92, E2
Ambalappuzha 42, B5
Ambalavayal 80, D4
Amballur 27, B4
Amballur 28, C3
Anakkulam 71, B2
Anappara 15, D4
Anchal 46, D3
Angadi 63, C2
Angadipuram 92, D5
Angamali 27, B2
Anikad 27, C4
Anjarakandi River 104, C4
Annur 104, A2
Anthikad 28, B3
Appupanthodu 63, D3
Aranmula 63, B2
Arattupuzha 49, B5
Areekode 92, C3
Arikkod 36, D5
Arpookkara 56, B3
Arthunkal 42, B3
Arur 49, A1
Aryankavu 46, F2
Ashoka Jn 71, B4
Athani 27, B2
Athani 28, B2
Athikad 88, E4
Athirampuzha 56, C2
Athirunkal 63, D3
Atholy 80, A4
Attingal 15, B2
Attipara 15, B3
Avanishwaram 46, C2
Ayarkunnam 56, C3
Ayiramthengu 42, C7
Aymanam 56, B3
Ayoor 46, D3
Ayyankunnu 104, E3
Ayyappankovil 71, C4
Azhikod 28, B2
Azhikode 104, B4

B
Badiaduka 111, B2
Balal 111, C4
Balaramapuram 15, C4
Balussery 36, B3
Bethel 71, C3
Beypore 36, B5
Bharanikkavu 46, B2
Bonacaud 15, D2

C
Chandanakavu 86, A2
Chadayamangalam 46, D3
Chalai 11, B6
Chalakayam 63, E2
Chalakudi 28, C4
Chalapuram 33, C4
Chaliyar 92, C2
Chalode 104, C4
Chambakulam 42, C5
Champakkara 49, A2
Chamravattom 86, A3
Chandanathode 80, A2
Changanacherry 56, C4
Chappathu 71, C4
Chathanur 46, C3
Chavadiyur 88, D1
Chavakkad 28 A2
Chavara 46, A3

Chavassery 104, D3
Chayamkod 111, C4
Chelakkara 28, C1
Chelambra 36, C5
Chemmanad 27, B3
Chengannur 49, C5
Chenkara 56, F2
Chenkulam 15, A1
Chennamkari 49, B4
Chenthitta 11, B5
Cherpulassery 88, C3
Cherthala 49, A2
Cherukattur 80, C2
Cherupuzha 104, B1
Chethalath 80, D2
Chettikulangara 42, C6
Chevayur 36, B4
Chingavanam 56, C4
Chinnakkanal 71, C2
Chinnar 71, C1
Chirayinkeezhu 15, A2
Chithirapuram 71, C2
Chittar 63, D3
Chittari 111, B3
Chitur 88, E4
Chiyyaram 28, B3
Chokad 92, D3
Choondal 28, B2
Chooralmala 80, D5
Chottanikkara 49, B1
Chullimanur 15, C2
Chundel 80, C4

D
Devikulam 71, C2

E
Edacheri 36, A2
Edakkad 104, C4
Edakkara 92, D2
Edakochi 42, A1
Edamon 46, D2
Edaneer 111, B2
Edapally 27, A3
Edappal 92, B6
Edathua 42, C5
Edavanna 92, C3
Edavilangu 28, B4
Elamkulam 56, D3
Elanad 28, C2
Elappara 71, B4
Elathur 36, B4
Enathu 63, B4
Engandiyur 28, B3
Eramallur 27, A4
Eranhipalam 33, C1
Erattupetta 56, D2
Eravallur 28, B2
Ernakulam 21- D2, 27- A4, 42- C1
Erumely 56, E4
Eruvessi 104, D2
Ettumanur 56, C2
Ezhattumukam 27, B1
Ezhimala 104, A3
Ezhukone 46, C3
Ezhumattur 63, B2
Ezhupunna 49, A1
Ezhupurapady 63, D3

F
Feroke 36, C5
Fort 11, A6
Fort Kochi 24

G
Gandhinagar 21, E3
Gavi 63, E1
Grampi 71, C5
Guruvayur 28, B2

H
Haripad 49, B5
Hosangadi 111, A1
Hosdurg 111, B4

I
Idukki 71, B4
Ilanthur 63, B2
Inchathotty 71, A2
Irikkur 104, D3
Iringal 36, A2

Irinjalakuda 28, B3
Iritty 104, D3
Irulam 80, D2

J
Jalsoor 111, D2
Jose Junction 22, C5

K
Kaachamkurichi 88, E5
Kabinigiri 80, D1
Kacherippady Junction 22, C1
Kadakkal 46, D4
Kadakkavur 15, A2
Kadampuza 86, A2
Kadanadu 56, D1
Kadangod 28, B1
Kadannamanna 92, C4
Kadannappally 104, B2
Kadavanthra 21, E3
Kadikkad 28, A1
Kaduthuruthy 56, B2
Kainakari 42, B4
Kaipamangalam 28, B3
Kaipattur 63, B3
Kakki 63, E2
Kaladi 92, B6
Kalamassery 27, A3
Kalikavu 92, D3
Kalkoonthal 71, C3
Kallai 36, B4
Kallana 28, E4
Kallar 111, C3
Kallar 15, D2
Kallar 71, C4
Kallara 15, C1
Kaloor 21, E1
Kalpetta 80, C3
Kambalakkad 80, C3
Kanchiyar 71,
Kangazha 56, C3
Kanhirakolly 104, D2
Kanjar 71, B4
Kanjikkuzhi 56, D2
Kanjikkuzhi 71, B3
Kanjirapally 56, D3
Kannadi Parammba 104, C3
Kannapuram 104, B3
Kannur (Cannanore) 104, B4
Kanthalloor 71, C1
Kanur 46, D4
Kappil 15, A1
Kappimala 104, C2
Karadka 111, C2
Karimannur 56, E1
Karimbam 104, B3
Karipur 92, B3
Karivellur 104, A2
Karthikappally 42, C6
Kartikulam 80, C1
Karukachal 56, C4
Karukutti 27, B2
Karumalur 27, A2
Karunagappally 46, A2
Karuvanchal 104, C2
Kasaragod 111, B2
Kattakkada 15, C3
Kattampara 63, D3
Kattappana 71, C4
Kattathipatra 63, E3
Kattippara 71, B3
Kavalam 42, C4
Kavalangad 71, A2
Kavalar 27, C1
Kavilumpara 36, C2
Kaviyoor 63, B1
Kayamkulam 49, C6
Kazhakkoottam 15, B3
Kidangoor 56, C2
Kilimanoor 15, B1
Kizhuparamba 92, C3
Kochi 20
Kodanad 27, C2
Kodanchery 36, D3
Kodangoor 56, D2
Kodasseri 27, B2
Kodikulam 27, D4

Kodimatha 42, C4
Kodungallur 28, B4
Koduvally 36, C4
Kolanchery 27, C3
Kolayad 104, E4
Kolazhi 28, B2
Kollam (Quilon) 46, B3
Kollappally 56, D1
Kollengode 88, D4
Kolukkumalai 71, C2
Kondotti 92, B3
Kongad 88, D3
Konnakad 111, D3
Konni 63, C4
Koodal 63, C4
Koodali 104, C3
Koonammavu 27, A3
Kootanad 88, B4
Koothattukulam 56, C1
Koothuparamba 104, D4
Koottikkal 56, E3
Koottupuzha 104, E2
Koratty 28, C4
Korom 36, C1
Kothamangalam 27, C3
Kottakkal 92, B4
Kottarakkara 46, C2
Kottayam 56, C3
Kottayi 88, D4
Kottiyoor 80, A1
Kovalam 98
Kovilkadavu 71, C1
Koyilandi 36, B3
Kozhencherry 63, B2
Kozhichal 104, C1
Kozhikode (Calicut) 36, B4
Kozhuvanal 56, D2
Kudayathur 71, A3
Kudiyanmala 104, C2
Kudlamogar 111, B1
Kulamavu 71, B4
Kulathupuzha 46, E3
Kulathur 92, C5
Kumarakom 42, C3
Kumbalangi 27, A4
Kumbanad 63, B2
Kumbazha 63, C3
Kumbla 111, B2
Kumily 66- B1, 71- C5
Kundala 71, C2
Kundara 46, B3
Kundupalli 111, D3
Kunjathur 111, A1
Kunnamangalam 36, C4
Kunnamkulam 28, B2
Kunnathunadu 27, C3
Kunnathur 46, B2
Kunnathur Padi 104, D2
Kunnukuzhi 11, A3
Kuppam 104, B2
Kurachundu 36, C2
Kurampala 63, B3
Kuravilangad 56, C2
Kuriyanad 27, C2
Kuruppanthara 56, C2
Kuruvattur 36, B4
Kuthattukulam 27, C4
Kuthiathodu 56, A1
Kuttamangalam 49, B4
Kuttiadi 80, A3
Kuttiattur 104, C2
Kuttichal 15, C3
Kuttichira Market 33, B4
Kuttikkanam 71, B5
Kuttippuram 92, C5
Kuzhithura 15, D5

L
Laha 63, D2
Lakkidi 80, C4

M
Madathara 15, C1
Madavoor 15, B1
Madhava Pharamcy Junction 22, B1
Mahe (UT) 104, C5
Makarachal 28, E4
Makki 80, C2
Mala 28, C4

142 | KERALA MAPS & MORE

Malappuram 92, C4, (88, A2)
Mallapally 63, B1
Mambaram 104, C4
Mananthavady 80, C2
Manarkadu 56, C3
Mangala Devi 71, D5
Mangalapuram 15, B2
Manimala 56, D4
Maniyar 63, D3
Manjallur 27, C4
Manjappara 71, C3
Manjapra 27, B2
Manjeri 92, C3
Manjinikkara 63, C3
Manjoor 56, C2
Mankada 92, D4
Mannanam 56, B2
Mannarassala 42, C5
Mannarkkad 88, C2
Mannuthy 28, C2
Maradi 92, D1
Maramon 63, B2
Marangattupally 56, C2
Mararikulam 49, A3
Marayoor 71, C1
Marottichal 28, C3
Mathamangalam 104, B2
Mathil 104, B2
Mattancherry 24, D2
Mattannur 104, D4
Mattupetty 71, C2
Mavelikkara 49, C5
Mavoor 36, C4
Mayyanad 46, B4
Meenangadi 80, D3
Meenkunnu 104, B4
Meenkutti 71, B1
Melattur 92, D4
Melukavu 56, D1
Meppadi 80, D4
Monipally 56, C1
Moolamattam 71, B4
Morayur 92, C3
Muhamma 42, B3
Mukkali 88, D2
Mukkam 36, C4
Mulakulam 56, B1
Mulavur 27, C3
Mulleria 111, C2
Mundakayam 56, E3
Mundan Kavu 63, B2
Mundur 88, D3
Munnamkal 36, B2
Munnar 71-C2, 74
Murinjakal 63, C3
Murinjapuzha 71, B5
Murukkumpuzha 15, B3
Muthalakulam 33, C3
Muthanga 80, F3
Muttil 80, D3
Muttom 71, A3
Muvattupuzha 27, C3

N
Nadakavu 33, B1
Nadapuram 36, A2
Naduvannur 36, B3
Naduvathumoozhi 46, D1
Nanmanda 36, B3
Nannambra 92, B5
Nattakom 56, C3
Nedumangadu 15, C3
Nedumbassery 28, C4
Nedumkandam 71, C3
Nedumpura 28, C1
Nedumudy 49, B4
Neendakara 46, A3
Neerettupuram 42, D5
Nellikunnam 46, C3
Nelliyampathy 28, E2
Nelluvaye 28, B1
Nemam 15, C4
Nenmara 88, D5
Neriyamangalam 27, D3
Nettur 42, B1
Neyyattinkara 15, C4
Nilambur 92, D2
Nilamel 46, D4

Nileswaram 111, C4
Njarakal 27, A2
Njeezhur 27, C4

O
Ochira 42, C6
Odayanchal 111, C3
Old Munnar 74, A5
Ollur 28, C3
Omallur 63, C3
Onamthuruthu 56, A2
Ottappalam 88, C3

P
Padagiri 88, E5
Padam 63, D4
Padichira 80, D2
Padma Junction 22, C2
Padmanabhapuram 15, D5
Paika 56, D3
Painavu 71, B4
Paivalike 111, B1
Pakku 56, C4
Pala 56, D2
Palakkad 88, D3
Palarivattom 21- E1, 27- A3
Palavayal 111, B4
Palisheri 28, B3
Pallana 42, C5
Pallikara 92, C6
Pallikkathodu 56, D3
Pallipuram 15, B3
Pallipuram 27, A2
Palode 15, C2
Pamba 63, E2
Pambadi 56, D3
Panamaram 80, C2
Panampilly Nagar 21, E4
Panathady 111, D3
Panayaal 111, B3
Pandalam 63, B3
Pandikkad 92, D4
Panmana 42, C7
Panthalayini Kollam 36, B3
Pathanamthitta 63
Panyannur 104, D5
Parakkod 63, C4
Parambikulam 88, E6
Parappanangadi 92, B4
Parassala 15, D4
Parassini Kadavu 104, C3
Parathodu 56, E3
Paravoor 27, A2
Paravur 46, B4
Paripally 46, C4
Pariyaram 104, B2
Pariyaram 28, D4
Parumala 63, A2
Pathanamthitta 63, C3
Pathanapuram 46, D2
Pathupara 27, D1
Pattambi 88, B3
Pattanakkad 27, A5
Pattekkudi 71, B3
Pattikadu 28, C2
Pattithanam 56, C2
Pavaratty 28, B2
Pavithreswaram 46, C2
Payippad 42, C5
Payyanur 104, A2
Payyoli 36, A3
Pazhanji 28, B1
Pazhayangadi 104, B3
Pazhayannur 28, D1
Peermede 71, B5
Perambra 36, B2
Peravoor 104, E4
Peringod 88, C3
Peringom 104, B1
Perinjanam 28, B4
Perinthalmanna 92, D5
Periya 80, A2
Perla 111, C2
Peroorkada 15, C3
Perumanna 92, B4
Perumanoor 21, E5
Perumbatta 111, C4
Perumbavoor 27, C3
Perumtodu 27, C2

Perumuzhi 71, A1
Perunna 49, C4
Peruvanthanam 71, B5
Perya 36, B3
Pezhumpara 63, C3
Piravam 27, C4
Piravanthur 46, D2
Plappally 63, D2
Poinachi 111, B3
Ponkandam, D3
Ponkunnam 56, D3
Ponnani 92, B6
Poochakkal 27, B5
Pookkottoor 92, C4
Poonchira 71, A3
Poonjar 56, E2
Poonkavu 49, A3
Poopara 71, C3
Poovar 15, C4
Pooyamkutti 27, D2
Pothanikad 27, D3
Pottanplavu 104, C2
Pudukad 28, C3
Puduppadi 80, B4
Pulamanthole 86, B2
Pulamanthole 92, D5
Pulingom 104, B1
Pulinkunnu 42, C4
Puliyanmala 71, C4
Pullad 63, B2
Pullu 28, B3
Pulluvila 15, C4
Pulpally 80, D2
Punalur 46, D2
Punnamada 49, B3
Punnasseri 36, B3
Punnayur 28, A2
Puthuppadi 36, C3
Puthur 46, C2
Puttadi 71, C4

R
Rajakkadu 71, C3
Ramanattukara 36, C5
Ramapuram 56, D1
Ranipuram 111, D3
Ranni 63, C2

S
Santhanpara 71, C3
Sasthamkotta 46, B2
Shenoys Junction 22, C3
Shoranur 88, B3
Sooranad North 46, B1
South Junction 22, D5
Sreekanteswaram 11, A5
Srikantapuram 104, C3
Sulthan Bathery 80, E3

T
Talapady 111, A1
Tannallur 46, B1
Tanur 92, B4
Teekoy 56, E2
Thaikandapuram 111, B4
Thalankara 111, B2
Thalassery 104, C5
Thalayolaparambu 56, B1
Thamarassery 80, B5
Thampanoor 11, B4
Thangasseri 46, B3
Thariode 80, D3
Tharuvana 80, B2
Thathamangalam 88, E4
Thattamala 46, B3
Thattampara 71, D1
Thattathumala 15, B1
Thavinhal 80, B1
Thazhakod 36, C4
Thekkady 66, D1
Thekkekkara 49, C6
Thenkurissi 88, D4
Thenmala 46, E3
Thidanad 56, D2
Thirunavaya 92, B5
Thirur 86, A2
Thiruvalathoor 88, E4
Thiruvalla 63, A2
Thiruvallam 15, B4
Thiruvambadi 36, D3

Thiruvananthapuram
 (Trivandrum) 15, B3
Thodikkulam 104, D4
Thodupuzha 71, A3
Thondernad 80, A3
Thonnallur 63, B3
Thoppumpadi 42, A1
Thottakara 27, C4
Thottappally Spillway 42, B5
Thrikkaavu 86, A3
Thrikkakara 27, B3
Thrikkunnapuzha 49, B5
Thrikovilvattom 46, C3
Thriprangode 92, B5
Thriprayar 28, B3
Thripunithura 27, B4
Thrissur (Trichur) 28, B2
Thrithala 88, B3
Thunneri 36, A1
Thuravur 27, A5
Thuvvur 92, D3
Thycaud 11, C4
Thykattusserry 42, B2
Tirur 92, B5
Tirurangadi 92, B4
Tiruvarpu 56, B3
Trikandiyur 86, A2
Trikaripur 111, C5
Turavur 49, A2

U
Udayagiri 104, C1
Udumbanchola 71, C3
Ulliyeri 36, B3
Ummannur 46, C3
Uppala 111, A2
Uppu 71, B3
Uppupara 71, C5
Urakad 27, B3
Uzhavoor 56, C1

V
Vadakkancheri 28, C1
Vadakkenchery 88, B4
Vadanapalli 28, B3
Vadasserikara 63, C2
Vadayambadu 27, B3
Vaduvanchal 80, D4
Vagamon 71, B4
Vaikom 56, B2
Valanchery 92, C5
Valapattanam 104, B4
Valayam 36, B1
Valikunnu 36, C5
Valiyashala 11, D5
Vallithodu 104, D3
Valluvambram 36, D5
Vamanapuram 15, B2
Vanchiyoor 11, A3
Vandanmedu 71, C4
Vandiperiyar 71, C5
Vanimel 36, B1
Varandarapilli 28, C3
Varapuzha 27, A3
Varkala 46, C4
Vatakara 36, A2
Vazhachal 27, C1
Vazhakkad 92, B3
Vazhakulam 27, D4
Vazhuthacaud 11, C2
Vechur 42, C3
Velangad 36, C3
Velanthavalam 88, E3
Vellamunda 80, B3
Vellar Junction 98, B2
Vellarada 15, D3
Vellayambalam 11, C1
Vellayil 33, B2
Vellinezhi 88, C3
Velur 28, B2
Venjaramoodu 15, B2
Vettikkod 42, B1
Vettilapara 27, C1
Vithura 15, C2
Vizhinjam 98, C5
Vythiri 80, C4
Vyttila 21- F3, 27- A4

W
Walayar 88, E3
Willingdon Island 21, C4

Stark World

Choosing the right destination book can be as difficult as making the choice of where to go. Moreover, books that give insights into the history and culture of a place, people's values and politics are rare. With its target-specific publications, Stark World addresses this need in the market.

All the information presented in Stark World books is researched by a team of insiders; people who know the ins and outs of the destination covered. The books combine a journalistic approach to description with a thoroughly practical approach to the reader's needs. By incorporating culture, history and contemporary insights with a critical edge, together with up-to-date, value-for-money listings, Stark World publications offer a complete package.

Stark World believes that visual images communicate the feel of the destination and the everyday life of the people who live there. Hence, you will find images playing a vital role in bringing out the essence of people and places in Stark World publications.

www.starkworld.net

Stark World – Kerala

Information used in this book is extracted from *Stark World – Kerala*, Edition 1.

Editor
Akber Ayub

Somebody who studied to be a mechanical engineer, then worked as a marine engineer and proceeded to become a project engineer for a hotel group before becoming an industrialist exporting goods to Europe, Akber Ayub has traversed many paths before settling down to what his heart indicated. Now a full-time freelance writer, travel writing is the forte of this poetic author – currently writing his first novel. After having travelled widely for the *Stark World – Kerala* Edition 1, where he contributed to the travel section, Ayub put together *Maps & More – Kerala*.

Project Co-ordinator
Robins V George

Robins, a postgraduate in tourism administration, more than proved his mettle when he worked on *Maps & More – Kerala*. After having worked tirelessly on the voluminous *Stark World – Kerala* Edition 1, Robins knew exactly how to plan and design this heavily condensed version. His earlier research for the Kerala book stood him in good stead when he set about validating facts, travelling across the State to collect information and verifying the information plotted on the maps. In addition to managing the cartography division, Robins also co-ordinated editorial content, design and production.